Intercultural Citizenship in Language Education

I0127582

LANGUAGES FOR INTERCULTURAL COMMUNICATION AND EDUCATION

Series Editors: **Michael Byram**, *University of Durham, UK* and **Anthony J. Liddicoat**, *University of Warwick, UK*

The overall aim of this series is to publish books which will ultimately inform learning and teaching, but whose primary focus is on the analysis of intercultural relationships, whether in textual form or in people's experience. There will also be books which deal directly with pedagogy, with the relationships between language learning and cultural learning, between processes inside the classroom and beyond. They will all have in common a concern with the relationship between language and culture, and the development of intercultural communicative competence.

All books in this series are externally peer-reviewed.

Full details of all the books in this series and of all our other publications can be found on http://www.multilingual-matters.com, or by writing to Multilingual Matters, St Nicholas House, 31-34 High Street, Bristol, BS1 2AW, UK.

LANGUAGES FOR INTERCULTURAL COMMUNICATION AND EDUCATION: 41

Intercultural Citizenship in Language Education

Teaching and Learning Through Social Action

Edited by
Kaishan Kong and Allison J. Spenader

MULTILINGUAL MATTERS
Bristol • Jackson

DOI https://doi.org/10.21832/KONG5768
Library of Congress Cataloging in Publication Data
A catalog record for this book is available from the Library of Congress.
Names: Kong, Kaishan, editor. | Spenader, Allison, editor.
Title: Intercultural Citizenship in Language Education: Teaching and Learning
  Through Social Action/Edited by Kaishan Kong and Allison Spenader.
Description: Bristol; Jackson: Multilingual Matters, [2023] | Series:
  Languages for Intercultural Communication and Education: 41 | Includes
  bibliographical references and index. | Summary: 'This book explores
  Intercultural Citizenship across a variety of US learning contexts. The
  chapters, which comprise both conceptual and empirical studies,
  represent a wide variety of languages at levels ranging from beginner to
  advanced. They urge us to look at how Intercultural Citizenship enhances
  and expands the work of world language educators' – Provided by
  publisher. Identifiers: LCCN 2023017993 (print) | LCCN 2023017994 (ebook) |
  ISBN 9781800415768 (hardback) | ISBN 9781800415751 (paperback) | ISBN
  9781800415775 (pdf) | ISBN 9781800415782 (epub)
Subjects: LCSH: Languages, Modern – Study and teaching – United States. |
  Multicultural education – United States. | Social justice and
  education – United States. | World citizenship in education – United
  States. | LCGFT: Essays.
Classification: LCC PB38.U6 I65 2023 (print) | LCC PB38.U6 (ebook) | DDC
  418.0071/073 – dc23/eng/20230613
LC record available at https://lccn.loc.gov/2023017993
LC ebook record available at https://lccn.loc.gov/2023017994

British Library Cataloguing in Publication Data
A catalogue entry for this book is available from the British Library.

ISBN-13: 978-1-80041-576-8 (hbk)
ISBN-13: 978-1-80041-575-1 (pbk)

Multilingual Matters
UK: St Nicholas House, 31-34 High Street, Bristol, BS1 2AW, UK.
USA: Ingram, Jackson, TN, USA.

Website: https://www.multilingual-matters.com
Twitter: Multi_Ling_Mat
Facebook: https://www.facebook.com/multilingualmatters
Blog: https://www.channelviewpublications.wordpress.com

The policy of Multilingual Matters/Channel View Publications is to use papers that
are natural, renewable and recyclable products, made from wood grown in sustainable
forests. In the manufacturing process of our books, and to further support our policy,
preference is given to printers that have FSC and PEFC Chain of Custody certification.
The FSC and/or PEFC logos will appear on those books where full certification has
been granted to the printer concerned.

Typeset by Riverside Publishing Solutions.

Contents

Contributors

Salah Ayari is currently Instructional Professor of Arabic and the Director of Language Instruction in the Department of Global Languages and Cultures at Texas A&M University. He has taught Arabic at all levels for more than 20 years. While leading short- and long-term study abroad programs for more than 10 years, Salah has conducted research on the impact of studying Arabic in an immersion environment on student language growth and intercultural competence. Since 2010, he has conducted more than 30 site visits to K–12 schools with different models of Arabic language programs for program evaluation and improvement, and for providing teacher training and mentoring. His areas of interest include curriculum development, evidence-based teaching practices, study abroad and language assessment.

Kevin Clancy, PhD, is the Director of the Center for Global Education at the College of Saint Benedict and Saint John's University (CSB and SJU). CSB and SJU are nationally recognized for their study abroad programs, specifically faculty-led semester programming. In addition to study abroad programs, the Center for Global Education hosts exchange students and scholars and it serves as the hub for CSB and SJU's internationalization efforts. Kevin received his PhD from the University of Minnesota with a research focus on the efficacy of contemplative pedagogy and mindfulness on study abroad programs.

Donna Clementi, PhD, lecturer in World Language Methods at Lawrence University, Appleton, WI, taught French and was the World Languages Program Leader in the Appleton Area School District (WI) for 33 years. She is a frequent workshop presenter and consultant nationally on best practices world language teaching. Since 2006, she has led the CARLA Summer Institute on Second Language Assessments at the University of Minnesota. She is co-author (with Laura Terrill) of *Keys to Planning for Learning: Effective Curriculum, Unit, and Lesson Design Second Edition* (ACTFL 2017). Her honors include: ACTFL's Florence Steiner Award for K–12 Leadership in Foreign Languages (2000); Distinguished Foreign Language Educator Award from the Wisconsin Association for

Language Teachers (2002); Supervisor of the Year Award by the National Association of District Supervisors of Foreign Languages (2004); *Les Palmes Académiques* from the French government (2008); Founders Award from the Central States Conference on the Teaching of Foreign Languages (2012).

Ana Fonseca Conboy is Associate Professor of French Language and Literature at the College of Saint Benedict and Saint John's University (St Joseph, MN). Research interests include 17th-century French literature, specifically hagiographic theater, meta-theater and theater within theater; contemplative pedagogy and mindfulness; and French language pedagogy, second language acquisition and phonetics. Ana also serves as the faculty adviser to the French Cultural Events Assistant and French Club of CSB and SJU and is part of the scientific committee for the Education and New Developments (END) annual conference. Recent publications include 'Where learning begins: Lessons from a pandemic' (*The French Review* 94 (3), 2021), 'Teaching and learning amid a pandemic: Reflections on spring 2020' (Teaching and Learning Culture Special Interest Group (ACTFL) *Newsletter*, July 2020), and 'Video-conferencing in the target language curriculum: Linguistic and cultural learning guaranteed' (with Esther Gimeno-Ugalde and Alexandra Reuber, Strengthening World Language Education: Standards for Success, ed. R. Terry and R. Fox, NECTFL *Review* Special Issue, 2017).

Cassandra Glynn is Associate Professor of Education and Director of Graduate Education at Concordia College, Moorhead, MN. She received her MA and PhD in Curriculum and Instruction from the University of Minnesota with a focus in second languages and cultures education. Her research interests center around the experiences of marginalized and under-represented students in world language classes and on world language teachers' experiences as they take critical approaches to teaching languages and cultures. Her work has been published in journals such as the *L2 Journal, Modern Language Journal, Language Teaching Research* and the *Journal of Curriculum and Pedagogy*. She is co-author (with Pamela Wesely and Beth Wassell) of *Words and Actions: Teaching Languages through the Lens of Social Justice* (ACTFL, 2014, 2018). Prior to starting at Concordia College, Cassandra taught middle school language classes and high school German, including dual credit, and worked in the German and French Villages at Concordia Language Villages.

Kaishan Kong is Associate Professor of Chinese at the University of Wisconsin-Eau Claire. She received her BA in English Education from Zhanjiang Normal University in China, her MA in Intercultural Communication from the University of Sheffield in England, and her PhD in Curriculum and Instruction from the University of Minnesota in the US. In addition to teaching language and culture courses on the UW-Eau Claire campus, she also teaches for the STARTALK program (through the National Foreign Language Center) and the CARLA Summer Institute (Center for Advanced Research on Language Acquisition). She is certified as an ACTFL OPI tester and IDI (Intercultural Development Inventory) administrator. She was recognized as both a Fulbright Scholar (2020) and a Wisconsin Teaching Fellow (2015) for her work on interculturalism and language education.

Brandon Locke is Director of World Languages and Immersion Programs for Anchorage School District, Anchorage, Alaska, a district of approximately 50,000 students. He provides leadership and professional development for ASD's 160 world language teachers, including K–12 language immersion programs in Chinese, French, German, Japanese, Russian and Spanish. He was recently awarded a second significant federal grant to continue the ASD's first Indigenous language immersion program – Yup'ik, one of Alaska's native languages. He is a frequent presenter at state, national and international conferences and has published a number of articles. He is a doctoral candidate in Literacy, Culture, and Language Education at Indiana University. His dissertation and research focuses on Indigenous language revitalization in urban settings.

Adriana L. Medina is Assistant Professor of Reading Education at The University of North Carolina at Charlotte. She teaches courses in language arts, reading comprehension, reading assessment and intervention, content area literacy, teacher identity through art, mindfulness and education, teaching reading to English language learners, and multicultural and global education. Every other year, she leads a Teacher Education in Germany study abroad program. Adriana's research interests include students who struggle with literacy, teacher education, global learning and educational program evaluation. She has co-authored (with Bobby Hobgood) the book *How to Study World Languages* (2021) and has published research on the impact of study abroad experiences on preservice teachers.

Allison J. Spenader is Professor of Education at the College of Saint Benedict and Saint John's University (St Joseph, Minnesota). Allison trains pre-service teachers in the areas of English as a second language and world languages education. She has led summer and semester-long study abroad programs in the United Kingdom, Australia, Sweden and Denmark. Her scholarship focuses on intercultural development in study abroad, and on critical content-based instruction in world language classrooms. Allison is a qualified administrator of the Intercultural Development Inventory and regularly uses the IDI in student and faculty development as well as in research. Her research has appeared in the journals *Foreign Language Annals*, *Frontiers: The Interdisciplinary Journal of Study Abroad*, *L2 Journal* and *Language Teaching Research*.

Manuela Wagner holds a PhD in English Studies with a specialization in linguistics from Graz University, Austria. Her research focuses on the integration of intercultural competence and intercultural citizenship (Byram, 1997, 2008) in (language) education and across the curriculum, from elementary school through post-secondary education. She is particularly interested in the interplay of theory and practice and has been part of and helped create communities of practice to implement theories of intercultural competence and citizenship as well as related theoretical frameworks (theories of criticality, intercultural communication, social justice, intellectual humility) in practice. The resulting book projects include the co-edited volumes *Teaching Intercultural Competence Across the Age Range: From Theory to Practice* (with Dorie Conlon Perugini and Michael Byram, 2018) and *Education for Intercultural Citizenship: Principles in Practice* (with Michael Byram, Irina Golubeva and Han Hui, 2017), and the co-authored book *Teaching Intercultural Citizenship Across the Curriculum: The Role of Language Education* (with Fabiana Cardetti and Michael Byram, 2019). She also investigates the role of educators as advocates for all (language) learners.

Acknowledgements

We are indebted to the authors of the individual chapters in this book, for sharing their profound visions of and illuminating approaches to teaching for intercultural citizenship. Their contributions present a wealth of opportunities to foster intercultural citizenship in a larger landscape of education. Their research would not have been possible without the engagement of many anonymous participants. We are grateful for the participants' dedication to learning languages and cultures, and their generous support to these chapters.

We are grateful to have Dr Michael Byram write a foreword for this book. We stand on his shoulders to gain a broadened view of intercultural citizenship. Dr Byram's seminal works continue to inspire us to question, explore, and reflect on our responsibilities as an educator, a professional, a global citizen and a lifelong learner in contributing to communities.

We would like to acknowledge the work of the anonymous reviewers of this book for their constructive feedback, as well as the thoughtful work from Anna Roderick and her team at Multilingual Matters. We appreciate their support in the publication process.

Finally, we would like to thank our families for their ongoing support.

Kaishan would like to thank her family for giving her wings to fly and supporting her decisions along the journey. When her father signed her up for an English summer camp in 1992, she was introduced to a new world of languages and cultures. She wishes to share this accomplishment with her parents (Qingli Kong and Huijuan Xie) and her two sisters (Kaiying Kong and Kaiwen Kong). 谨以此书献给我的父母和两位姐姐！

Allison extends many thanks to family for always encouraging her pursuits of language learning and intercultural risk-taking. She recognizes the tremendous role that Concordia Language Villages has played in her growth as a citizen of the world and as a language teacher. Additionally, she acknowledges the important work of AFS Intercultural Programs (and other wonderful organizations) for facilitating study abroad at the secondary level.

With gratitude to the great interculturalists who have come before us, and to my family and friends who have supported this endeavor, let us all work towards becoming better intercultural citizens!

Foreword

I would like to begin with my thanks to Allison and Kaishan for their invitation to write a foreword. Secondly, I would like to thank them and the contributors to the book for demonstrating so persuasively how the theory of intercultural citizenship can be realized in practice in US American language teaching.

Let me say immediately to readers that this is not a book only for US teachers: there is every possibility of transferring and translating the examples given here to many other locations and education systems. Naturally, this requires a degree of that intercultural competence which is at the heart of the book itself, for it requires readers to use the intercultural skills, attitudes and knowledge to imagine how they can benefit from the experience of teachers in another country.

I am of course pleased and flattered that the work of my colleagues and myself has been used by the editors and contributors. At the same time, I hope that readers remember that intercultural competence includes the notion of 'critical cultural awareness', and that they will critique and improve practice and theory as they transfer it to their own contexts.

For my part, reading these excellent descriptions of teaching and research, so ably framed in terms of theories by Cassandra Glynn and Manuela Wagner, has led me to think back over some of the theory, and I take this opportunity to re-consider some of the issues that have become clearer to me in the hope that these thoughts will help readers as they proceed through the book.

The notion of intercultural citizenship was developed in part from my becoming familiar with the German tradition of *politische Bildung* and in part from the developments in education in England stimulated by the Crick Report on education for citizenship (Qualifications and Curriculum Authority, 1998). The crucial notion of 'community involvement' was used in the Crick Report. It is worth reminding ourselves of the answer the Report's authors give to their own rhetorical question 'What do we mean by "effective education for citizenship"?':

We mean three things, related to each other, mutually dependent on each other, but each needing a somewhat different place and treatment in the curriculum: social and moral responsibility, community involvement and political literacy. (Qualifications and Curriculum Authority, 1998: 11)

They then define community involvement:

learning about and becoming helpfully involved in the life and concerns of their communities, including learning through community involvement and service to the community. (Qualifications and Curriculum Authority, 1998: 12)

This is followed by a crucial statement about the relationship of learning in school to experience in the community whilst they simultaneously clarify what they mean by 'political':

This, of course, like the other two branches of citizenship, is *by no means limited to children's time in school*. Even if pupils and adults perceive many of the voluntary groups as *non-political, the clearer meaning is probably to say 'non-partisan'*: for voluntary bodies when exercising persuasion, interacting with public authorities, publicising, fund-raising, recruiting members and then trying to activate (or placate) them, all such bodies are plainly *using and needing political skills*. (Qualifications and Curriculum Authority, 1998: 12, emphasis added)

The implication seems to be that activity in the community would be working in a voluntary capacity in non-governmental organisations. In this book, and projects described elsewhere, activities have been much more than this, reflecting an imaginative, creative interpretation of political, non-partisan activity and a much richer understanding of 'community'.

Throughout the Crick Report, the word 'community' collocates most frequently with 'local' and occasionally with 'wider'. This was a time when young people were citizens of the United Kingdom *and* the European Union and 'wider' implied a recognition of their European status. In contrast, there are only three references to the 'global community'. It is stated that young people should know about and understand issues such as 'sustainable development, economic interdependence, heavily indebted countries, and the work of United Nations organisations and major non-governmental organisations' (1998: 52), but nothing more. There is nothing on how they might be involved in this global community. 'Community involvement' remains, above all, local and – in the context of rights and responsibilities – national/European.

Much the same can be said of the other source of the theory of intercultural citizenship, i.e. *'politische Bildung'* in Germany, and the work of Gerhard Himmelmann on *'demokratie Lernen'* (Byram, 2008). It is frequently, if not always, the case in other countries too that citizenship education, or its equivalent, is focused exclusively on local and national communities.

What my colleagues and I added to this was the notion that citizenship can be related to communities beyond the national, through work in the world/foreign language classroom. At the same time this raises the questions addressed in this book about how linguistic and communicative competence can be learnt and used simultaneously with intercultural citizenship, through scaffolding and translanguaging. Furthermore, what has also become clear and is made explicit in this book is that intercultural citizenship is important within national boundaries too, for there are many communities within any country and, moreover, many languages used in them.

Neither the theory in England nor in Germany took into consideration the need for communicative competence and intercultural communicative competence, when a wider and more subtle understanding of 'community' is in place. Yet community involvement or 'action in the [any] community' – the phrase used in many projects including the ones described in this book – presupposes mutual intelligibility.

It is the notion of 'mutual intelligibility' that strikes me as important as I read, in particular, the chapters where Arabic and Chinese are the languages in question. Other projects and earlier publications have brought together students learning European languages, usually Romance and Germanic. For speakers of European languages – not least English in the US American education system – Arabic and Chinese are 'difficult' and 'distant' languages, and languacultures. Creating a convergence of understanding (Risager, 2006) is likely to be much more problematic. Furthermore, this also reminds us that we may have a false impression of the degree of mutual intelligibility among speakers of Romance or Germanic languages, even for those who speak English, the creole created from both.

Language teachers may be aware of the issues through their knowledge of the Sapir–Whorf hypothesis: that language and thought are inextricably related, that language determines the limits of thought and that mutual intelligibility is not assured. This can lead to a relativist view that, ultimately, mutual intelligibility is not possible, a view that language teachers would find depressing and even devastating because it undermines their professional purposes.

On the other hand, in practice and in empirical research studies, we find that, with the help of imaginative insight (Berlin, 1990) and with careful analysis (Lloyd, 2014), we can 'stretch' our own concepts and ways of thinking and, provided we are willing to do so, we can access the meaning of others to some – and usually a large – degree. In his analysis of how we can understand texts from ethnographies of 'exotic' societies, and from Ancient Greek and Chinese writings – where the 'difficulty' or 'distance' is even greater – Lloyd says that there is no 'unmediated access', but he uses a turn of phrase that is familiar to those who seek to teach intercultural communicative competence to argue that:

> it is up to observers, to us, to see what we can learn from the exercise of investigating their ways of being in the world. That means suspending

disbelief and being prepared to revise just about everything we normally take for granted. (Lloyd, 2014: 231)

What does this mean for practice? I think, teachers might be expected – and helped through teacher education – to engage with these matters as part of their professionalism, because they are crucial to understanding intercultural (communicative) competence and communication. It is not a perspective that is easy for learners to engage with but we must remember that the teaching of philosophy in schools is possible (e.g. Naji & Hashim, 2017), and there is potential for cross-curricular cooperation here.

'Activity in the community' – which includes ensuring or making an effort to create mutual intelligibility – has thus become a crucial element of intercultural citizenship. It incorporates the implicit expectation that young people will take action, become 'engaged' or '*engagé*', in other words become politically active. That 'expectation' raises many issues. Some are methodological: for example, in how teachers persuade learners to take action. Others are ethical: for example, with respect to the responsibilities of teachers in 'transforming' learners (Byram *et al.*, 2021). Yet others are ideological: for example, with respect to how teachers who are employed by a public authority – a national or federal state, for example – think about encouraging their learners to critique the society in which they live. Teachers who are civil servants and declare loyalty to the state, as in Germany, might have particular concerns about this. There is still much work to do on these issues, especially by teacher educators.

But what about those learners who, despite their teachers' expectations, do not wish to become active and engaged? In a discussion of some of the work of Bernard Crick – the man behind the Crick Report – Hiruta (2021) distinguishes between Hannah Arendt's conception of 'freedom through politics' and Isaiah Berlin's notion of 'negative freedom'. For my purposes here, it is sufficient to say that Arendt, Crick and – in a more modest way – my colleagues and I, assume that freedom comes through political activity, through being involved in community life. Berlin, on the other hand, believes that ('negative') freedom comes from the absence of interference or constraint on the individual – for example, by a teacher, we might say – and the freedom to choose. The individual might choose to become active in their community/ies, but they may also choose not to.

Behind these two concepts of freedom, there are two conceptions of what it is to be human: the Arendtian view that being human comes only through political engagement, and the Berlinian view that the fundamental characteristic of being human is that human beings understand plurality and make choices, including the choice not to be politically active (Hiruta, 2021: 84). On an Arendtian view, encouraging and expecting learners to become politically active is to help them to realize their human potential. On a Berlinian view, teachers should not expect or encourage or teach their learners to be active in the community but should ensure they understand the notion of choice and that being active in the community is one, but not the only, choice. Which should a teacher pursue?

I have no answer to offer. Probably every teacher has to decide for themselves. I cannot go further than this but I hope that these thoughts will help readers to think about the huge responsibilities taken by the contributors to this book. Such responsibilities are of course not unfamiliar to teachers as they seek the best for their learners, to help them reach their potential, to be human in the deepest sense. 'Taking action in the community' simply brings the issues into sharper focus. That the contributors to this book have not shirked these responsibilities as they teach and assess, research and evaluate, is to their credit. Their work deserves the fullest appreciation and admiration of readers, not least myself.

Michael Byram
February 2023

References

Berlin, I. (1990) *The Crooked Timber of Humanity*. Princeton, NJ: Princeton University Press.

Byram, M. (2008) *From Foreign Language Education to Education for Intercultural Citizenship: Essays and Reflections*. Bristol: Multilingual Matters.

Byram, M., Porto, M. and Wagner, M. (2021) Ethical issues in teaching for intercultural citizenship in world/foreign language education. *TESOL Quarterly* 55 (1), 308–321. https://doi.org/10.1002/tesq.3008.

Hiruta, K. (2021) *Hannah Arendt and Isaiah Berlin*. Princeton, NJ: Princeton University Press.

Lloyd, G.E.R. (2014) On the very possibility of mutual intelligibility. *HAU: Journal of Ethnographic Theory* 4 (2), 221–235.

Naji, S. and Hashim, R. (2017) *History, Theory and Practice of Philosophy for Children: International Perspectives*. London: Routledge.

Qualifications and Curriculum Authority (Crick Report) (1998) *Education for Citizenship and the Teaching of Democracy in Schools*. London: Qualifications and Curriculum Authority. (See especially pp. 7–21 and 44–45.)

Risager, K. (2006) *Language and Culture Pedagogy: From a National to a Transnational Paradigm*. Clevedon: Multilingual Matters.

Preface: Intercultural Citizenship – A Passion Project

Kaishan Kong and Allison J. Spenader

When we first conceptualized this volume, the editors came together through a mutual passion for language teaching and a commitment to fostering intercultural development in students. We had both found our excitement ignited by the recent publication of Wagner, Cardetti and Byram's *Teaching Intercultural Citizenship Across the Curriculum: The Role of Language Education* (2019). We share a deep commitment to teaching for intercultural development and, upon ACTFL's publication of this piece, were excited to see a focus on interculturality in language teaching validated at the national level. Within this important publication, Kaishan immediately found herself drawn to the four classroom projects described. In fact, as the current manuscript was taking shape over the summer of 2022, Kaishan was participating in a Fulbright Scholar program in Malaysia, and the only physical book she took in her luggage was the Wagner *et al.* (2019) volume! Likewise, Allison was highly enthusiastic when she first heard about the book and she immediately purchased it and read it cover to cover. At the annual ACTFL conference in 2019, Allison tracked down Manuela Wagner, peppering her with questions to learn more about her work on intercultural citizenship. By summer 2021 we had conceptualized this edited volume, aiming to share the synergy that we were seeing among our colleagues in the field of world language. We saw a great deal of energy around the confluence between intercultural development and language teaching and learning. We wanted to contribute to the momentum that we saw in this important and evolving educational framework. We held inclusivity of diverse voices as an explicit goal, aiming to incorporate a wealth of languages, program types, as well as author backgrounds and perspectives. While most of the contributing authors have deep connections to the Upper Midwest, the volume simultaneously reflects the work and voices of teachers and researchers from all over the US as well as several other countries.

Introduction: Diverse Perspectives on Intercultural Citizenship

Kaishan Kong and Allison J. Spenader

Background and Aim

Globalization and cultural diversity propel the field of language teaching and learning towards developing culturally appropriate communication skills. Byram's intercultural communicative competence (ICC) framework (2021) has inspired language educators to empower learners with intercultural knowledge, attitudes and skills to explore a culture through understanding others' perspectives and solving problems. As Wagner *et al.* (2019: vii) aptly state, it is significant for educators 'to create learning experiences that lead students to "go outside" in order to discover "what's inside"'. They suggest teaching intercultural citizenship across the curriculum as a pathway to foster learners' self-reflection and self-awareness, making connections between subjects, contents, communities and cultures. We find ourselves in a tumultuous moment of politicization of education, particularly in the US. Following a decade of progress towards developing critical stances in learners, US schools today are witnessing culture wars around notions of social justice and critical approaches. Although teaching for multiculturalism has been politicized, it is more important than ever to infuse critical thinking, critical cultural awareness and interculturality into the curriculum. For these reasons, our gaze shifts to the framework of intercultural citizenship as a viable pathway to transforming language education, with important implications for other subject areas as well.

Rooted in the ICC framework, intercultural citizenship stresses the agency within learners, highlighting learners' endeavors in communities as bridge-builders, problem-solvers and advocates. *From Principles to Practice in Education of Intercultural Citizenship* (Byram *et al.*, 2017) presented theoretical frameworks and examples of collaboration on fostering intercultural citizenship, illuminating a new direction of language research. A special issue of the *Foreign Language Annals* included numerous articles calling on foreign language educators to embed intercultural citizenship goals in language teaching, highlighting the community engagement of students, and articulating an innovative research agenda for language learning in various contexts (Byram & Wagner, 2018; Marijuan & Sanz, 2018; Palpacuer *et al.*, 2018). Recently, *Teaching Intercultural Citizenship across the Curriculum* (Wagner *et al.*, 2019) exemplified interdisciplinary collaboration and gave prominence to preparing students linguistically and interculturally. Further, Porto (2019: 142) implemented these intercultural citizenship goals in a service-learning project, addressing 'the affordances, complexities and challenges that intercultural citizenship poses to teachers and teacher education'. We recognize scholarship on cross-cultural and intercultural competency that, while related to intercultural citizenship, advances models in which language learning may be an important but not a required component. This scholarship has helped us distill core aspects of interculturality and includes models such as Bennett's Developmental Model of Intercultural Sensitivity (Bennett, 1993), Cultural Intelligence (Ang *et al.*, 2007), and Deardorff's framework of Intercultural Competence (2006). This exciting body of literature inspired this edited collection of scholarship, which seeks to further this line of discussion and inquiry.

Focus, Purpose and Potential Contribution

This book represents scholarship at the intersection of two critical areas: language education and intercultural citizenship. The contributors address the importance of curriculum design, second/world/foreign language learning, dual language and immersion education, culture, teacher education, social justice, peer interaction and study abroad, in fostering language learning collectively. Embracing contemporary conceptual and empirical chapters, this collection situates intercultural citizenship in a variety of research spheres, addressing language education both within and beyond the US context, as well as across educational settings.

The purpose of this book is to advance the discussion of what intercultural citizenship means, its application, challenges, pedagogical significance, and its connection with social justice. We agree strongly with Fantini who reminds us that our pursuit of intercultural teaching and learning will '... lead us toward what we most desire – peace, social justice and equality' (Fantini, 2020: 60). We draw on Byram's (2006) position that the word 'citizenship' is not referring to allegiance to a specific country but, rather, to students' curiosity, willingness and competence to undertake a journey towards global competence and to reflect on ways of thinking and doing. This conceptualization of 'citizenship' aligns with PISA's (Programme for International Student Assessment; OECD, 2018) definition of global competence, wherein cultural awareness and the ability to interact effectively with peers from a variety of backgrounds are intentionally supported by schools, preparing young people to engage with global issues (see oecd.org/pisa/innovation/global-competence/). The scholarship in this collection investigates and expands our conceptualization of the characteristics of intercultural citizenship, exploring language education related to advancing social justice, fostering questioning attitudes, promoting a willingness and ability to engage in intercultural dialogue with others, and cross-cultural collaboration (Porto, 2019; Wagner *et al.*, 2019).

This book will contribute to the field in two important ways. First, the contributors represent diverse cultural and linguistic backgrounds, bringing profound expertise and innovative findings and implications. We are thrilled to have Manuela Wagner – a leading figure in intercultural citizenship – champion this discussion through two collaborative chapters. Other contributors include language assessment expert Donna Clementi and her colleague Salah Ayari who is a leader in the field of Arabic language teaching. Additionally, this book features the work of recognized teacher educator and social justice expert Cassandra Glynn, dual language and immersion expert Brandon Locke, and dedicated researchers in study abroad Ana Conboy, Kevin Clancy and Adriana Medina. Their important contributions form a powerful foundation for future discussion in the field.

Second, the wide variety of topics and language representations (Arabic, Chinese, French, Japanese, Spanish and Yup'ik) will benefit a broad audience. The chapters embrace inquiries in language acquisition, interculturality, bilingualism, literacy, culture and teacher education, through various lenses and in contexts ranging from primary grades to professional development for in-service teachers. A diverse set of theoretical perspectives and research methods addresses the relationships, innovative practices and assessment of intercultural citizenship in language education. In sum, this timely book will benefit the field of language learning more broadly by exploring why, how and what to teach for intercultural citizenship, propelling this important field forward through profound and stimulating discussion. The use of diverse angles for examination of intercultural citizenship (henceforth ICit) will entice readers including, but not limited to, language instructors, researchers, interculturalists, teacher educators, language program administrators and study abroad professionals.

As the volume editors we have had the privilege of reading each of the chapters and we have identified a number of recurring themes for consideration. We invite you to join us in noting and reflecting upon how these examples of teaching with ICit are connected and how they expand our understanding of this powerful educational framework.

The need for professional development for intercultural citizenship

Because the ICit framework is new to many teachers, it is imperative that teaching resources are shared and that professional development addresses how to infuse ICit learning goals into our instruction. Chapter 1, by Glynn and Wagner, presents a conceptualization of the confluence between social justice education and ICit. The authors provide several lesson examples that can be applied to a variety of classroom contexts, giving readers valuable tools for infusing ICit and social justice learning goals into classrooms. In Chapter 2, Clementi, Ayari and Wagner describe a model for professional learning communities that focuses on developing units of study that allow for the exchange of ideas across Arabic-speaking communities. Both chapters include detailed descriptions of effective strategies for creating and sustaining professional development opportunities for teachers.

Looking at ICit from early learners through adulthood

The diversity of contexts included brings perspectives spanning from kindergarten to in-service teacher professional development. Building on important works by Wagner and others (Byram & Wagner, 2018; Wagner et al., 2019), the chapters expand into younger grades as well as adulthood, providing for new understandings of how ICit is enacted at each developmental stage. This volume adds to our understanding of how teaching for ICit occurs with learners as young as kindergarten (Chapter 3 by Spenader & Locke) and reveals some of the challenges related to developmental traits of younger children (see Feinauer & Howard, 2014). What kind of understanding of culture (our own and others) is possible in primary grades? Spenader and Locke explore how conceptualization of one's own and other cultures is not always distinguishable. Not only do younger learners have a less robust conceptualization of racial, ethnic and national identity than older children (Barrett, 2007; Davis et al., 2007), students in an ethnically diverse dual-language immersion program may feel strong identification with more than one cultural group. At the other end of the age range is ICit development in young adults/college students. This volume presents multiple research projects focused on university level learners (Chapter 4 by Kong; Chapter 5 by Spenader & Medina; Chapter 6 by Conboy & Clancy). Each of these chapters describes traits of ICC and ICit development in adult learners.

Fostering ICit through thoughtful program design in study abroad

This volume distinguishes itself from others in examining ICit in a wider landscape of education – both within and beyond the classrooms. While ICit has been widely researched in classroom practice and sometimes in relation to peers from other contexts, there is a lacuna in the field of international education and study abroad. As Conboy and Clancy argue in Chapter 6, the experiential nature and intercultural learning opportunities offered by study abroad programs are affordances to foster students' ICit. Hence, they focus on metacognition and critical reflection to identify students' increased ICit during and after their sojourner. Their chapter, representing a collaboration between a language professor and a study abroad administrator, exemplifies an orchestrated effort to adopt contemplative pedagogy to nurture ICit in study abroad programs (Jackson, 2011). The chapter examines the following questions: Is ICit limited to a specific duration of a study abroad program? What can propel the continuous development of ICit? What can be done to interweave ICit, language education and study abroad to maximize learning?

An interesting duality is noted in the work by Spenader and Medina (Chapter 5), who examine how teachers both develop traits of the ICit framework (along with ICC) in themselves while simultaneously planning and delivering instruction that enacts the ICit framework for their students. Is it possible to teach for ICit without first developing ICC and the capacity for ICit in oneself? The authors of Chapter 5 argue that a precursor to fostering ICit in K–12 students is to foster ICC in pre-service teachers, which is realized through semester-long study abroad as part of teacher preparation. The findings illuminate the potential of study abroad in developing pre-service teachers' ICit and the suggestions echo Conboy and Clancy's work (Chapter 6) on the importance of intentionality and purposefulness in study abroad program design.

In a similar light, in Chapter 4 Kong discovers Chinese international students' ICit through intercultural virtual pen pal exchange with local students. In contrast to Chapters 5 and 6 discussed above that investigated outbound study abroad participants, Kong's chapter inspires language educators to consider how to foster inbound study abroad students' ICit. Although Kong's study occurred within the US, her participants included Chinese students who were studying abroad in the US. How do educators within the US create opportunities to foster international students' ICit through collaboration with local students? Because international students and native speakers are often invited to interact with local students, Kong's chapter reminds us all to design mutually beneficial activities to benefit both local and international students, which is an effective way to avoid those 'instrumental, utilitarian and uncritical orientations' (Porto, 2019: 150) that would tokenize the international students. Despite their varied focus, all of these chapters remind us of the importance of intentional and thoughtful design that can support students' ICit during their study abroad.

Students' language proficiency in ICit

Is students' proficiency in the target language high enough for a profound discussion on difficult topics? This is a prominent concern that prevents many language instructors from delving into difficult topics. Many of the chapters in this volume address this complexity. In Chapter 1, Glynn and Wagner shed light on the value of translanguaging, which empowers students to use their linguistic capabilities in developing their ICit. Their support of translanguaging in ICit teaching resonates with Boonsuk and Fang's (2021) notion that 'The recognition of translanguaging in settings for intercultural citizenship education also promotes equality from a critical perspective' (2021: 14), allowing students 'to imagine new ways of being and languaging' so that they 'can begin to act differently upon the world' (García & Li, 2014: 138). On the other hand, in Chapter 4 Kong accentuates the significance of language scaffolding when facilitating students' intercultural discussion. These chapters acknowledge the limits and complexity of students' language proficiency in fostering ICit; however, as Wagner *et al.* (2019) argue that 'more is possible than at first seems likely' (2019: 123), these authors suggest using different techniques to support students' development of ICit.

It is our hope that you will find these contributions to the field to be illuminating. We are grateful to the authors for engaging in this important scholarship and for sharing their findings with our professional community. We all understand the value of language education for preparing the next generation of competent and thoughtful leaders, and we see ICit as a viable and exciting means to realizing that shared goal.

References

Ang, S., Van Dyne, L., Koh, C., Ng, K., Templer, K., Tay, C. and Anand Chandrasekar, N. (2007) Cultural intelligence: Its measurement and effects on cultural judgment and decision making, cultural adaptation, and task performance. *Management and Organization Review* 3, 335–371.

Barrett, M. (2007) *Children's Knowledge, Beliefs and Feelings about Nations and National Groups*. Hove: Psychology Press.

Bennett, M.J. (1993) Towards ethnorelativism: A developmental model of intercultural sensitivity. In R.M. Paige (ed.) *Education for the Intercultural Experience* (2nd edn, pp. 21–71). Yarmouth, ME: Intercultural Press.

Boonsuk, Y. and Fang, F. (2021) Re-envisaging English medium instruction, intercultural citizenship development, and higher education in the context of studying abroad. *Language and Education* 1–17. https://doi.org/10.1080/09500782.2021.1996595.

Byram, M. (2006) Developing a concept of intercultural citizenship. In G. Alred, M. Byram and M. Fleming (eds) *Education for Intercultural Citizenship: Concepts and Comparisons* (pp. 109–129). Clevedon: Multilingual Matters.

Byram, M. (2021) *Teaching and Assessing Intercultural Communicative Competence: Revisited*. Bristol: Multilingual Matters.

Byram, M. and Wagner, M. (2018) Making a difference: Language teaching for intercultural and international dialogue. *Foreign Language Annals* 51 (1), 140–151.

Byram, M., Golubeva, I., Hui, H. and Wagner, M. (eds) (2017) *From Principles to Practice in Education for Intercultural Citizenship*. Bristol: Multilingual Matters.

Davis, S.C., Leman, P.J. and Barrett, M. (2007) Children's implicit and explicit ethnic group attitudes, ethnic group identification, and self-esteem. *International Journal of Behavioral Development* 31 (5), 514–525. https://doi.org/10.1177/0165025407081461.

Deardorff, D. (2006) The identification and assessment of intercultural competence as a student outcome of internationalization at institutions of higher education in the United States. *Journal of Studies on International Education* 10 (3), 241–266.

Fantini, A. (2020) Reconceptualizing intercultural communicative competence: A multinational perspective. *Research in Comparative and International Education* 15 (1), 52–61.

Feinauer, E. and Howard, E.R. (2014) Attending to the third goal: Cross-cultural competence and identity development in two-way immersion programs. *Journal of Immersion and Content-Based Language Education* 2 (2), 257–272.

García, O. and Li, W. (2014) *Translanguaging: Language, Bilingualism and Education.* Basingstoke: Palgrave Macmillan.

Jackson, J. (2011) Cultivating cosmopolitan, intercultural citizenship through critical reflection and international, experiential learning. *Language and Intercultural Communication* 11 (2), 80–96.

Marijuan, S. and Sanz, C. (2018) Expanding boundaries: Current and new directions in study abroad research and practice. *Foreign Language Annals* 51 (1), 185–204.

OECD (2018) *Preparing our Youth for an Inclusive and Sustainable World. The OECD PISA Global Competence Framework.* Paris: OECD.

Palpacuer Lee, C., Curtis, J.H. and Curran, M.E. (2018) Shaping the vision for service-learning in language education. *Foreign Language Annals* 51 (1), 169–184.

Porto, M. (2019) Affordances, complexities, and challenges of intercultural citizenship for foreign language teachers. *Foreign Language Annals* 52 (1), 141–164.

Wagner, M., Cardetti, F. and Byram, M. (2019) *Teaching Intercultural Citizenship across the Curriculum: The Role of Language Education.* Alexandria, VA: American Council on the Teaching of Foreign Languages (ACTFL).

1 The Why and How of Teaching Languages for Social Justice and Intercultural Citizenship

Cassandra Glynn and Manuela Wagner

Introduction

Moving beyond the traditional and familiar

We, the authors, work in different contexts in language education: as language teachers, researchers, advisors to graduate students, and guiding pre-service and in-service teachers through licensure coursework and professional development. We are afforded many opportunities to peer inside classrooms and to hear and see what language teachers across the country are doing in their classrooms. It is clear that language teachers' approaches to teaching their students falls on a spectrum, from sticking to a more traditional approach to disrupting the status quo of (language) education. At one end of the spectrum, we find learners engaged in exercises to practice verb conjugation and paging through readers. We hear the teacher telling a light, humorous, 'by the way' cultural story and students laughing about their teacher's experience. We listen to students navigate a menu and figure out what they would order in the restaurant. To be clear, none of these examples of 'typical' language classroom activities is a 'bad' practice *per se*, and we do not mean to suggest that teachers should never facilitate these activities. At the other end of the spectrum, we see teachers aiming to delve deeper with students into topics about injustice, examining topics like sustainable tourism and how to support communities that are trying to preserve their customs in the face of colonization and tourism. We listen to teachers talk about discussions they have had with their classes as they wrestled with complex issues and topics around the world.

We work with teachers in a variety of contexts ranging from professional development to mentoring new teachers and graduate students in their teaching. In this work, we find teachers who, for a variety of reasons, are afraid of talking about difficult topics, such as racism, poverty, war, and we meet others who are frustrated because doing this in a way that is meaningful is difficult and comes with many challenges and sometimes even the danger of losing their jobs. Manuela finds herself urging graduate students – some of whom might have prior teaching experience and some not – to scaffold the target language and to avoid using English in order to work through complex topics. At the same time she supports translanguaging and students' use of other languages. This is one example of the complexities we face as educators, and we will try in this chapter to provide some tools to address these complexities. Meanwhile, Cassandra struggles to help pre-service language teachers consider an approach to teaching that is different from how they were taught when they were high school language students. What they, and we, often notice is that addressing the missing elements of digging deeper to uncover how people experience things in different ways, examining complex topics that move beyond safe, tangible cultural topics, and making connections to the student's role in their communities, can be fraught with challenges.

Despite these challenges, we propose that it is time that we move beyond a focus in teaching language for the mere purpose of learning the formal aspects of language, and instead teach languages to enable our students to critically investigate the world around them and their role in it. One way to go about this endeavor, that we found helpful, is through social justice education (e.g. Glynn *et al.*, 2018; Nieto, 2010; Osborn, 2006) and interdisciplinary intercultural citizenship education (Byram, 2008; Wagner *et al.*, 2019). Using a framework that combines social justice education and intercultural citizenship helps highlight the role of language education in educating students who can apply what they learn in language classrooms to the real world, hence highlighting the role of language education in the larger endeavor of educating our students for life.

Around the world, communities are navigating complex issues on a daily basis, issues like xenophobia, racism and homophobia (Ennser-Kananen, 2016), that further exacerbate problems such as hunger, environmental issues, lack of healthcare, poverty, access to education and inequities in a variety of contexts. Becker *et al.* (2022) refer to these topics as 'taboo issues' and posit that including 'taboos' in teacher education can encourage teachers to go 'beyond simply maneuvering through taboos and to move from a "Don't Ask, Don't Tell" towards a "Do Ask and Do Tell" approach to foreign language learning' (2022: 10). To ignore these issues in order to focus on language or cultural topics that are perceived as safe or 'light, curious, and often pleasantly amusing' (Ennser-Kananen, 2016: 557) is to completely ignore important aspects of cultures and the experiences of groups of people and individuals within that culture. Furthermore, to ignore these topics is to ignore the experiences of our students, who may face some of these issues at home, in school and in their communities. By bringing social justice topics into the classroom, we provide an opportunity for students to see their own lives and experiences reflected in the lives and experiences of people living in other cultures, and we also open students' eyes to experiences and perspectives they might not have considered before. In the process of uncovering some of these complex topics in another context, students can examine actions that citizens in different contexts are taking to address the issues, encouraging our students to develop their own agency to act and to become intercultural citizens.

Within the US context, ready-made and teacher-made instructional materials tend to be geared toward preparing students to travel, study or live abroad. Simply put, this is a practice that we must stop. Study abroad numbers have indeed increased, and approximately 10.9% of community college students and 16% of baccalaureate students do opt to study abroad at some point during their post-secondary education (Redden, 2019). In the 2018–2019 academic year, 347,099 American students studied abroad but, of that number, only 6.5% were black or African American (*Journal of Blacks in Higher Education*, 2021). In 2019–2020, study abroad participation decreased in the spring of 2020 due to Covid-19 but 70% of study abroad participants were white, while approximately 5.5% were African American, almost 10.6% were Latino and 8.6% were Asian American or Pacific Islander (NAFSA, n.d.). These study abroad numbers mirror enrollment, in general, in world language where an over-representation of white students and under-representation of black students, in particular, can be found (Glynn & Wassell, 2018; Glynn *et al.*, 2022). Ultimately, what this means is that the curriculum in our field has long been aimed at white students who will study abroad, leading teachers to continue activities like planning a school schedule, renting an apartment, shopping in a store and ordering off a menu. Osborn (2006) poses the question, 'Who cares what my school schedule would look like in Germany? – *U.S. students do not go to school there*! They do not receive daily weather briefings in French, and they do not normally inquire of their Spanish-speaking classmates as to what hobbies they have' (2006: 59, italics original). Yet, here we are, in the midst of Black Lives Matter and Women's Rights protests, war in Ukraine, school shootings in the US, global warming and ongoing inequalities throughout our communities, still wondering why these activities are more the norm than the exception. Why does it matter what a student's schedule would look like when there are more pressing, more relevant topics to explore? We have long been mired in approaches to language teaching that use resources presenting 'the absurd, essentialized world of those who speak the language as depicted in textbooks' (Osborn, 2016: 59) rather than focusing on the intersectionality of students' social identities and how those identities relate to relevant, current topics in their own communities and in communities around the world. Hines-Gaither *et al.* (2022) argue that to do otherwise is to present an inauthentic view of target culture communities. Further, it sets us up to present culture as something that 'happens only in "other" places or "over there" rather than within our own communities' (Conlon Perugini & Wagner, 2022: 52).

We must begin to develop our world language courses with the mindset of creating intercultural citizens and with the aim of meeting our students where they are at right now, rather than on planning lessons that might prepare only a fraction of our students to perhaps someday travel or study in a target culture of the language we teach. Kramsch (2014: 98) argues that students must be prepared for the world in which they live, requiring a more reflective, interpretive, historically grounded and politically engaged pedagogy. Meanwhile, Cammarata *et al.* (2016: 9) underscore the importance of 'learning to use language for meaningful communication about relevant content'. In doing so, there is hope of 'tapping into the full awareness raising potential that the language learning experience can offer' (Cammarata *et al.*, 2016: 9). The aim of this chapter is to challenge teachers to become transformative intellectuals (Kumaravadivelu, 2003, as cited in Wooten *et al.*, 2022). A transformative intellectual acknowledges how hierarchies, world events and power are at play in their teaching practices; they intend to 'effect change in the world through their work in the classroom' (Wooten *et al.*, 2022: 181). A language teaching approach that brings together tenets of social justice education and intercultural citizenship provides a pathway for becoming a transformative intellectual as a teacher and inspiring students to be responsibly engaged in the world.

Our proposed framework: Connecting social justice education and intercultural citizenship

Education for intercultural citizenship (ICit)

Byram (1997) emphasized that in order for students to engage in intercultural dialogue, i.e. to become intercultural speakers or mediators, we need to intentionally and systematically teach and assess the knowledge, skills and attitudes involved in intercultural communicative competence (ICC). Byram (1997, 2021) describes five dimensions of intercultural competence that students need to master in addition to the three linguistic skills we usually teach in language education, i.e.

linguistic, sociolinguistic and discourse competences. The five dimensions of intercultural competence are described as follows:

- Attitudes: curiosity and openness, readiness to suspend disbelief about other cultures and belief about one's own.
- Knowledge: specific knowledge of social groups and their products and practices in one's own and in one's interlocutor's country, and a general knowledge of processes of societal and individual interaction.
- Skills of interpreting and relating: the ability to interpret a document or event from another culture, to explain it and relate it to documents from one's own.
- Skills of discovery and interaction: the ability to acquire new knowledge of cultural practices and the ability to operate knowledge, attitudes and skills under the constraints of real-time communication and interaction.
- Critical cultural awareness/political education: an ability to evaluate, critically and on the basis of an explicit systematic process of reasoning, values present in one's own and other cultures and countries.

(Byram, 2021: 62–67)

Intercultural *communicative* competence consists of the linguistic competences and intercultural competence (knowledge, skills of interpreting and relating, skills of discovery and interaction, attitudes and critical cultural awareness). Critical cultural awareness plays an important role in linking education for ICit, which we introduce in the next section, and social justice education. Guillherme (2000) pointed out that critical cultural awareness provides a natural link to critical pedagogy, and a 'pedagogy of praxis, where reflection and action take the lead, …' (2000: 13). This is in line with our view of the constant interplay of theory and practice, in which theory informs practice and, in turn, practice has an important impact on how we read and understand theory. While Byram (1997) already introduces criticality and reflection, his work did not originally contain an action component. That additional connection to civics education is described in the framework of ICit (Byram, 2008, 2021).

Building on teaching languages for intercultural communication and on the political dimension of intercultural communicative competence, Byram (2008) made an important observation: most national curricula ask educators to develop students' abilities to be good (national) citizens. Pointing to the interconnectedness in today's world, Byram offers a framework that provides a framework for (language) educators to help students become intercultural citizens. This framework develops five orientations for intercultural citizenship, namely the evaluative, cognitive, comparative, communicative and action orientations.

Critical cultural awareness also plays a crucial role here as Byram (2008) emphasizes that, upon leaving an education system, students should have a 'critical cultural awareness of the particular nature of sociopolitical action and interaction in international and intercultural contexts' (2008: 185).

In a nutshell, ICit means that students develop knowledge, skills and attitudes related to intercultural communicative competence combined with an action component, or 'active citizenship', which means that students use their intercultural communicative competence (ICC) to address a societal problem of their choice. The ICit framework has been applied in numerous contexts, ranging from early language and elementary immersion programs to post-secondary language classrooms. Units developed by educators who collaborated in international projects showed that ICit education lends itself to investigate social justice and human rights issues (Byram *et al.*, 2017). Wagner *et al.* (2019) also emphasized the meaningful relationship between ICit and social justice education by listing the following characteristics of ICit:

- a concern about social justice and a belief in the values of humanistic thought and act,
- a readiness to encourage a questioning attitude which recognizes the positive and negative in a social group's beliefs, values and behaviors when evaluated against humanistic standards,
- and a willingness to promote social action in the world and the creation of identification with others beyond the limits of national boundaries. (Wagner *et al.*, 2019: 24)

In the next section we explore some of the common tenets of education for ICit and social justice education (SJE).

Common tenets of education for ICit and SJE

Osborn (2006: 29) describes social justice education as a 'framework for inquiry, not a pedagogical end in itself' and Nieto (2010: 46) refers to SJE as a 'philosophy, an approach, and actions that embody treating all people with fairness, respect, dignity, and generosity'. A helpful framework comes from Nieto (2018) in the way she conceptualizes multicultural education, noting '[b]ecause it uses critical pedagogy as its underlying philosophy and focuses on knowledge, reflection, and action (praxis) as the basis for social change, multicultural education promotes democratic principles of social justice' (2018: 31). In other words, as described by Nieto, multicultural education is social justice education (and, as she points out, also antiracist education). Moreover, as can be seen in the quotes above from Nieto, the components mentioned – i.e. knowledge, reflection, and action – align with the framework of ICit.

Osborn (2016) also lists several features of SJE that can readily be compared to important aspects of ICit:

- Teaching world languages for social justice is not the end (in the sense of a goal) of education; it is the beginning. The world is changed by teaching world languages for social justice—that becoming the goal of teaching and learning.
- Teaching world languages for social justice is not linear, it is recursive.
- Teaching world languages for social justice involves inquiry *with* (not about or on) the students and the community, which may be focused on problems.
- Teaching world languages for social justice does not elevate action above listening. Learning to hear those around us is not a passive skill, it is activism.
- Teaching world languages for social justice is connected to other, broader social movements.
- Teaching world languages for social justice is not conforming; it is confrontational.

(Osborn, 2016: 31–36).

Osborn and Wagner (2023) consider SJE and ICit education 'two sides of the same coin' and pointed out that all these tenets of SJE are well connected with tenets of ICit. It would go beyond the scope of the current chapter to provide more detail about each of the connections. Teaching for ICit aims to have an impact on the student and the world beyond the immediate goals of language teaching; learning to engage in intercultural dialogue and become an intercultural citizen is a life-long process; teaching for ICit involves engagement and listening to the community; ICit education also disrupts beliefs of what are norms and it connects to societal problems and social movements.

Additionally, as both approaches clearly require educators to acknowledge the political (but not partisan political) nature of teaching for ICit and SJE, educators who teach through this philosophy reject the myth of neutrality in teaching (see also Kubota, 2016) . They also reflect critically on practices in language education that can be harmful to students as the practices perpetuate views that exclude or exoticize parts of the population, as will be explored in more detail below.

That critical reflection or constant development of critical cultural awareness, in our opinion, is an important prerequisite for and link between SJE and ICit education. Some topics for educators' reflection include their positionality, which can be a difficult task. Preliminary analysis of a study that investigates the affordances and challenges of teaching with critical approaches shows that educators teaching through critical approaches often struggle with the challenges of others or their own doubts concerning their positionality (Osborn & Wagner, unpublished manuscript). Developing critical cultural awareness also requires constant interrogations of our own biases, reactions and actions. This in turn entails accepting our vulnerabilities. Ideally, then, teaching for ICit that acknowledges the important connections with SJE enables teachers to '... promote criticality in that educators enable students to reflect critically on language, discourse, and culture with regard to power and inequality' (Byram & Wagner, 2018: 147). The ultimate goal is to use education for students to find their place as active and critical citizens.

The connections between SJE and aspects of intercultural competence have also been pointed out in the context of dual language education (DLE), a form of bilingual education that promotes grade-level academic achievement, bilingualism and biliteracy, and sociocultural competence (SCC). In DLE, researchers suggest that practitioners use the social justice standards to promote SCC in their students. In fact, Manuela is involved in a study in which a research team is developing a measure of SCC that integrates intercultural competence via the Reference Framework of Competences for Democratic Culture (RFCDC) (Council of Europe, 2018), sociopolitical awareness, and the social justice standards in addition to a wide body of related bodies of literature. The research team made the decision to combine intercultural competence and the social justice standards because they also saw (1) strong connections between these concepts and (2) the necessity for teachers and students to understand them to foster their own identities and understand and respect those around them.

This goes to show that SJE and education for ICit not only have common tenets but, as we intend to illustrate in this chapter, can be applied in practice to (1) teach world languages (WL) for all students (i.e. to sustain our students' diverse backgrounds and open them up to exploring their diverse identities and those of others); (2) break down borders, both between subjects and disciplines and those between communities, locally, nationally and internationally; (3) disrupt hurtful myths (e.g. related to language education, but also linguistic, cultural, societal, etc.) and understand the role of power in intercultural dialogue; and (4) help students gain the knowledge, skills and attitudes to address issues of injustice.

In the following section we share some examples of how language educators can use frameworks from SJE and ICit in different contexts.

Moving from theory to practice: Activities for engaging students in social justice and intercultural citizenship

Hackman (2005) identified five components for effectively adopting a SJ approach to teaching and felt that work in any of the five components would be beneficial but that, when combined, all five together would provide an environment in which SJE could thrive. Hackman's five components include (1) content mastery, (2) tools for critical analysis, (3) tools for social change, (4) tools for personal reflection and (5) an awareness of multicultural group dynamics that connects the other four components together. Although Hackman's framework is not related to world language teaching specifically, it provides a strong foundation for considering activities that would ensure that teachers are working toward all five components. Social justice standards do exist and were developed by Learning for Justice (2018); those standards have four domains: identity, diversity, justice and action, all of which can be met through this framework from Hackman. The framework focuses more on the teacher's approach to integrating social justice education into the classroom and curriculum and less on specific standards.

While we will not analyze connections between Hackman's (2005) approach and ICit education in detail, it is clear that the frameworks complement each other. Hackman's *content mastery and factual information* can be found in the *knowledge* dimension in ICit; *Tools for critical analysis* and *tools for personal reflection* are represented throughout ICit but perhaps most prominently in *critical cultural awareness; multicultural group dynamics* clearly play an important role in ICit; finally, *tools for action and social change* are reflected in the *action in the community* dimension of ICit.

Concepts from Glynn *et al.*'s (2018) work around social justice in world language education (WLE) and Wagner *et al.*'s (2019) work around ICit can be used to build on Hackman's framework to merge world language teaching approaches and the World-Readiness Standards (ACTFL, 2015) with components of SJE and the development of ICit. Glynn *et al.* (2018) describe how the Communication Standards can be used to dialogue about and listen to a variety of perspectives and viewpoints within the class and in materials and resources from outside of the class, necessitating the importance of cultivating a classroom community where civil discourse and careful listening can take place. An awareness of multicultural group dynamics is key to this community: therefore Glynn *et al.* (2018) and Wagner *et al.* (2019) underscore the value of both teachers and students reflecting on and understanding their own identities and how their identities intersect. Wagner *et al.* (2019) note that although teachers are concerned about how students might communicate and dialogue about more complex topics, they believe that with mediation and effective scaffolds, it is possible. The ACTFL Cultures Standards and Connections Standards serve as a framework for employing critical thinking, accessing diverse perspectives, drawing on knowledge from other content areas, and engaging in critical analysis of topics and resources in order to understand the perspectives and experiences of others (Glynn *et al.*, 2018). Wagner *et al.* (2019) posit that students can become ethnographers in this process, knowing that it is acceptable to have more questions than answers. Additionally, teaching for SJ and ICit is interdisciplinary in nature: 'Applying content-based language instruction (CBI) approaches, there is no limit regarding the topics that can be covered in our classes and connections that can be made with other subjects and with the real world' (Wagner *et al.*, 2019: 11). The Comparisons Standards are necessary for reflecting on one's own identities, background and experiences as they relate to the identities, backgrounds and experiences of individuals and groups within the target cultures (Glynn *et al.*, 2018). In teaching for ICit, it is important that students be able to compare their own experiences, issues and actions taking place in their communities with experiences, issues and actions in communities other than their own (Wagner *et al.*, 2019). Lastly, the Community Standards pave the way for action through collaboration and interaction with others in a variety of contexts and communities at home and in target cultures (Glynn *et al.*, 2018). This is where ICit is put into practice as students investigate solutions and develop a plan for action that would have a positive impact on communities in a variety of contexts, whether it be within their own school, the community near the school, their home communities, or communities further away (Wagner *et al.*, 2019).

As we merge teaching for SJ and for ICit, we suggest five types of activities that will allow us to put these concepts and theories into practice: (1) activities for understanding the role of identity; (2) activities for critical analysis of topics and resources; (3) activities for dialogue and listening; (4) activities for developing the agency to act; and (5) activities for reflection. We now describe each of these activities in further detail and, in the section thereafter, we provide examples of what these types of activities might look like at different proficiency levels.

Activities for understanding the role of identity

ICit asks students to develop an understanding of their social responsibility as citizens of their communities, and teachers play a distinct role in that process of encouraging learners to become involved in their communities (Wagner *et al.*, 2019). In the process, students examine a variety of complex topics in different cultural contexts, and stereotypes and prejudice can arise. In both teaching for SJ and ICit, we are asking students to engage in dialogue with diverse perspectives. It is vital therefore that students and teachers understand their frames of reference: 'Each of us enters into the classroom with unique perspectives about the world that are informed by our ethnicity, sexuality, religion, socioeconomic status, place of origin and current residence, political views, education, age, immigration status, home language(s), and other dimensions' (Glynn *et al.*, 2018: 16).

We suggest engaging students in target language activities that allow them to explore their own identities, and we recommend that teachers engage in these activities alongside their students. In these activities, it is also important to help students to reflect upon and to articulate their current engagement in the different communities to which they belong. We always try to get to know our students and help our students get to know each other first. Too often we emphasize 'the target language identities', whatever that may be, instead of really seeing who the students in our classrooms are. In our opinion, this attitude also has a negative impact on student recruitment as it offers a view of language education that can be considered 'elitist' and exclusionary rather than what we clearly intend: language education in which all students are welcome and work together to investigate, understand and sustain their diverse identities. In many contexts that means plurilingual and pluricultural identities. The Council of Europe (2020) considers plurilingualism an important component of the competences for democratic culture. noting that plurilingualism does not merely mean speaking multiple languages but bringing 'the whole of one's linguistic equipment into play' (2020: 30), among other characteristics (see also the concept of translanguaging: Flores, 2016; García & Li, 2014). Similarly, pluricultural attitudes allow us to use all our cultural repertoire (for more information see Council of Europe, 2001).

At a conference, Manuela learned about an easy activity for classrooms in which there are students with multiple home languages: We can ask students to use the home language – whatever that might be and whether the teacher understands the language or not – to write a sentence (in elementary school) or a paragraph (from middle school on) about a topic of the student's choice and to share it in class. Although the student reflected upon and/or journaled about the topic in their home language, the student then has the opportunity to explain a word, a concept, a custom, something that is important to them, in the target language. The teacher can provide sentence frames to scaffold the language for the students to allow them to share it with everyone. The activity does not take much time and, when done well, celebrates different aspects of students' lives at home that they otherwise might not be inclined to share, especially since our educational system often prioritizes the dominant language and neglects the students' home languages.

Activities for addressing the role of identity can meet a variety of World-Readiness Standards. It is possible that students are reading or listening to profiles of people with diverse identities and backgrounds, engaging in interpretive communication. Students will also likely share details about their own and other's identities, using interpersonal and presentational communication. These kinds of activities are also an effective way to meet school and global communities as it is possible to invite guest presenters into the classroom to share about themselves and provide another diverse point of view.

Activities for a critical analysis of topics and resources

Glynn *et al.* (2018) suggest using the 3 Ps (products, practices and perspectives) for taking a critical eye to topics and resources. Let us consider how we might use the 3 Ps for engaging in a critical analysis of cultural topics and for understanding one's individual role in a community. Products: Food is a typical cultural topic in any given world language class. However, rather than just learning about traditional foods, where to buy foods, and eating habits, a teacher might focus on a community's efforts to grow and eat sustainable food sources or on access to fresh food in communities, depending on where one lives. A product then becomes much more than just learning *about* a certain product: rather, students examine how a community engages with a particular product, how the product impacts groups of people within a community, and how access to the product can vary among communities. Practices: practices may be 'issues that arise from how people interact' (Glynn *et al.*, 2018: 9). Returning to the example of access to food, students can explore how individuals and groups of people address issues of access: chefs in communities turn to sustainable food sources and, in some cases, revitalize Indigenous and cultural sources of food; groups of people develop community gardens to combat food deserts in their communities; organizations in communities develop strategies for providing food to those struggling with housing and food insecurity. Finally, perspectives: perspectives may be 'issues stemming from attitudes and values' (Glynn *et al.*, 2018: 9). Students might explore how perspectives about access to food in general, and access to fresh food, are influenced by socioeconomic status and demographics or how colonization has impacted sustainable food sources in communities.

Using the 3 Ps as a guide, teachers can engage students in a variety of critical analysis activities. One option is problem-posing in which students pose questions about cultural products, practices and/or perspectives from their own culture and other cultures. Wagner *et al.* (2019) suggest that students can be ethnographers as they examine topics, asking more questions than they provide answers. In order to engage in critical analysis, students must first gather information from a variety of sources and perspectives. Then, students identify the way in which different individuals or groups interact with products in communities and/or engage in practices and action in communities. Next, they interpret how these products and practices affect the perspectives and experiences of individuals and groups within different communities, by developing hypotheses, drawing conclusions and posing questions. As a last step, they evaluate their interpretations by comparing their own perspectives and experiences with those in their own communities and in other communities. The initial gathering of information and engaging with it – i.e. suspending judgment until we have more knowledge and hopefully have become aware of the complexity of an issue (fostering interpreting and relating, discovery and interaction, attitudes, and knowledge dimensions of Byram, 1997, 2021) – is an important component of being able to develop critical cultural awareness where students are asked to use evidence and reasoning to make a judgment.

Regarding the World-Readiness Standards, these types of activities clearly address the culture standards: Relating Cultural Products to Perspectives and Relating Cultural Practices to Perspectives. Students also have an important opportunity with activities for critical analysis to engage in interpretive communication and build their interpretive reading, listening and viewing skills. Further, they are able to interact with a variety of authentic resources of different genres, meeting the Acquiring Information and Diverse Perspectives standard. Finally, there are possibilities to meet the Cultural Comparisons standard as students are using the 3 Ps to critically examine a variety of topics.

Activities for dialogue and listening

Suspending judgment and using the skills of interpreting and relating (Byram, 1997, 2021) seems to be more important than ever since there is some evidence that it might become harder to engage with people who have different opinions as can be seen in the many divisive issues introduced above. There are numerous helpful activities and frameworks used to teach the skills necessary to engage in dialogue. Sarrouf (2022) provides a number of tools to invite all students to share their reflections. For example, rather than asking a question and expecting an immediate answer, students are asked to reflect on the question and write about it for two minutes. Sarrouf also suggests time-limited speaking so that every student has a chance to speak and to be listened to. Other tools are to agree on a pause between speakers to honor and reflect on what has been said. Finally, the 'go-round', in which students know that they each go in order and share their comments, helps them listen to one another as they do not need to think of a way to 'get the floor'.

Often, when we think about dialogue for the purpose of discussing complex topics, we think about preparing students to engage in civil discourse. United States Courts (n.d.) provide a roadmap for teachers to set ground rules for civil discourse with their students. One example they provide underscores the importance of relying on the truth, using a non-aggressive tone, controlling facial expressions, being attentive to others' points of view, and using a variety of evidence to make one's points. However, it is also important to note that calls for civility have been used as a form of oppression 'to avoid difficult conversations – particularly about race – or to mask acts and policies that denigrate marginalized populations' (Dillard, 2018: para. 5). Before we ask our students to engage in civil discourse, we need to interrogate what is meant by a 'non-aggressive' tone or controlled facial expressions. Who decides what is non-aggressive or which facial expression is civil? Dillard (2018) suggests that it is vital to differentiate between civility and politeness and to focus on respect for others' identities, needs and beliefs. In doing so, teachers can also help students to understand the history behind how calls for civility have silenced voices and have been used as a tool of power. As a class, the teacher and students can work together to create a class charter and to agree on norms that do not silence voices in the classroom and do not serve to control reactions in order to make those with more privilege feel safer as the class navigates complex topics.

Finally, it is vital that students (and the teacher) learn to 'listen with intention' (Howell, 2020). Howell (2020) proffers that in order for students to feel safe to share their perspectives and experiences, the teacher needs to model this for them by sharing their own perspectives and experiences and by providing opportunities for students to practice receiving information from others. In this process of receiving, students have to be taught to take it in as 'true and valid' rather than debating it or rejecting it because it does not match their own experiences (Howell, 2020: para. 9). Howell (2020) shares that students can practice demonstrating that they have received what their classmate told them by paraphrasing it back to them, taking the lead in doing so instead of the teacher paraphrasing. Another suggestion Howell (2020) makes for building the capacity to listen with intention is to have students share something about themselves and ask students to write down what they remember about each classmate. When they identify the classmates about whom they could not remember anything, the teacher can encourage them to seek out opportunities to get to know that person better and to learn something new about them. It allows them to see how carefully they were listening and to whose experiences or thoughts they were listening to most closely and could remember. Ultimately, practicing the skill of listening carefully and openly receiving information from others as true and valid takes practice as a class.

Of course, we also see that these activities are helpful for practicing skills that increase language acquisition, e.g. using language to argue, discuss, explain, describe, etc., while also developing discourse competence. Of the World-Readiness Standards, students are most directly engaged in Interpersonal Communication; however, developing the ability to listen with intent and to engage in civil discourse also clearly meets the Lifelong Learning standard.

Activities for developing the agency to act

One of the key components of Hackman's (2005) SJE Framework is action. Additionally, Standard 20 under 'Action' in the Learning for Justice Social Justice standards reads: 'Students will plan and carry out collective action against bias and injustice in the world and will evaluate what strategies are most effective' (Learning for Justice, 2018). This connects directly with the action component in ICit in which students are asked to consider the role that they play in working toward equity and justice in the communities to which they belong. This requires students to identify steps that they can take to accomplish these goals. It is important to note that the component of action is perhaps the most elusive and difficult for teachers to imagine implementing but, in order to meet the goals of SJE and ICit, it is also vital.

Activities that include action can be conceptualized in a variety of ways. They might be activities that the class does together, which results in some kind of change, such as writing a petition or engaging in an activity to support members of a community in some way. It need not always be a case of a teacher leading the students in action: rather, the teacher can provide opportunities for students to practice steps for engaging in action. Activities such as the following could allow students to develop the agency to act: (1) writing social media posts to draw attention to an issue and to engage in discussion of the issue in a more public way; (2) engaging in hypothetical situations to identify steps they would take when they witness inequities, discrimination or injustice in their communities; (3) planning engagement in a protest about a topic about which they feel strongly; (4) creating public service announcements as a way of drawing attention to an issue.

These are just a few examples of how students can engage students in action, and they can and should be done in the target language, using a variety of scaffolds to allow students to feel successful. For example, in novice levels, students could be given multiple-choice options to identify steps for action, or they can be provided with sentence frames to help them create their social media posts. There are many possibilities, and as students gain confidence in understanding the role they can play in making a difference in their communities, they can take the lead on making suggestions for how they can take action. Ultimately, the most important thing is that teachers include actionable elements in their units and lessons so that students develop the capacity not just to identify injustice but also to act and address the injustice, even in small ways that will positively impact the communities to which they belong. In our experience, learning about what other communities have done and what had an impact can also help students feel empowered in their own contexts.

A variety of World-Readiness Standards can be met through activities for action, most notably Presentational Communication as students demonstrate their knowledge through action. However, Lifelong Learning is another key standard being met as students gain skills that have the potential to impact their own and others' lives within and outside the classroom.

Activities for reflection

Finally, activities for reflection are crucial as they are a necessary tool for students to develop critical cultural awareness, which is an important prerequisite for meaningful and thoughtful action in the community.

In other words, students need to have ample opportunity to reflect on their own biases and preconceptions, to learn what they know and what they do not know yet. Becoming aware of and acknowledging the complexity of issues lowers the risk of oversimplifying issues and of holding blind convictions and therefore can enable us to step back and be open to learning more about the topic at hand, which might in turn create conditions under which we are able to discuss issues from different perspectives rather than merely seeking confirmation or confrontation when facing difficult issues. Self-assessment and reflection also can be used to 'empower students by giving them responsibility for evaluating their own progress and encouraging them to question the bigger picture of how their perspective on social justice affects their work' (Osborn, 2006, as cited in Glynn *et al.*, 2018: 90).

Excellent activities for reflection include journaling, self-assessment of growth in understanding topics, and peer and group assessment. Glynn *et al.* (2018) and Wagner and Tracksdorf (2018) recommend that journaling take place frequently and should be ungraded and uncorrected in order to encourage students to just write what they are thinking and feeling without worrying about accuracy. They can be encouraged to translanguage, using all their linguistic capabilities to express themselves, writing in one language or multiple languages. Journaling can also take place in the form of vlogs, blogs and podcasts (Glynn *et al.*, 2018). Another example related to the concept of journaling is the *Autobiography of Intercultural Encounters* (Byram *et al.*, 2009) that guides students to think and write about an encounter they had with someone from a different cultural background. Two further tools have since been made available: the *Autobiography of Intercultural Encounters through Visual Media* (AIEVM) and the *Autobiography of Intercultural Encounters through the Internet* (AIETI). All three tools come in two versions, for older and younger learners, and can be found at https://www.coe.int/en/web/autobiography-intercultural-encounters. By asking students to reflect on an intercultural encounter, students develop their intercultural competence further. Thereby, in addition to providing information related to assessment, portfolios also help students and teachers see the progress of students over time, thereby documenting how students think about topics at specific times and how their perspectives might have changed if a portfolio is used over a longer period of the student's education.

In addition to journaling, self-assessments can be a powerful tool for both students and teachers to better understand the gains they made in grasping the content. One example includes self-assessments that are aligned with the social justice objectives of the lessons. Teachers can ask students directly about the extent to which they were able to internalize the content and make sense of it. Prompts like 'If I had to explain [insert concept] to a friend who doesn't take this class, I'd know what to say' can be used and students can be given forced-choice items in order to respond to the prompt (Glynn *et al.*, 2018: 91). Open-ended questions should also be included in self-assessments to allow students to write more about their thoughts and consider things that surprised them, areas where they grew, action they could take, and things that were interesting and challenging in the unit (Glynn *et al.*, 2018).

The World-Readiness Standards are perhaps more difficult to attain with these kinds of activities as we do not require students to use the target language to engage in reflection. Students, no matter their proficiency level, often hit their ceiling with the language and benefit from being able to reflect about complex feelings and topics in the language with which they are most comfortable, or with a variety of languages or images in order to best express themselves.

Putting the Activities into Practice: Examples from a Novice Unit

Although we acknowledge that many teachers do not use a textbook, there is still a significant number of programs that rely on the scope and sequence of a textbook to determine the types and order of thematic units. In order to illustrate how these theoretical frameworks can be put into practice, we have chosen to focus on a novice mid to novice high unit from a first-year language class. Often, a first-year textbook encompasses topics that include greetings, descriptions of people, careers, school, family, things in the home, weather, ordering in a restaurant and shopping for food, transportation, staying in a hotel and traveling, and sometimes, depending on the textbook, environment and media. We like the idea of choosing one overarching theme to focus on for the entire year and fitting each of the individual thematic units under that overarching theme. Taking into account our desire to develop units around both social justice goals and ICit, we have, therefore, chosen the overarching theme of migration. If a first-year class focused on the topic of migration, it would be possible to still get at the scope and sequence by focusing on identity, languages (majority and minority languages and power and language), stereotypes, geography, climate and weather, clothing, housing, food and transportation and travel. However, by focusing on migration and integrating SJE and ICit into each of these topics, we are able to come at a typical scope and sequence from a different angle that will allow us to meet our goals and dig more deeply into typical topics with students. After identifying our overarching topic, we must develop essential questions that can be understood in the target language by students. Some examples of possible 'essential questions'[1] are as follows:

- Who migrates? Why do people migrate?
- How does movement affect the lives of people around the world in different contexts?

These essential questions can be used to drive the unit, and we suggest returning to them regularly with the class to answer and discuss them as the class keeps learning new information that could inform how they answer the question(s). Well-designed essential questions are aimed at 'uncovering the depth and richness of a topic that might otherwise by obscured by simply covering it' (McTighe & Wiggins, 2013: 3). Cassandra had a graduate student who discovered the power of an essential question with a French class. The graduate student kept the essential question 'What is worth fighting for?' front and center in her unit on revolutions and, as students examined revolutions and protests around the world from historical and contemporary perspectives, they kept returning to the question, answering it in different ways as they gained new ideas and understandings. Eventually, the students began asking their own questions, such as 'Does someone have to die in order for it to be considered a revolution?'. This French teacher discovered that the essential question caused her class to engage and think more deeply, and she was more encouraged than ever before to use essential questions to drive the unit. Manuela, in her role as co-director of the German Language and Culture Program at her university, co-designed the program in such a way that each semester students individually, or in small groups, think about how they wish to address the essential question throughout the semester. Reflections in the form of journals, homework and group work, guide students to make connections between each unit and the essential question. Individualized research helps students gain new knowledge from different perspectives. A midterm and a final in the form of an integrated performance assessment (IPA) prepare students for their final project in which they apply their ICC in an action project, hence engaging in an ICit project.

In this section, we provide one example of how a year-long ICit sequence of a first-year world language course can be planned (see Table 1.1). We provide thematic units that are usually covered during a first-year world language class and present related topics that students can consider using their critical thinking. We will show how the dimensions of ICC (attitudes of open mindedness, tolerance of ambiguity, and creativity; knowledge; skills of interpreting and relating; skills of discovery and interaction; and critical cultural awareness) can be used to transform typical topics.

Finally, we will connect ICC with: (1) understanding the role of identity; (2) critical analysis of topics and resources; (3) dialogue and listening; (4) developing the agency to act; and (5) reflection. Although we provide one example of each at a novice mid to novice high proficiency level, these examples can be adapted to other proficiency levels. Also, there are many possibilities for each of these five activities, and our examples, too, may need to be adapted to fit the needs of teachers' own students and teaching contexts. In Table 1.1, column 1 provides an overview of typical textbook topics in first-year language, column 2 lists the transformed topics in which students used their ICC, which they also applied in the examples of the five activities we share in column 3. After each topic, we share reflection questions that help students think critically about the topics and that also guide students to connect what they learn with the essential question. The reflection questions can also serve to remind students to think about the action component they plan for the end of the year.

In this next section, we expand on the ideas above and share some examples of activities that prepare students for their ICit project toward the end of the year. Although these descriptions of possible activities are not extensive, and we only focus on three of the topics above (greetings and names; geography, climate and weather; descriptions of people), they provide snapshots that can give teachers an understanding of how the theoretical framework we shared can be implemented in practice.

Greetings and names

This unit can start as world language units often start: with greetings used in the target language. We strongly recommend exposing students to a number of different regional varieties as well as greetings with different levels of formality. There are many resources available online. For example, Langmedia (https://langmedia.fivecolleges.edu/) offers different greetings in a number of different languages being taught. Showing greetings in different contexts of the target language lends itself to practicing such greetings and getting a feeling for language variation from the very beginning. This is also an opportunity to do an Identity Activity to explore how one's identity influences greetings the students use in different contexts. These can be influenced by age, occupation, status, and even home languages. In some countries, second-generation immigrants have melded multiple languages together that are used in their community to communicate with each other, including using different greetings.

Reflection Activities at the end of class or in a journal at home can help elicit students' impressions of language variation and can also help them think about the role of greetings in their own contexts. These activities also practice the ICC dimensions of interpreting and relating, knowledge, as well as attitudes of curiosity, open mindedness and tolerance of ambiguity. Manuela loves using journals in which students reflect in the target language, but also in other languages of their choice to reflect more deeply on the topics covered in class. Students can think critically at any age and proficiency level but they cannot always express complex thoughts in the target language. Journals can get students interested and find out more information which they can then share in

Table 1.1 Example of a year-long ICit sequence for a first-year world language course

Year-long overarching theme: Migration
Essential question (EQ): How does movement affect the lives of people around the world in different contexts?

Typical Textbook Topics in First-year Language	Transformed Topics	ICC activities
Greetings and names (pronouns)	identity, power, language awareness, gender	• Identity • Critical analysis of topics and resources • Reflection

Reflection questions related to EQ:
• How does our name reflect our cultural background and heritage?
• How does naming and being misnamed and misgendered influence our identity?
• How do different regional greetings reflect or represent different communities?
• How does how we greet others create community and connections?
• How does moving to or living in a different context influence names?

Geography, climate, weather	sustainable activities, climate change and comparisons, (in)equity, natural catastrophes, climate refugees, languages, topography, important landmarks	• Identity • Critical analysis of topics and resources • Developing the agency to act • Reflection

Reflection questions related to EQ:
• How does climate change affect people?
• How is climate change related to issues of equity and justice?
• How does climate change affect migration?
• What do people in different parts of the world do to combat climate change?

Descriptions of people	gender, sexuality, religion, cultural and linguistic backgrounds, race and ethnicity, stereotypes, clothing, hobbies and sports, likes and dislikes, influence of culture and identities on preferences and participation in hobbies/sports	• Identity • Critical analysis of topics and resources • Dialogue and listening • Developing the agency to act • Reflection

Reflection questions related to EQ:
• What is the relationship between our appearance and our identities?
• How do our identities influence our preferences and activities?
• How do our identities and cultural backgrounds influence how we present ourselves to the world?
• How do our perspectives influence how we describe people's appearances?
• What stereotypes are there concerning people's appearances?
• What consequences can these stereotypes have on minoritized groups of people in different cultures?

Family, friends and home	gender roles in homes, cultural and linguistic backgrounds, linking back to geography and stereotypes about homes in different parts of the world, circles of care, meaning of 'home'	• Identity • Critical analysis of topics and resources • Dialogue and listening • Developing the agency to act • Reflection

Reflection questions related to EQ:
- How do the people in our circles of care influence our identities?
- What role does gender play in homes in different cultures?
- How do stereotypes influence how we think about homes in our own and other cultures?
- What differences are there between life at home and life at school?
- What does home mean to people in different cultures and contexts?
- What is the role of language and culture in the different contexts we live?

Careers and school	socioeconomic status and prejudice, cultural values related to work and spare time, unseen/unsung heroes in our communities, who does what kind of work in different cultures and why, access to education	• Identity • Critical analysis of topics and resources • Dialogue and listening • Developing the agency to act • Reflection

Reflection questions related to EQ:
- What is the role of work in the contexts you know?
- What did you learn about the role of work in the cultural contexts you researched?
- Who are the workers in our communities who are overlooked or undervalued? How do they contribute to our communities?
- How does culture influence the way in which different kinds of careers are valued or not valued?
- What kinds of barriers prevent students from our community and communities around the world from gaining an education?
- What kinds of practices in schools benefit students and which ones marginalize students? Which practices are fair or unfair?

Transportation and travel	availability and cost of public transportation (infrastructure), sustainability and tourism, sustainability and transport, engaging responsibly with other cultures	• Identity • Critical analysis of topics and resources • Dialogue and listening • Developing the agency to act • Reflection

Reflection questions related to EQ:
- How can one prepare to engage responsibly and ethically with other cultures, whether one is traveling close to home or further away?
- How can we cause the least amount of damage to areas we visit?
- What impact does travel and/or transportation have on climate and geography? (returning to a previous topic)
- What do cultures around the world with travel destinations do to promote sustainable tourism? How can tourists aid them in this process?
- What are the reasons why one chooses to travel and one is forced to travel?

Possible Action Components	• Students create and disseminate information on their topic on a webpage or with pamphlets, by giving presentations • Students can decide to organize an awareness day on their topic together with other classes or community members • Students can organize an event with an action, e.g. a food drive or volunteering with an organization that helps immigrants to their community to settle • The class, as a whole, could partner with classes of English learners or newcomers in their district to build relationships • Students can write to their administration about an issue related to naming and pronouns or lack of representation in case they identified issues of inequity • College students could decide to write to their representative in government and demand action on an issue: for example, related to the environment.

class in the target language with scaffolding by the teacher. Sample reflection questions include: How do you greet different people in your life, whatever the language is? Can the wrong greeting have negative consequences in different contexts? What special greeting could we have in class?

In class, the students can engage in an interpersonal activity to discuss the greetings they use in different contexts in their own lives using a graphic organizer with a partner. They can compare notes and see visually the different kinds of greetings they use. The teacher can facilitate a conversation about how different kinds of greetings can build community in different ways and lead the students in a negotiation of a new, special greeting in the target language they would like to develop to use just in their class. This lesson could not only lead to community building in the classroom, but also to build awareness about the importance and diversity of greetings. The teacher can provide scaffolding so that students can give reasons for their choices.

Geography, climate, weather

The role of geographical location as it relates to stereotypes and (in)justice can be examined at multiple points in the first year. Interesting combinations with geography include climate, weather, and related topics such as climate change, sustainability, natural catastrophes and climate refugees. In most textbook sequences, numbers are covered early on. As soon as students know the numbers, they can analyze statistics in the target language and talk about complex topics without having to know much grammar or vocabulary. Students can interpret and create infographics, for example. We find these tools (numbers, pictures and visual representations such as mind maps, etc.) helpful when we want to scaffold critical thinking about topics in the target language.

Throughout this unit on geography, climate and weather, students can engage in a Critical Analysis of Resources. For example, after students are introduced to the weather, they can analyze how the temperatures have changed over the past 100 years. They can look at statistics of refugees related to climate and can think about locations that are in danger due to climate change. Students can research a related topic of their choice outside class and bring interesting facts to class. When Manuela taught beginning German at university level, her students were at first surprised to find themselves analyzing statistics but they soon brought up interesting facts and numbers related to the topics they learned about in class. With the teacher's help, students can present their findings in a couple of sentences or in the form of a visual in class. This can be done in group work, to promote more interaction, or as short presentations in front of the whole class. Students who are listening to the presentation should have tasks, such as deciding what was surprising to them, what they already know, etc.

This topic also lends itself well to Developing the Agency to Act. Students can do a gallery walk to examine simple profiles, with pictures of people around the world who are taking steps to address climate change. After completing a comprehension guide as they walk through the gallery of change makers, they can debrief, and the teacher can provide scaffolded questions via a technology tool, such as Mentimeter or Peardeck, that will allow students to consider steps they can take to address climate change. To scaffold the language for the students, the teacher might provide options for students in a multiple-choice format, providing a menu of good ideas for taking action in small and large ways from which students can select. One of Manuela's students, for example, went plastic-free for a month, which meant she decided to avoid using plastic for a whole month, documenting the experience and providing recommendations for those who want to limit their use of plastic.

Descriptions of people

In a first-year language class, students can often be seen building their repertoire of adjectives to describe people, places and things. As the students are learning adjectives to describe themselves and others, the teacher can ask them to complete an Identity Activity such as Circles of My Multicultural Self (Gorski, n.d.) that includes Reflection Activities that can be done both in English and in the target language, depending on the activity. These reflection questions ask students to tell a story about a time when they were proud to be associated with one of their identifiers and a time when they felt misunderstood. This is a good Identity and Reflection Activity for a journal. The next step is for students to write 'I am (a/an) _____, but I am not (a/an) _____' (Gorski, n.d.).

In pairs or small groups, students tell their stories about when they were proud to be associated with an identifier and when it was difficult to be associated with an identifier. At a novice level, sharing their stories likely would need to be done in English, but it is also a time to practice Dialogue and Listening. Before sharing their stories, the teacher would need to prepare the class by reviewing the class norms for dialogue and listening and by helping the class to generate some questions they could ask each other about their stories or some responses they could make in order to help others in their group feel heard. Then, the students can share their 'I am _____, I am not _____' statements in the target language, and they can respond to each other using gambits in the target language provided by the teacher.

This can be followed with a Critical Analysis of Resources. There are a number of projects around the world that have been created to address stereotypes, and many of these projects use images and signs to disrupt stereotypes or encourage people to look beyond the surface. One example is a project called 'Ich bin anders als du denkst' [I am different than you think] (Wir Sind die Zukunft, 2018). This project, for example, has a gallery of signs created by children, teenagers and adults that include statements such as 'Ich bin Ausländer aber kann gut Deutsch' [I am an immigrant but can speak German well] and 'Ich sitze im Rollstuhl aber habe dadurch viele besondere Menschen kennengelernt' [I am in a wheelchair but have met many special people because of it]. This critical analysis could be followed by further Reflection, asking students to journal about how stereotypes affect not only them but also other people in their circles of care and in their communities.

Next, the students could create their own signs and take pictures to make their own gallery, similar to projects that have been undertaken around the world. To expand it beyond their classroom, they could share the gallery with the school and create a large bulletin board space outside the classroom – on the walls, for example – to hang their signs and encourage other students to stop and add their own statements, in whatever language they would like. This could be a first step in Developing the Agency to Act and to disrupt stereotypes in the spaces in which they learn, work and live.

Next Steps and Moving Forward

As with anything new that we try in the classroom, it is important first to step back and examine and reflect on our current practices. Teachers should ask themselves the following questions:

(1) What am I already doing that meets the goals of SJE and ICit?
(2) Which of the five activities am I already doing well with students?
(3) How can I draw on what I am already doing with students to strengthen SJE and ICit in the units and lessons I am teaching?

Although this chapter is full of ideas that may be new to you, we want you to begin by acknowledging the things you are already doing with students in the classroom that fit with the goals of SJE and ICit. As a teacher, it is possible to build from there to strengthen connections to SJE and ICit.

Next, begin with just one curricular unit that you teach and examine it carefully. It is extremely difficult and time-intensive to make changes across multiple units at one time without beginning to feel overwhelmed. Give yourself permission to take one step at a time in your units and lessons; there is no need to throw out everything and start over from the beginning. If you choose one unit with which you feel comfortable and enjoy teaching, examine your unit themes and goals: How can you adapt these to better fit SJE and ICit? Then, examine your assessments: How do those assessments allow you to see that your students are meeting the SJE and ICit goals? Finally, examine your current activities: Which activities can you keep? Which activities can you adapt to better fit the goals?

We also strongly recommend that you collaborate with colleagues. Ideally, you can plan curriculum with colleagues and discuss your ideas with each other. We find that units always come out better when we collaborate with colleagues: (1) more people are likely to have more ideas; (2) collaborators can ask critical questions and we can think through answering them and finding solutions for possible problems; (3) it's just much more fun! If you cannot collaborate on the whole unit, we still suggest talking to colleagues about your unit to benefit from the points we mentioned at least in some way. Collaboration with teachers of other subjects would be wonderful for interdisciplinary units.

Finally, know that it will not be perfect the first time you try new things: some things may not work well with your students or you might make some missteps when navigating more complex topics with your students. Do not give up when an activity flops or you make some mistakes. This is part of the process. Step back and reflect on the activity and consider how you could improve it when you try it again. We would even go as far as to say that, in many of our projects, what seemed bumps in the road turned out to be the best learning opportunities.

Note

(1) 'Essential questions' are open-ended, provocative questions that encourage inquiry and are used to guide units and lessons. Good essential questions lead to more questions and stimulate careful thought among students (McTighe & Wiggins, 2013).

References

ACTFL (American Council on the Teaching of Foreign Languages) Guiding principles: Facilitating target language use. Retrieved from https://www.actfl.org/resources/guiding-principles-language-learning/target-language (Accessed 1 June 2022).

Becker, D., Ludwig, C. and Summer, T. (2022) Taboos in ELT through the lens of critical pedagogy: A short introduction. *Teacher Development Academic Journal* 2 (2), 9–16.

Byram, M. (1997) *Teaching and Assessing Intercultural Communicative Competence.* Clevedon: Multilingual Matters.

Byram, M. (2008) *From Foreign Language Education to Education for Intercultural Citizenship: Essays and Reflections.* Clevedon: Multilingual Matters. https://doi.org/10.21832/9781847690807.

Byram, M. (2021) *Teaching and Assessing Intercultural Communicative Competence: Revisited* (2nd edn). Bristol: Multilingual Matters. See https://doi.org/10.21832/9781800410251.

Byram, M. and Wagner, M. (2018) Making a difference: Language teaching for intercultural and international dialogue. *Foreign Language Annals* 51 (1), 140–151.

Byram, M., Barrett, M., Ipgrave, J., Jackson, R. and Méndez García, M.C. (2009) *Autobiography of Intercultural Encounters*. Strasbourg: Council of Europe Publishing.

Byram, M., Golubeva, I., Han, H. and Wagner, M. (eds) (2017) *From Principles to Practice in Education for Intercultural Citizenship*. Bristol: Multilingual Matters.

Cammarata, L., Tedick, D. and Osborn, T. (2016) Curricular reforms and content-based instruction: Issues and goals. In L. Cammarata (ed.) *Content-Based Foreign Language Teaching: Curriculum and Pedagogy for Developing Advanced Thinking and Literacy Skills* (pp. 1–21). London: Routledge.

Conlon Perugini, D. and Wagner, M. (2022) Enacting social justice in world language education through intercultural citizenship. In B. Wassell and C. Glynn (eds) *Transforming World Language Teaching and Teacher Education for Equity and Justice: Pushing Boundaries in US Contexts* (pp. 41–64). Bristol: Multilingual Matters.

Council of Europe (2001) *Common European Framework of Reference for Languages: Learning, Teaching, Assessment (CEFR)*. Cambridge: Cambridge University Press. Available at www.coe.int/t/dg4/linguistic/source/framework_en.pdf (Accessed 13 June 2022).

Council of Europe (2018) *Reference Framework of Competences for Democratic Culture* [3 volumes]. Strasbourg: Council of Europe.

Council of Europe (2020) *Common European Framework of Reference for Languages: Learning, Teaching, Assessment: Companion Volume with New Descriptors*. Strasbourg: Council of Europe.

Dillard, C. (2018) Who decides what's civil? *Learning from Justice*, 1 August. Retrieved from https://www.learningforjustice.org/magazine/who-decides-whats-civil (Accessed 22 June 2022).

Ennser-Kananen, J. (2016) A pedagogy of pain: New directions for world language education. *Modern Language Journal* 100 (2), 556–564.

Flores, N. (2016) Combatting marginalized spaces in education through language architecture. *Perspectives in Urban Education* 13 (1), 1–3.

García, O. and Li, W. (2014) *Translanguaging: Language, Bilingualism and Education*. London: Palgrave Macmillan.

Glynn, C. and Wassell, B. (2018) Who gets to play? Issues of access and social justice in world language study in the U.S. *Dimension* (Spring), 18–32.

Glynn, C., Wesely, P. and Wassell, B. (2018) *Words and Actions: Teaching Languages through the Lens of Social Justice* (2nd edn). Alexandria, VA: ACTFL.

Glynn, C., Hines-Gaither, K. and Jenkins, T. (2022) Increasing black representation in languages: Lessons from the past and present. *The Language Educator* 17 (1), 40–44.

Gorski, P. (n.d.) *EdChange*. Retrieved from http://www.edchange.org/multicultural/activities/circlesofself.html (Accessed 22 June 2022).

Guillherme, M. (2000) Critical cultural awareness: The critical dimension in foreign culture education. Doctoral thesis, Durham University, School of Education, Durham, England.

Hackman, H. (2005) Five essential components for social justice education. *Equity & Excellence in Education* 38 (2), 103–109.

Hines-Gaither, K., Perez, N.S. and Torres Melendez, L. (2022) Voces invisibles: Disrupting the master narrative with Afro Latina counterstories. In B. Wassell and C. Glynn (eds) *Transforming World Language Teaching and Teacher Education for Equity and Justice: Pushing Boundaries in US Contexts* (pp. 85–102). Bristol: Multilingual Matters.

Howell, C. (2020) To sustain the tough conversations, active listening must be the norm. *Learning for Justice*, 12 November. Retrieved from https://www.learningforjustice. org/magazine/to-sustain-the-tough-conversations-active-listening-must-be-the-norm (Accessed 24 June 2022).

Journal of Blacks in Higher Education (2021) The Black percentage of all U.S. students who studied abroad took a big hit from the pandemic [Online]. Retrieved from https://www.jbhe.com/2021/11/the-black-percentage-of-all-u-s-students-who-studied-abroad-took-a-big-hit-from-the-pandemic/.

Kramsch, C. (2014) Teaching foreign languages in an era of globalization: Introduction. *Modern Languages Journal* 98 (1), 296–311. See https://doi. org/10.1111/j.1540- 4781.2014.12057.x.

Kubota, R (2016) The multi/plural turn, postcolonial theory, and neoliberal multicultural-ism: Complicities and implications for applied linguistics. *Applied Linguistics* 37 (4), 474–494.

Kumaravadivelu, B. (2003) A postmethod perspective on English language teaching. *World Englishes* 22 (4), 539–550. See https://doi.org/10.1111/j.1467-971X.2003.00317.x.

Learning for Justice (2018) *Social Justice Standards*. https://www.learningforjustice.org/ frameworks/social-justice-standards.

McTighe, J. and Wiggins, G. (2013) *Essential Questions: Opening Doors to Student Understanding*. Alexandria, VA: ASCD (Association for Supervision and Curriculum Development).

NAFSA: Association of International Educators (n.d.) Trends in U.S. study abroad [Online]. Retrieved from https://www.nafsa.org/policy-and-advocacy/policy-resources/ trends-us-study-abroad.

Nieto, S. (2010) *Language, Culture, and Teaching*. London: Routledge.

Nieto, S. (2018) *Language, Culture, and Teaching* (3rd edn). London: Routledge.

Osborn, T.A. (2006) *Teaching World Languages for Social Justice: A Sourcebook of Principles and Practices*. Mahwah, NJ: Lawrence Erlbaum.

Osborn, T. (2016) Architects wanted for professional remodeling: A response to Ennser–Kananen. *The Modern Language Journal* 100 (2), 568–570.

Osborn, T. and Wagner, M. (2023) Revisiting 'foreignness': Nationalism and language education. *Language and Intercultural Communication* 23 (3), 1–13. https://doi.org/ 10.1080/14708477.2023.2175847.

Redden, E. (2019) Study abroad numbers continue steady increase. *Inside Higher Ed*, 17 November. Retrieved from https://www.insidehighered.com/news/2019/11/18/ open-doors-data-show-continued-increase-numbers-americans-studying-abroad?v2.

Sarrouf, J. (2022) In pursuit of the dialogic classroom: Designing spaces for conviction. In A. Finger and M. Wagner (eds) *Bias, Belief, and Conviction in an Age of Fake Facts* (pp. 181–201). London: Routledge.

United States Courts (n.d.) Setting ground rules - Civil discourse and difficult decisions [Online]. Retrieved from https://www.uscourts.gov/educational-resources/educational-activities/setting-ground-rules-civil-discourse-and-difficult (Accessed 24 June 2022).

Wagner, M. (eds) (2022) *Bias, Belief, and Conviction in an Age of Fake Facts*. London: Routledge.

Wagner, M. and Tracksdorf, N. (2018) ICC online: Fostering the development of intercul-tural competence in virtual language classrooms. In M. Wagner, D. Conlon Perugini and M. Byram (eds) *Teaching Intercultural Competence Across the Age Range: From Theory to Practice* (pp. 135–154). Bristol: Multilingual Matters.

Wagner, M., Conlon Perugini, D. and Byram, M. (eds) (2018) *Teaching Intercultural Competence Across the Age Range: From Theory to Practice*. Bristol: Multilingual Matters.

Wagner, M., Cardetti, F. and Byram, M. (2019) *Teaching Intercultural Citizenship Across the Curriculum*. Alexandria, VA: ACTFL.

Wir Sind die Zukunft (2018) Foto Aktion: Ich bin anders als du denkst [Online]. Retrieved from: https://www.wir-sind-die-zukunft.net/aktionen/2018-foto-aktion/beitraege-ich-bin-anders-als-du-denkst/ (Accessed 22 June 2022).

Wooten, J., Randolph Jr, L.J. and Johnson, S.M. (2022) Enacting social justice in teacher education: Modeling, reflection, and critical engagement in the methods course. In B. Wassell and C. Glynn (eds) *Transforming World Language Teaching and Teacher Education for Equity and Justice: Pushing Boundaries in US Contexts* (pp. 179–202). Bristol: Multilingual Matters.

2 Developing a Professional Learning Community to Teach Arabic for Intercultural Citizenship

Donna Clementi, Salah Ayari and Manuela Wagner

Introduction

Concordia Language Villages is a nationally recognized language and cultural immersion program for language learners of all ages. Founded in 1961, it added professional development for world language educators in 1988, sharing how language learning is experienced throughout the day at the Language Villages along with implications for classroom instruction. In 2011 Salah Ayari, designer of the original Arabic Language Village curriculum, and Donna Clementi, a long-time staff member at Concordia Language Villages, introduced the first professional development program specifically for teachers of Arabic at the Language Villages. Ayari and Clementi proposed a program where Arabic educators at all levels of instruction from across the US could work collaboratively to explore how strategies, including immersion methodologies, could be applied to the teaching of Arabic. An important goal of the proposal was to break the isolation that Arabic teachers often feel when they are the only Arabic teacher in a school or at a particular level of instruction. Concordia Language Villages implemented the professional development proposal and received ongoing support from Qatar Foundation International.

The first workshops for teachers of Arabic (2011 and 2012) combined participation in a summer institute at the Center for Advanced Research in Language Acquisition (CARLA) at the University of Minnesota with participation in a summer session at Al-Waha, the Arabic Language Village. Starting in 2014, the workshops transitioned to professional learning communities (PLC) with two in-person workshops, one in the fall and one in the spring, and three related webinars to bridge the time between the fall and spring in-person workshops. Since inception, 150 Arabic language educators in grades K–16 from 30 different states have participated in the workshops. The participants represent a variety of K–12 education settings including public, magnet, private, religious, charter, independent, language immersion and Saturday schools. Post-secondary participants teach in public and private colleges, universities and community colleges. In the early years, priority was given to first-time participants in the workshops. Because many participants were interested in returning to continue their professional development, the emphasis shifted to balance first-time participants with returning participants. As of 2021, more than half the attendees have participated in two or more of the yearly workshop series.

Workshop themes selected each year by Ayari and Clementi emphasized new understandings of standards-based second language teaching and learning with application to Arabic classroom instruction. Among the topics explored were 21st-century skills, global literacy, thematic unit design and high-leverage teaching practices. Beginning in 2016 each workshop series included a book study. A complete list of topics and book studies is listed in Appendix A.

For the 2019–2020 workshop series, Ayari and Clementi selected *Teaching Intercultural Competence Across the Age Range* (Wagner *et al.*, 2018) for the book study and invited Manuela Wagner, a co-editor of the selected book, to present at the fall workshop. The workshop participants considered how to plan, teach and assess intercultural communicative competence (ICC) in their Arabic language and cultures classes. It was clear that this topic was extremely rich and needed further exploration. Wagner agreed to continue collaborating in the workshops. Consequently, the book study for the 2020–2021 workshop focused on *Teaching Intercultural Citizenship Across the Curriculum: The Role of Language Education* (Wagner *et al.*, 2019), co-authored by Wagner. For the 2021–2022 series, the workshop leaders (Ayari, Clementi, Wagner) connected intercultural citizenship (ICit) to learner engagement, referencing *Engaging Language Learners in Contemporary Classrooms* by Mercer and Dörnyei (2020) for the book study.

In this chapter, we report on this ongoing initiative. We share how we planned and implemented extended professional development for teachers of Arabic throughout a school year and how the learning continued across several years. Specifically, we share how the PLC participants explored how ICit could be taught intentionally and systematically at all educational levels as well as with all levels of proficiency and in different modalities (traditional/immersion classrooms, traditional learners/heritage learners). Questions we address include, How can the framework of ICit be applied to different contexts of Arabic language teaching? What does this way of teaching afford teachers, students and society as a whole? What challenges did participants of the PLC face, and what solutions were considered? Finally, we provide practical tools (sample objectives, lesson plans, activities, assessments) that we developed together with the participants.

We hope that this chapter will be helpful for language educators who wish to embark on the journey of teaching languages for ICit. We hope that language teacher educators and/or program administrators see the benefits of extended professional development to integrate ICit into their programs and make language learning more meaningful and purposeful.

The Theoretical Framework: Intercultural Communicative Competence and Intercultural Citizenship

Intercultural communicative competence (ICC)

Byram's (1997, 2021) 'model' of intercultural communicative competence (ICC) provides a description of the knowledge, attitudes and skills that students need to engage in meaningful intercultural dialogue in addition to the linguistic skills we usually teach in language education, i.e. linguistic, sociolinguistic and discourse competences. It is important to note that these skills should be integrated intentionally and systematically. The model describes five dimensions of intercultural competence (IC):

- *Attitudes*: curiosity and openness, readiness to suspend disbelief about other cultures and belief about one's own.
- *Knowledge*: specific knowledge of social groups and their products and practices in one's own and in one's interlocutor's country, and of the general knowledge of processes of societal and individual interaction.
- *Skills of Interpreting and Relating*: ability to interpret a document or event from another culture, to explain it and relate it to documents from one's own.
- *Skills of Discovery and Interaction*: ability to acquire new knowledge of cultural practices and the ability to operate knowledge, attitudes and skills under the constraints of real-time communication and interaction.
- *Critical Cultural Awareness/Political Education*: an ability to evaluate, critically and on the basis of an explicit, systematic process of reasoning, values present in one's own and other cultures and countries.

(Byram, 2021: 62–67)

To reiterate, intercultural communicative competence (ICC) includes both intercultural competence (IC) (attitudes, knowledge, skills of interpreting and relating, skills of discovery and interaction, and

```
┌─────────────────────────────────────────────┐
│        INTERCULTURAL COMMUNICATIVE            │
│                 COMPETENCE                     │
└─────────────────────────────────────────────┘

   ┌──────────────┐  ┌──────────────┐  ┌──────────────┐
   │  linguistic  │  │sociolinguistic│  │  discourse   │
   │  competence  │  │  competence  │  │  competence  │
   └──────────────┘  └──────────────┘  └──────────────┘
```

INTERCULTURAL COMPETENCE

skills of interpreting/ relating
(savoir comprendre)

knowledge
(savoirs)

critical cultural awareness
(savoir s'engager)

attitudes – curiosity/ openness
(savoir être)

skills of discovery/ interaction
(savoir apprendre/faire)

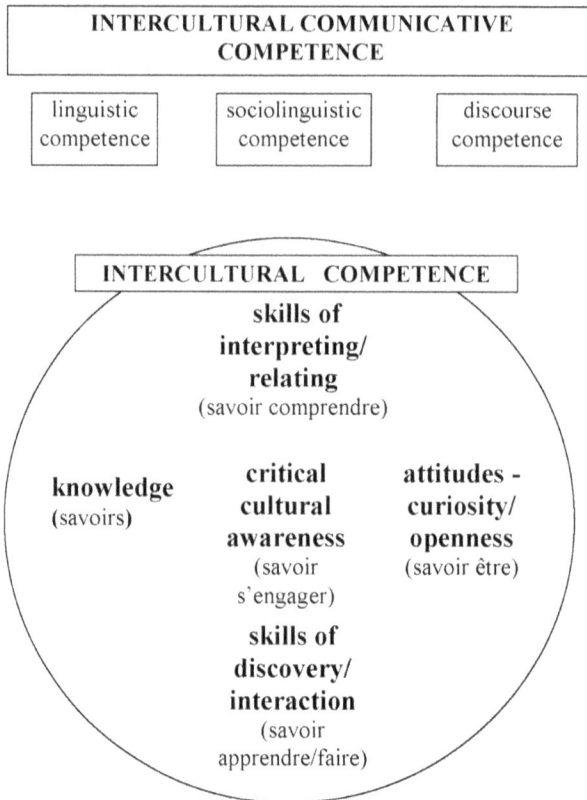

Figure 2.1 Byram's model of intercultural communicative competence

critical cultural awareness) and linguistic, sociolinguistic and discourse competences.

An important aspect of the ICC model is *critical cultural awareness*. In representations of the model (e.g. Byram, 1997, 2021), critical cultural awareness is depicted at the center of the ICC model (Figure 2.1).

This critical evaluation based on specific criteria and using reasoning is essential in order for students to take different perspectives into account, to understand the world around them and to refrain from merely seeking confirmation of what they already believe. Initially, the teacher plays a more important role in helping define the criteria. For example, it is crucial that the resources used are reliable, that sources present different viewpoints, and that students use their logical reasoning, initially withholding their judgment, in order to be able to make a judgment after considering the evaluated, analyzed and discussed information. Critical cultural awareness is also an important aspect of the connections between teaching for intercultural dialogue and teaching for social justice (see Glynn & Wagner, Chapter 1 this volume). Finally, the notion of critical cultural awareness has been further developed in Byram's (2008) framework of ICit, which is introduced in the next section.

Intercultural citizenship (ICit)

Byram (2008) introduced the framework of intercultural citizenship (ICit), building on teaching languages for intercultural communication. Rather than being concerned with educating students to identify with and become citizens of their own country, language educators have the opportunity and, we believe, a responsibility to help students understand the interconnectedness of today's world and to help them find their place in it. This entails the acquisition and implementation of the skills of ICC combined with 'active citizenship', i.e. being involved in the life of one's local, national or international community. In other words, an educator who teaches for ICit designs opportunities for students to develop the skills they need to engage in intercultural dialogue which students then apply to a societal problem of their choice. The connection between ICC and an action component highlights the role of language in this endeavor for projects that are carried out in world language education.

In 2019, Wagner, Cardetti and Byram published *Teaching Intercultural Citizenship Across the Curriculum* with the American Council on the Teaching of Foreign Languages (ACTFL) in which they introduced units for interdisciplinary ICit. The premise is that students should use their knowledge and skills from other subjects as well as from their life experiences to investigate and address a societal issue they deem important. Through this approach, students can apply their whole selves while we break down and challenge borders: those between subjects, between the school and the community, and even those between national borders.

The Why and How of Teaching Arabic for Intercultural Citizenship

ICit is 'being active in one's community – local and beyond the local – and using one's linguistic and intercultural competence to realize and enrich discussion, relationships, and activities with people of varied linguistic and cultural backgrounds' (Wagner *et al.*, 2019: xv). When driven by the notion of ICit as defined above, teaching Arabic could be a transformative experience, with a lasting impact on student knowledge, skills and attitudes. Turning the Arabic language classroom into a space conducive to the development of ICit, however, hinges upon consideration of the broader contexts surrounding Arabic teaching and learning, including the sociopolitical status and social capital of the Arabic language. A careful examination of those contexts allows the Arabic teacher to design meaningful learning experiences for his/her/their students as well as to identify and harness available resources to foster language growth and intercultural dialogue.

Being the language of the Qur'an – the language of prayer and other acts of worship – in addition to being the language of growing numbers of immigrants from Arab countries to the US, Arabic has a growing presence in private and public schools and colleges across the US. According to the Pew Research Center (2016), Arabic has become the fastest growing language in the US due to the continued immigration from the Middle East and North Africa and the growing US Muslim population. The Pew Research Center report reveals that 'the number of people ages 5 and older who speak Arabic at home has grown by 29% between 2010 and 2014 to 1.1 million, making it the seventh most commonly spoken non-English language in the U.S.' (Brown, 2016: 3).

The growing number of Arabic-speaking communities in the US means that there is an increase in the number of Arabic heritage speakers and Arabic-speaking communities present within and near schools where Arabic is taught, giving language learners opportunities to engage with Arabic-speaking communities around them and use their linguistic and intercultural competence to realize and enrich discussions, relationships and activities with those diverse Arabic-speaking communities.

Another important factor contributing to the demand for learning Arabic has to do with the events of September 11, 2001, and the subsequent military involvement of the US in the Arab region, leading to exponential growth in Arabic language enrollment at all levels of instruction, but especially at the post-secondary level (Looney & Lusin, 2019). Following this growth in student enrollment, the need to break the stigma around the Arabic language and its speakers became more urgent. There is a recognition that students of different ages and backgrounds come to the Arabic classroom with different motivations, including heritage, friends, community and/or curiosity about the Arabic language, people and cultures. These motivations lead to a wide range of impressions, stereotypes and misconceptions, and to questions about the language and the culture that could impact the level of motivation and engagement students exhibit in the Arabic classroom and beyond. Participants in the workshop series came to recognize that they were faced with the daunting task of addressing those preconceived notions; and what better ways to do so than to intentionally and systematically design learning experiences for students so that they can develop the knowledge, skills and attitudes required to engage in intercultural dialogue within and beyond the classroom.

Making Arabic Familiar: Intercultural Communicative Competence

The positive impact that familiarity can have on people's feelings and attitudes towards a particular group of people highlights the pivotal role that the Arabic language teacher can play in breaking the stigma about 'the Arabic culture' by carefully and systemically designing experiences for their students to learn about, meet and interact with Arabic speakers and to learn about the diversity and complexity of cultures connected to Arabic.

During her first workshop in integrating ICC into Arabic language teaching in the fall of 2019, Wagner started by asking the participants why they would want to teach Arabic for intercultural dialogue. Wagner was impressed with the deep conversations with and among participants that followed. While there was general excitement about teaching for ICC, there was also some skepticism whether such an approach would indeed have an impact, specifically on the attitudes of Americans towards speakers of Arabic or on the inability of people with different opinions on important topics to talk with each other. There were also questions about how to introduce complex topics in Arabic, especially for young learners and learners at the novice language level. Wagner shared some examples from her work with classroom teachers and, as a group, we discussed how those examples might by adapted to the Arabic language classroom, including which topics were appropriate for novice learners and which topics were appropriate for more advanced learners. We also discussed the appropriateness of topics for different age groups. Afterwards, Wagner shared with Clementi and Ayari that it was clear to her that there was a dynamic in the group that allowed for criticality and the open exchange of ideas. The rest of the day, and the following day, there were additional workshops by Clementi and Ayari, including significant time for group work to start designing or revising units with attention to the components of ICC. For example, in a middle school Arabic language class, students prepared a fashion show for the entire school explaining different types of clothing in the Arab world. A high school Arabic language class learned about different foods in the Arab world and prepared authentic dishes for the community at a weekend fair. Another class of novice language learners compared their family tree to a family tree for an Egyptian family along with activities that each family did together. Through the exploration of these topics, learners used the Arabic language purposefully to learn more about the Arab world. The participants also discussed how the positive impact of exposure and familiarity can be maximized by having students reflect critically on their interactions with both Arabic-speaking and non-Arabic-speaking communities in reflection journals.

The Power of Reflection

Considering the power of reflection on student learning and its role in helping them to identify and dispel stereotypes they may have about the Arab world, teachers attending the 2019 fall workshop examined sample reflection journals collected from Arabic language learners at Texas A&M University following their study abroad experiences (Ayari, 2014). In one of these reflection journals, a student described the transformative impact of her study abroad experience in Tunisia, and how that experience allowed her to reconstruct her prior understanding of the water situation in the Arab world which she had formed following her study abroad experience in Jordan:

> Our experience studying in Jordan did not help us completely as some of our preconceived notions were apparently very wrong, and as it turns out entertaining and slightly offensive for our Tunisian host family. At supper our first night, we were trying to figure out the show-ering situation. The places where my roommate and I had each stayed in Jordan had water tanks supplying the whole apartment building with water. If the building used up all the water that was in the tank, there would not be any more until the next week when the tank was refilled. Making assumptions, which is a bad thing and should not be done as we soon found out, my roommate and I figured that this was just the way of the Arab world. We did not want to use up our family's weekly water supply, so we asked them about the size of their water tank. Our host brother explained in Arabic to our mom and sisters what we meant and soon the whole kitchen had erupted in gales of laughter...

Another student described his transformative study abroad experience in Tunisia and how it had allowed him to dispel some negative perceptions about the Arab world. 'I always felt Arab countries are hostile to America...', wrote the student in his reflection journal, 'but we were actually greeted with open hands ... The media really shapes the way you think about other people'. Another student wrote in his journal: 'Pulling into the driveway on May 21st, I definitely felt nervous. I was in a foreign land and staying with a family I had no idea about. As soon as I pulled up to the house though, I was greeted with smiles and hugs...'.

Using the ICit framework to guide the discussion about the value of student reflection, teachers considered how the sample reflections allowed students to broaden and consciously reconstruct their knowledge about the Arab world. They discussed how doing reflection as part of teaching for ICit could lead their students to reflect critically on their assumptions about the Arab world and be more sophisticated in their understanding of a region as diverse as the Arab world. Finally, and as part of maximizing the benefits of reflection in developing ICit, teachers discussed the importance of having students conduct reflection (written and/or oral) in L1 and L2. Doing so contributes to linguistic growth in the target language and allows them to talk deeply and thoroughly about their experiences and to draw conclusions in their first language.

Teaching Arabic for Intercultural Citizenship

After the initial exploration of ICC during the 2019–2020 workshop series, the subsequent year of workshops took ICC one step further to think about the role of ICit. The essential question guiding this second year was: How are ICC and ICit linked? Because of the complexity of these approaches to teaching Arabic, it was important to provide teachers with concrete examples showing how learning Arabic could serve as a springboard for active community involvement.

To address this question, Ayari described and discussed with the teachers a joint project launched by the Arabic program and the English Language Institute at Texas A&M University. The project, called Language Exchange, allowed students to utilize their linguistic and intercultural competence to have a positive impact on the community. Language Exchange served as a service–learning opportunity pairing international and domestic students in weekly conversations. The objective was to promote linguistic and cultural exchanges between international and domestic students by having conversation groups meet for one hour of conversation each week (i.e. half an hour in English and half an hour in Arabic for 12 weeks). The Exchange provided direct and personal access to speakers of the language. Students participating in the Language Exchange went beyond practicing pronunciation to focusing on communication and thereby developing fluency in the target language. Arabic language learners were introduced to the target language community, consisting of international students from different Arabic-speaking countries who were pursuing their studies at Texas A&M Universities. The purpose of the encounter was to learn about those language partners while helping them learn about life in the US and making them feel welcome. Language learners on both sides viewed themselves as students and teachers at the same time, and the struggle to build target language proficiency was shared by both parties. To ensure accountability, students participating in the exchange were required to submit written and oral projects that demonstrated reflection on and growth in their communication and critical thinking skills. Furthermore, the exchange helped to prepare US students learning Arabic for 10 weeks of study abroad in Jordan or Morocco each summer.

The Language Exchange helped to promote diversity and global learning by building camaraderie between US students learning Arabic and Arabic-speaking students learning English, giving the participants first-hand access to other cultures and worldviews. As a result, many of the international and domestic students who participated in the Exchange were able to build relationships that endured after the semester ended. Several of the original participants continued to meet with their conversation partners after they were no longer required to do so. As such, while Arabic language learners were afforded cultural and communicative preparation for study abroad, the Arabic-speaking students felt a greater sense of integration into the university community, ameliorating some of the isolation that is commonly felt by students studying abroad.

Building on the success of the program in the first two years, the program was later expanded to include a virtual exchange with college students from the University of Mohamed V in Rabat, Morocco. Built around the same principles and pedagogical approach as the in-person exchange, the virtual language exchange conversation allowed US and Moroccan students to gain a virtual international experience by helping each other learn about college life and about how life in their respective countries was impacted by the Covid-19 pandemic. In order to ensure accountability and linguistic and cultural growth, students were expected to reflect on and describe their learning experiences by giving a PowerPoint presentation as part of their final project, describing what they had learned from their language partners.

The virtual experience served as a reminder for the teachers participating in the workshop series that engaging in intercultural dialogue could take place virtually with other schools and universities. It also emphasized that even virtual exchanges can be service oriented. In Ayari's example, both the US and the Moroccan students improved their language skills while gaining important information about college life and the impact of Covid in their countries.

After discussing how the Language Exchange utilized linguistic and cultural competence to make a positive difference outside the classroom, workshop teachers worked in small groups to grapple with the purpose for the instructional units they designed: Could the knowledge and understandings they gained in the classroom extend beyond the classroom?

In response to that question, teachers from the Dearborn Michigan Schools developed a unit based on the essential question (EQ): How does weather affect your daily lifestyle? Some of the ICC goals for the unit included:

- Keep a chart of weather conditions in different states/countries around the world for several days.
- Convert temperatures in Celsius to Fahrenheit and vice versa for a weather forecast.
- Create a short weather forecast.
- Describe the weather in different places around the world and suggest appropriate activities for the weather using the sentence pattern: The weather today is __; therefore, I am going to __.
- Draw a favorite seasons/scene and share it with classmates.

The teachers added the following ICit goals:

- Create posters in Arabic for the community with safety tips in the event of severe storms.
- Organize food and clothing donations to help students and their families following a flood in their community.

The students used what they learned in Arabic to provide a service to their community through the creation of safety posters. The learning became even more personal and powerful when their classes collected food and clothing for people in their community impacted by a flood. The students applied their learning beyond the classroom bringing the concept of ICit to life.

Analyses: What Was the Impact of this Professional Development Model on the Teaching of Arabic? Discussion: What Does this Mean for Other Languages?

We now turn to questions related to the impact of the professional development model on our participants, their students and their communities in general, and we reflect on the conditions needed for such benefits to occur. We also share some of the challenges that participants faced and offer suggestions for ways forward.

We first share a sample unit developed by workshop participants to show the impact that the PLC had as well as providing an example for how teachers can collaborate in the planning of ICit curricula. Beginning during the fall workshop in 2019, participants applied the workshop goals systematically by designing lessons and units with a focus on ICC. In year two, ICit was added. During the third year, we decided to create a whole unit that would integrate ICit in meaningful ways to increase learner engagement. For that purpose, we created working groups: one for elementary and middle school, two high school groups and one higher education group. The rationale was that the units could be planned in more detail with attention to age- and level-specific considerations. We present one example in some detail here, and provide overviews of four additional units in Appendix B.

It is important to note that the development of these units was a year-long process that was scaffolded by the facilitators. The first task was to come up with a theme and an essential question. Then, the participants were asked to design a summative assessment for this unit based on the principles of backwards design (Wiggins & McTighe, 2005). Finally, participants looked for resources and planned the different activities, which prepared the students to complete the summative assessment and action component. They were asked to carefully consider what students needed to know and be able to do to develop critical cultural awareness on the issue, i.e. How could they gain enough knowledge from different perspectives to use their reasoning to make a judgment on the issue? This step entails scaffolding activities that allow students to gain knowledge by:

- interpreting information about the issue in different contexts and relating it to their own situation;
- interacting with others to discover new knowledge, being openminded and tolerant of ambiguity when faced with surprising information;
- making a critical cultural judgment on the issue, knowing that at the same time there is always more to know.

Participants reviewed examples of units with similar components that they were asked to include in the units they were designing. The summative assessment included the integration of ICC in the form of an Integrated Performance Assessment (IPA) as shared in Wagner *et al.* (2019) and based on a model unit plan by Clementi and Terrill (2017).

As workshop facilitators, we were not all able to participate in person at both the fall and spring workshops. Those of us who were not on site benefitted from Zoom, allowing all three of us to move from group to group to provide feedback, mostly in the form of questions to consider as we listened to the group interactions. We also answered questions and clarified concepts for the groups. As will be discussed later, there was an obvious development of understanding that occurred as the participants and the facilitators worked through the units. Planning for ICit is complex: the structure of the workshops and the group work helped participants face the challenge together. Participants and facilitators worked together to overcome the various hurdles in the planning as well as working through the logistical challenges they faced in their schools. The collaboration also fostered the sharing of ideas and building upon each other's ideas, which resulted in a more comprehensive unit that considered critical questions from a variety of perspectives.

Sample unit: Food waste

As they met in the 2020 fall workshop to discuss how student projects could be designed to address societal problems, teachers examined and discussed a project designed by students learning Arabic at Cholla High School in Tucson, Arizona, that was meant to make a positive difference in their community. In 2015 and 2016, a community of refugees from Syria and Iraq was resettled, mostly in family units, with children attending schools as English Language Learners (ELL). The Arabic teacher and her students at Cholla High School where Ayari visited several times, saw an opportunity to design meaningful learning experiences where they could utilize their Arabic language and culture skills to make a positive difference in the lives of those refugees. They helped to provide school supplies and supported families in bake sales by helping them sell their homemade pastries to the local community (This is Tucson, 2021). Using their linguistic and cultural skills, they also visited schools attended by refugee children to converse with them in Arabic and make them feel welcome. 'When I was speaking with the Syrian refugees, it was very surreal,' said Adriana Noriega, a junior at Cholla High School. 'I've heard about it before, all the problems they're going through ... and being able to speak to someone who has been going through this their whole life really made me want to give back more.' Noriega collected school supplies and more than $300 to purchase educational necessities. She was featured in a local newspaper telling the story of her impactful volunteer work.

Analyzing a real-world example of a unit that included ICit was an important first step in empowering teachers to design their own ICit unit. After discussing the example from Cholla High School, one group of high school teachers decided to work on the global challenge of food waste. The unit was created for grades 9–12 targeting novice high to intermediate low language proficiency. The overarching essential question guiding the unit was: How does food waste contribute to social injustice in the world? Supporting questions included: What can we do, as students, to find solutions to food waste and food shortage? Why do some countries waste food while people in other parts of the world die of hunger? From the overarching essential question, students can be asked to think about an action component related to food waste which is part of active citizenship in ICit. This encourages learner engagement as students suggest potential action projects and then select the project they will implement. Taking ownership and responsibility for the action project is a critical component of learner engagement and ICit.

We would like to note here that although the overarching goal is always ICit, enabling students to come up with a project that addresses a societal issue, realistically it is difficult for every unit to have an action component. In our experience, there are several reasons for this:

(1) Action components need to be planned very well. If they are not, the projects can fail and students and or the community partners with whom they engage can be harmed in the process.
(2) Following from point (1), there are a number of logistical issues that need to be considered: e.g. making and maintaining contacts with partners locally, nationally or transnationally; resolution of technical issues; obtaining permissions to conduct the action component; maintaining communication with all participants, just to name a few examples.

(3) Students need to develop the knowledge, skills, and attitudes to be able to engage thoughtfully in an action project. What that means in practice is that, even though the aim is ICit, students do engage in aspects of ICC in all their units.

What we would recommend, then, is to remind students throughout all units about possible actions if it is not feasible to conduct action projects in every unit. In the university German program that Manuela Wagner co-directs, for example, students plan one action project throughout the whole semester that is realized at the end of the semester. In every unit, they think about connections to ICit but the action project occurs as a culminating project at the end of the semester.

The group came up with the following action goals for the unit on food waste:

- Students design infographic posters to raise awareness of the crises and display them widely in the school and the community.
- Students create a video and make it available to the school community on the school TV on YouTube.
- Students organize a food drive to engage all students from different disciplines.

The summative performance assessment tasks followed the IPA format. As can be seen in Table 2.1 (and in the unit in Appendix B), for the interpretive task students read information, watched videos and analyzed visual data representing different perspectives about food waste. In the presentational task, students prepared a multimedia

Table 2.1 Summative assessment tasks

SUMMATIVE ASSESSMENT TASKS	
INTERPRETIVE: LISTEN, READ, VIEW	
1. Read, in small groups, different articles on food waste/solutions in various countries. Complete a graphic organizer about food waste and solutions in the countries studied. 2. Watch, in small groups, different videos on food waste and identify the nature of the problem and possible solutions. 3. Summarize information on various charts, showing parts of the world with different levels of food waste and the reasons for food waste.	
PRESENTATIONAL: WRITE OR SPEAK FOR AN AUDIENCE	*INTERPERSONAL – INTERACT WITH OTHERS IN PAIRS, SMALL GROUPS*
Work in small groups to design a multimedia presentation on the effect of food waste and food shortage on regions, countries and peoples. Use summaries from reading and videos, as well as representations about different solutions that raise awareness and offer suggestions on ways to stop food waste.	Survey others about the reasons for food waste. In an open discussion, share findings from the surveys, and ideas about reducing food waste.

presentation to share what they learned with their school community. Finally, the interpersonal task included collecting opinions about reasons for food waste via an oral survey followed by an open discussion of their findings.

There were many learning activities leading up to the summative assessment and the action component. Activities related to learning information (gaining knowledge) about food waste included interpreting information about food waste in other locations and relating it to their own location, interacting with other students locally and from the Arab world about food waste, and discovering new information, showing and practicing their open-mindedness, curiosity and tolerance of ambiguity. The teachers curated helpful authentic resources on the topic of food waste. They modeled for students how to find and evaluate relevant information found on the internet. They reminded students that the information they learned could be used for projects in other classes and beyond. Students also conducted surveys investigating food waste in their context and shared the results with each other. In many activities students learned from each other by exchanging the information they found. Rather than all students learning the same information at the same time, students chose resources from the curated collection and also completed independent investigations on topics they found personally interesting related to food waste. This independent exploration facilitated real-world collaboration as each student contributed unique findings and understandings in small group work and in creating the multimedia presentation.

As we mentioned before, the workshop groups received feedback from the facilitators several times. They also presented their units on two different occasions during the year-long process in order to benefit from feedback from their workshop colleagues. As they worked in groups over the course of the year to develop instructional units within the ICC and ICit framework, teachers grappled with the question of how to simultaneously develop their students' linguistic skills and IC as well as how to stay in the target language while providing comprehensible input. Working in groups by instructional level enabled teachers to exchange ideas, suggestions and opinions about how best to integrate ICC and ICit while considering the proficiency level of the learners. The challenging nature of simultaneously developing linguistic skills, cultural knowledge and understandings, and ICit transpired during a focus group discussion where participants were invited to reflect on the challenges associated with the integration of ICit into their Arabic language programs in terms of planning, teaching, assessment. Dedicated time for collaboration among teachers to address these challenges is critical to the successful integration of ICit action goals.

As can be seen from the sample unit we have shared, participants were able to plan ICit units at the end of the three years of workshops.

It is important to note that participants came up with activities and lesson plans throughout the three years. However, we noticed that by continuously discussing, reflecting upon and co-creating activities, and reflecting upon them, there was a notable shift in the thinking of most participants in that they truly thought about how they could help students use their Arabic and their ICC to become intercultural citizens. In other words, we noticed that there was a shift in the participants' teaching philosophy.

The gradual shift in teachers' thinking was evident from a focus group discussion conducted during the spring workshop of 2022. During this discussion, teachers had an opportunity to reflect on how the workshop series and webinars focusing on intercultural communication and citizenship had impacted their teaching practices. One of the participants who has attended the workshops regularly since 2013 noted:

> I used to conduct projects outside of the classroom as an extra thing, but when I learned about the new concepts of ICC and ICit, I realized that they need to be an integral part of my unit and lesson plans, and those projects have become more organized and more grounded in theory as I work with other schools on joint projects.

Another participant who was a new participant in the ICit workshop described the impact of his experience working with other teachers to develop a thematic unit within the ICit framework:

> Meeting with teachers from different backgrounds who teach in different schools, with different experiences and use different curricular materials allowed me to go back with a wide variety of ideas. I started to think about abandoning the textbook and using thematic units instead. I am so intrigued by the concepts of thematic units and backward design even though this has been my first year.

He went on to describe the importance of the ongoing work on building a unit that integrates the notions of ICit and engagement:

> We started the unit in our past meetings and today we are still working on it. I feel that building a thematic unit is a work in progress, with a lot of ideas and a wide variety of experiences that we are trying to put and integrate in one document. We have a chance to discuss concepts and share experiences and the theme this year having to do with engagement is very important and challenging.

The high impact of the workshop series on teacher practices goes beyond the classroom. One teacher described how the exchange of ideas with other teachers as they worked to develop thematic units inspired him to create a model lesson for the Annenberg Library to promote the integration of dialects into the Arabic classroom: 'When I created a lesson for the Annenberg Library about integrating Arabic dialects, the idea came from this group'.

Wagner observed that for her it was helpful that workshop participants had prior knowledge and strategies for using themes to teach languages, integrating high-leverage teaching practices and other useful tools from their participation prior to the in-person workshops at the Language Villages. It was also clear that the participants had formed a community. There was a sense that teaching Arabic is a common endeavor, that knowledge and resources should be shared, that those who join later are to be welcomed into the community and updated on what they have missed. The continuity of the professional learning community played an important role in allowing participants to develop and refine their knowledge, skills and attitudes. It also allowed the past participants to become informal mentors to those who were participating for the first time in the workshop series. As the saying goes: you truly understand a concept when you have to teach it to someone else. First-time participants asked excellent questions and offered perspectives that enhanced the learning experience for both the returnees and the new participants. As Clementi noted, the reality that each year's workshop series included new participants as well as returnees became a strength of the program rather than a limiting factor.

Another affordance that the participants as well as the facilitators observed was that the participants themselves were from so many diverse Arabic-speaking backgrounds that they not only prepared to teach intercultural communicative competence but also practiced it themselves through their interactions in their workshops. Understanding language and culture varieties, the power dynamic and the underlying preconceptions and stereotypes, is a critically important part of ICit. Ayari observed that participants in the workshops had – and took advantage of – ample opportunities to grapple with questions about language variation and cultural diversity. One teacher described how the whole group had enjoyed learning about and from each other by playing games: 'Coming here, we used to sit outside and play games, different types of games, and one of those games was about understanding the vocabulary in different dialects'. This type of interaction led some teachers to integrate the teaching of dialects into their teaching in order to prepare their students to engage more effectively with Arabic-speaking communities who speak different dialects. 'I've learned so much about the Arab world. It's an intercultural exchange – the idea of pushing dialects in the classroom came from this group,' noted one teacher during the focus group discussion.

Even the workshop facilitators experienced the benefits of participating in the PLCs. Wagner, for example, never imagined learning so much about the linguistic and cultural aspects of different parts of the Arabic-speaking world as she did during her first weekend on site at the Language Villages when workshop participants shared their knowledge so freely. The awareness that it is important to draw from all linguistic and cultural resources surely also benefited the workshop participants' students as well as their communities. Learning to appreciate cultural and linguistic diversity means that we first need to understand that there are different varieties, that they are important in their own rights, that they are connected to identities, and that often misconceptions and stereotypes about linguistic and cultural diversity have to do with power.

Another outcome of the diverse community of educators of Arabic coming together in the PLC was that educators from elementary school, middle school, high school, college, adult education as well as those teaching different levels of Arabic or even Arabic literature, film etc., came together and talked about their experiences, successes and challenges, which often turned to the topic of articulation. *Articulation is such an important and yet evasive topic in language education.* Through the workshop series, there is now a significant group of educators of Arabic who are in touch about articulation issues and who can help each other respond to questions that arise, including the creation of a Facebook page to discuss topics relevant to Arabic language teaching (https://www.facebook.com/search/top?q=arabiclangchat). That has an impact on the overall conversation about Arabic language education in the US.

Conclusion

We have shared how a group of educators and researchers came together in a PLC to learn how to teach languages for ICit. We found that using ICit as a framework helps solidify the purposeful use of language. It takes language learning beyond the classroom and into the community, connecting what students learn in Arabic to their real world and to the world beyond the classroom and school walls. It emphasizes the transfer of learning: while using the Arabic language is of primary importance, there is much learning through the study of Arabic that can be applied to help understand/resolve contemporary issues that our students are facing today.

Bringing together Arabic language teachers of diverse backgrounds allows them to become learners, curious about Arabic countries and cultures that were unknown to them. It encourages them to reach out to their community and beyond to find native speakers of Arabic from around the world who are willing to share their cultures with the students. While travel to the Arab world may be an ultimate goal, there is much to be learned about interacting with others locally and beyond via technology, and in one's local community.

We hope that this chapter will be helpful for language educators who wish to embark on the journey of teaching languages for ICit and for language teacher educators and/or program administrators who plan to integrate intercultural citizenship into their programs and make language learning more meaningful and purposeful through extended professional development opportunities. Some lessons learned and related recommendations include:

(1) Creating a community that collaborates over an extended period has many advantages compared to one-time workshops on a topic, especially when a topic is complex and requires understandings of a number of related topics.

(2) Building upon prior knowledge is crucial when we embark on re-designing curricula. The fact that each year's workshop series brought together returning participants with 'first-timers' provided the opportunity for the returnees to act as informal mentors as they shared what they had learned in prior workshops with the 'first-timers'. This allowed the returnees to solidify their understanding of past topics, an unintended positive consequence of blending the 'first-timers' with the returning participants.

(3) Providing enough opportunities for participants to learn with and from each other is crucial. Even if there are some detours in the sense that not everyone will be on board with a new concept from the very beginning, it is crucial that participants can bring themselves into the process and consider their contexts and share their ideas as well as their concerns with each other.

(4) Related to (3), we suggest always leaving room for participants to challenge a new concept and to critique it. There are so many 'fads' in education that teachers are asked to join that it is important to leave room for a conversation of how this new approach/concept/ teaching philosophy can help us and the challenges that are part of implementing new approaches. This is related to building community and to the need for extended collaborations mentioned in (1).

(5) If possible, it is helpful to provide resources for teachers when we ask them to consider something new. Now, more than ever, educators are stretched in their time and energy. They need the gift of time to learn, discuss and reflect upon new strategies and concepts with colleagues and the opportunity to collaborate to apply their learning to the classroom.

(6) If the time to collaborate, the professional development opportunities to build common understandings among collaborators, and colleagues willing to collaborate are in place, truly wonderful results can happen. We can wrap our minds around complex topics and help our students use what they learn in their language classes to find their place in the world and thereby also highlight the important role that language education plays.

Appendix A: History of Concordia Language Villages Professional Development for Teachers of Arabic

- 2011–2012: Participation in a CARLA Summer Institute and residency at the Arabic Language Village during the summer to observe and assist with instruction.
- 2012–2013: Collaboration with CARLA Summer Institute and residency at the Arabic Language Village during the summer continued.
- 2013: Workshop 'Integrating the Common Core and 21st Century Skills into Units of Instruction for the Arabic Language Classroom'.
- 2014–2015: First 'series workshop' (fall and spring in-person, 3 webinars to bridge fall and spring workshops) 'Strategies to Facilitate Language Learning'.
- 2015–2016: Workshop Series: 'Global Literacy'.
- 2016–2017: Workshop Series: 'Learner Engagement Through Thematic Unit Planning'; first book study to accompany workshop series: Clementi, D. and Terrill, L. (2017) *The Keys to Planning for Learning: Effective Curriculum, Unit, and Lesson Design.* American Council on the Teaching of Foreign Languages (ACTFL). 1001 North Fairfax Street Suite 200, Alexandria, VA 22314.
- 2017–2018: Workshop Series: 'New Literacies for a Globally Connected World: Strengthening Communication Skills'; Book study: VanPatten, B. (2017) *While We're on the Topic: BVP on Language, Acquisition, and Classroom Practice.* American Council on the Teaching of Foreign Languages (ACTFL). 1001 North Fairfax Street Suite 200, Alexandria, VA 22314.
- 2018–2019: Workshop Series: 'High Leverage Teaching Practices'; Book study: Glisan, E. W. and Donato, R. (2017) *Enacting the Work of Language Instruction: High-Leverage Teaching Practices.* American Council on the Teaching of Foreign Languages (ACTFL). 1001 North Fairfax Street Suite 200, Alexandria, VA 22314.
- 2019–2020: Workshop Series: 'Intercultural Communicative Competence: Linking Language and Culture'; Book study: Wagner, M., Conlon Perugini, D. and Byram, M. (eds) (2018) *Teaching Intercultural Competence Across the Age Range: From Theory to Practice.* Languages for Intercultural Communication and Education series, vol. 32. Bristol: Multilingual Matters.
- 2020–2021: Workshop Series: 'Intercultural Citizenship'; Book study: Wagner, M., Cardetti, F. and Byram, M. (2019) *Teaching Intercultural Citizenship Across the Curriculum: The Role of Language Education.* American Council on the Teaching of Foreign Languages (ACTFL). 1001 North Fairfax Street Suite 200, Alexandria, VA 22314.
- 2021–2022: Workshop Series: 'Learner Engagement and Intercultural Citizenship'; Book study: Mercer, S. and Dörnyei, Z. (2020) *Engaging Language Learners in Contemporary Classrooms.* Cambridge: Cambridge University Press.

Appendix B: Intercultural Citizenship Unit Overviews

Elementary Group: Amani Mandil, Sawsan Darwish, Layali Eshqaidef, William Bice, Eman Altayyeb, Wael Fawzy

Grade /Language Level	Grades 5–6 Novice mid/High
Theme/Topic	Contemporary Life: The Clothes We Wear
Essential Question	*How do clothes reflect who we are?*
ICC Unit Goals	Learners will be able to: • Watch a video showing traditional Arab clothing. • Identify various traditional clothes from Arab countries. • Gather information about traditional clothes from Arab countries. • Share information with classmates about traditional clothes from the Arab countries. • Compare changes in clothing from traditional to modern styles. • Ask and respond to simple questions about clothing preferences (color, patterns, style). • Give examples of how clothing reflects who people are. • Describe an outfit that reflects their personality.
Intercultural Citizenship Action How can goals of this unit be connected to the community beyond the classroom (learning activities that contribute to engagement with people outside the classroom)?	To bring awareness about traditional and modern clothing in the Arab world and the value they bring to the people who wear them, students will present a fashion show of traditional and modern clothes from Arab countries for the school community.

SUMMATIVE PERFORMANCE TASKS
Interpretive (Listen, Read, View)
Read descriptions of various outfits and match the descriptions to the images described. Watch a video showing people wearing different traditional Arab clothing from different Arab countries. Match the country to the image of the outfit.

Presentational – Write or Speak for an Audience	Interpersonal – Interact with Others in Pairs, Small Groups
In small groups choose one Arab country and research traditional modes of dress in that country, distinguishing between the cultural functions of each article of clothing. Present your research as part of a fashion show about Arab clothing.	Students interview each other about clothing they learned about from the Arab world, asking and responding to questions about their favorite and least favorite styles.

High School Group: Nabila Hammami, Nawf Abou-Dib, Rafef Saed, Batol Alizairij

Grade/Language Level	Grades 9–12 Novice high/Intermediate low
Theme/Topic	Global Challenges – Weather/Climate
Essential Question	*How does weather affect your daily lifestyle?*
ICC Unit Goals	Learners will be able to: • Keep a chart of weather conditions in different states/countries around the world for several days. (Geography) • Convert temperatures in Celsius to Fahrenheit and vice versa for a weather forecast. (Math) • Create a short weather forecast. (Science) • Describe the weather in different places around the world and suggest appropriate activities for the weather: The weather today is __; therefore, I am going to __. (Science, Geography, Language Arts) • Draw a favorite season/scene and share it with classmates. (Art) • Discuss how severe weather conditions could affect people's lives. (Geography, Science) • Write a reflection about the impact of weather on people's lives. (Language Arts, Science)
Intercultural Citizenship Goals How can goals of this unit be connected to the community beyond the classroom (learning activities that contribute to engagement with people outside the classroom)?	To provide service to the local community, students will create posters in Arabic for the community with safety tips in the event of severe storms. Because of a recent flood in the community, students will organize food and clothing donations to help students and their families in their community following a flood.

SUMMATIVE PERFORMANCE TASKS

Interpretive (Listen, Read, View)

1. Watch short videos/documentary on changes of weather conditions in different seasons in order to match the weather condition to the season.
2. Listen to a live weather forecast in Arabic in order to suggest what to wear.
3. Read a weather forecast and select weather symbols that reflect the forecast.

Presentational – Write or Speak for an Audience	Interpersonal – Interact with Others in Pairs, Small Groups
Prepare a visual presentation showing how the lives of people are affected by catastrophic weather conditions.	Exchange information about extreme weather conditions around the world. Discuss ways of assisting community members during bad/catastrophic weather conditions they have experienced.

High School Group: Fadi Abughoush, Sanaa Jouejati, Hadia Al Alabdullah, Almutazbe Alabd, Mona Badawy, Abdulnasser Ahmed, Alice Saba

Grade/Language Level	Grades 9–12 Novice high/Intermediate low
Theme/Topic	Global Challenges – Food Waste
Essential Question	*How does food waste contribute to social injustice in the world? What can we do, as students, to find solutions to food waste and food shortage? Why do some countries waste food while people in other parts of the world die of hunger?*
ICC Unit Goals	Learners will be able to:

	• Read and identify key words about food waste from a text.
	• Identify the main topic of a text/video about food waste.
	• Summarize using simple sentences a text/video about food waste.
	• Ask and answer questions about food waste.
	• Analyze diagrams and reflect in writing about food crises.
	• Present orally and in writing to others what they learned about the food crises to raise awareness.
	• Create a culture triangle about bread
	  Product: Bread
	  Practice: Pick up any piece of bread from the floor, put the leftover bread in a separate container.
	  Perspective: The importance of the bread for everyone regardless of socioeconomic level.

Intercultural Citizenship Goals How can goals of this unit be connected to the community beyond the classroom (learning activities that contribute to engagement with people outside the classroom)?	**Empathy:** Students will show and express empathy regarding the marginalized and less-privileged people in their own context and in other parts of the world. **Justice:** Students will reflect on and deepen their knowledge and practice of social justice principles and the equitable distribution of food around the world. **Action:** Students plan, present and carry out collective actions toward food crises in the world. Students will design infographic posters to raise awareness of the crises and display them in school and the community. Students create a video and make it available to the school community on the school TV on YouTube.
SUMMATIVE PERFORMANCE TASKS	
Interpretive (Listen, Read, View)	

1. Read, in small groups, different articles on food waste/solutions in various countries. Complete a graphic organizer about food waste and solutions in the countries studied.
2. Watch, in small groups, different videos on food waste solutions and identify the nature of the problem and possible solutions
3. Summarize information on various charts showing parts of the world with different levels of food waste and the reasons for food waste.

Presentational – Write or Speak for an Audience	Interpersonal – Interact with Others in Pairs, Small Groups
Work in small groups to design a multimedia presentation on the effect of food waste and shortage on regions, countries and peoples. Use summaries from reading and videos, as well as representations about different solutions that raise awareness and offer suggestions on ways to stop food waste.	Survey others about the reasons for food waste. In an open discussion, students share findings from the surveys, and ideas about reducing food waste.

Key Learning Activities/Formative Assessments	Mode of Communication
Meet other students from the Arabic-speaking world and talk about food waste in their country and come up with ideas and potential solutions.	Interpersonal
Design posters about how NOT to waste food. Share solutions with the school community.	Presentational
Describe pictures about food waste.	Presentational
Conduct a survey about their own food waste by asking and answering questions and find commonalities in behaviors.	Presentational Interpersonal
Organize a community evening to raise awareness on reducing food waste in the community.	Presentational
Watch a video about food waste in the world and identify words about food waste; present the information from the video in a table/chart.	Interpretive Presentational
Watch a video about the significance/value of food, especially bread, in the Arab world where throwing it is considered almost a sin/taboo and then compare that concept to the importance of food in their own culture.	Interpretive Interpersonal

Resources
https://www.damas24.com/wp-content/uploads/2017/04/58d2abeec461889a108b462a.jpg https://alkssr.com/portal/wp-content/uploads/2017/09/000-5475128001505916897357.jpg http://www.alriyadh.com/media/thumb/67/1d/750_2e407a6eb8.jpg https://i.ytimg.com/vi/jQ0jyF25OWE/maxresdefault.jpg https://gulfopinions.com/ar/wp-content/uploads/2019/05/WhatsApp-Image-2019-05-09-at-3.56.32-PM-660x330.jpeg

Post-Secondary Group: Asma Ben Romdhone, Samir El Omari, Youness Mountaki

Grade/Language Level	Third-year university
Theme/Topic	Contemporary Life: Arab Women Higher Education in the MENA region
Essential Question	*How are Arab women represented in higher education in the MENA region?*
Unit Goals - ICC	Learners will be able to: • Increase awareness about the situation of women's education in the MENA region through reading articles and watching videos. • Identify Arab women's rights in higher education. • Identify issues Arab women face in higher education. • Conduct interviews with Arab women faculty in different fields. • Participate in virtual exchanges with Arab speakers to learn about women in higher education in different Arab countries. • (For heritage learners) Interview their parents or family members about experiences with Arab women in higher education.
Intercultural Citizenship Goals How can the goals of this unit be connected to the community beyond the classroom (learning activities that contribute to engagement with people outside the classroom)?	Students organize a panel discussion to make the population on campus aware of the rights of Arab women in higher education and the issues facing Arab women in higher education.

SUMMATIVE PERFORMANCE TASKS
Interpretive (Listen, Read, View)

Listen to مى امانى video on Al Kitaab.
Listen to a podcast on songs like "سعيدة فكري"
Read about نوال السعداوي and فاطمة المرنيسي -فاطمة الفهرية
Listen to Arab voices اصوات عربية about كولييت خوري

Presentational – Write or Speak for an Audience	Interpersonal – Interact with Others in Pairs, Small Groups
Students will be divided into three groups (North Africa, the Levant and the Gulf Region) to research and give a presentation about the MENA region and Arab women in higher education.	Participate in a debate about issues facing Arab women in higher education.

References

Ayari, S. (2014) Studying Arabic abroad: A transformative experience. In A. Hodges and L. Seawright (eds) *Going Global: Transnational Perspectives on Globalization, Language, and Education* (pp. 128–147). Newcastle upon Tyne: Cambridge Scholars Publishing.

Brown, A. (2016) The challenges of translating the U.S. census questionnaire into Arabic. *Pew Research Center*, 3 June. See https://www.pewresearch.org/fact-tank/2016/06/03/the-challenges-of-translating-the-u-s-census-questionnaire-into-arabic/).

Byram, M. (1997) *Teaching and Assessing Intercultural Communicative Competence.* Clevedon: Multilingual Matters.

Byram, M. (2008) *From Foreign Language Education to Education for Intercultural Citizenship: Essays and Reflections.* Clevedon: Multilingual Matters. https://doi.org/10.21832/9781847690807.

Byram, M. (2021) *Teaching and Assessing Intercultural Communicative Competence: Revisited* (2nd edn). Bristol: Multilingual Matters. https://doi.org/10.21832/9781800410251

Clementi, D. and Terrill, L. (2017) *The Keys to Planning for Learning: Effective Curriculum, Unit, and Lesson Design.* Alexandria, VA: American Council on the Teaching of Foreign Languages (ACTFL).

Looney, D. and Lusin, N. (2019) *Enrollments in Languages Other Than English in United States Institutions of Higher Education, Summer 2016 and Fall 2016: Final Report.* New York, NY: Modern Language Association of America. See https://www.mla.org/content/download/110154/2406932/2016-Enrollments-Final-Report.pdf.

Mercer, S. and Dörnyei, Z. (2020) *Engaging Language Learners in Contemporary Classrooms.* Cambridge: Cambridge University Press.

This is Tucson (2018, January 1, updated June 21, 2021) 5 Tucson kids who make us optimistic about the future [Online]. *This is Tucson*, 1 January (rev. 21 June 2021). See https://thisistucson.com/tucsonlife/5-tucson-kids-who-make-us-optimistic-about-the-future/collection.50c479e2-e5ba-11e7-bd51-a73553b6ef3f.html#1.

Wagner, M., Conlon Perugini, D. and Byram, M. (eds) (2018) *Teaching Intercultural Competence Across the Age Range: From Theory to Practice.* Bristol: Multilingual Matters. http://dx.doi.org/10.21832/WAGNER8903.

Wagner, M., Cardetti, F. and Byram, M. (2019) *Teaching Intercultural Citizenship Across the Curriculum: The Role of Language Education.* Alexandria, VA: American Council on the Teaching of Foreign Languages (ACTFL).

Wiggins, G.P. and McTighe, J. (2005) *Understanding by Design.* Alexandria, VA: Association for Supervision and Curriculum Development (ASCD).

3 Dual Language and Immersion Programs: Naturally Fostering Intercultural Citizenship

Allison J. Spenader and Brandon T. Locke

Introduction

Dual language and immersion (DLI) programs have been flourishing in North America since their beginnings in Canada in the late 1960s, providing students with opportunities for advanced levels of language proficiency as well as opportunities for profound academic and cultural learning. One of the three fundamental, overarching goals of dual language and immersion programs is that of developing a greater sense of cross-cultural understanding, or intercultural competence (Curtain & Dahlberg, 2016). However, many programs tend to overlook this goal, citing that language instruction and academic content take priority. Cross-cultural understanding has not been a consistent focus of immersion education (Met & Lorenz, 1997; Wesely, 2012). This lack of prioritization can be traced to intercultural competence being seen as a less important outcome. A compounding challenge has been the lack of consensus within the field as to what cross-cultural learning is and how it should be operationalized within immersion programs (Feinauer & Howard, 2014). The concept of *intercultural citizenship* provides a new framework with which to examine dual language and immersion programs, building on Byram's model of intercultural communicative competence by infusing a focus on social justice, questioning attitudes and a desire to make changes for the better (Byram, 1997; Wagner *et al.*, 2019).

With calls for the development of intercultural citizenship in all US language learners, it is time for dual language and immersion programs to take a closer look at how to realize this goal. Previous research has shown that immersion students struggle to define and describe culture(s), and that advanced levels of language proficiency do not automatically lead to high levels of intercultural development (Wesely, 2012). Dual language and immersion programs have the potential to naturally and intuitively serve as the building blocks for fostering true intercultural citizenship, especially those programs that start in the early elementary grades.

This chapter examines and describes intercultural citizenship development in dual language and immersion programs in the Anchorage School District (Alaska). Using non-participant classroom observations, focus groups and individual interviews with dual language and immersion practitioners, we show how the intercultural citizenship framework is enacted in these settings. The findings illustrate the necessity for intercultural citizenship to be intentionally included as an important goal of dual language and immersion programs. The potential for enacting the intercultural citizenship framework within this educational context is great – but it is not guaranteed. Intercultural citizenship should be prioritized for all immersion programs, receiving attention and focus on a par with both academic content learning and language instruction.

Literature Review

Immersion education in the US

Since their inception more than 50 years ago in Canada, language immersion programs have grown in both popularity and numbers, not only in North America but also around the world (Howard *et al.*, 2018; Johnson & Swain, 1997). While we do not have an exact number of reported Dual Language Immersion (henceforth DLI) programs in the US to date, according to the 2011 *Directory of Foreign Language Immersion Programs in U.S. Schools*, formerly maintained by the Center for Applied Linguistics, there was a total of 510 DLI programs in 22 different languages identified. Of these, 81.5% of programs were in Spanish, French, Mandarin, Hawaiian and Japanese. A variety of models of immersion exists to meet different but related goals, all with the aim to foster multilingualism through content-based instruction. But what of the third goal: that of fostering greater cross-cultural understanding?

While the focus of this chapter is not to explain the various models of DLI programs, it is important to have a general understanding of the most common types of DLI programs, in order to comprehend and consider how intercultural citizenship fits. DLI program models vary depending on the amount of instructional time in the second language (total or partial), as well as in the population of the students who are served in the program (one-way or two-way). The level of entry into the program also needs to be considered, such as early entry, secondary continuation or late entry.

One-way programs are designed for students who share a majority language (i.e. English) and who are all learning the second language (i.e. Japanese) together for the first time. Two-way immersion programs (TWI), while similar in outcomes to one-way programs, differ based on the number of native speakers in both languages. The ideal percentage breakdown in two-way programs is 50% native speakers of one language (i.e. English) and 50% native speakers of the other language (i.e. Spanish); however, it is not uncommon to see programs with up to 70% in one language and 30% in the other. In order to have a two-way program, it is critical that there is a significant number of speakers of both languages. It is also important to note that the two population groups are co-seated/co-educated, allowing for native language models for both student groups. It is also important to mention that TWI programs have, over the years, been referred to as both 50/50 programs (referring to the breakdown of student groups) and dual language programs (referencing both languages). This can be confusing since it is more common to use 50/50 to refer to instructional time (see below), and the term 'dual language' (DLI) is now used to refer to all immersion models since they all teach two languages.

Total or full immersion programs are sometimes called 90/10 programs, which refers to the amount of instructional time in the language. In such programs, the immersion (second or new) language is used for instruction for the entire school day for the first few years, typically grades K–2. Content areas such as art, music and physical education are typically the exceptions and fall into the 10% of the instructional day. Typically, English is introduced in grade 3, and is taught by an English teacher (specialist) outside the immersion classroom. Partial immersion programs are sometimes called 50/50 programs (not to be confused with two-way models), which refers to programs where half the core academic content is taught in one language (i.e. English) and the other half is taught in the immersion language. Ideally, this is shared between two teachers: the immersion language teacher and the English partner teacher. In the Anchorage School District (ASD), showcased in this chapter, the elementary programs are all partial immersion programs. The content is shared among two teachers. The English partner teacher is responsible for English language arts and mathematics, while the immersion teacher teaches science and social studies in addition to literacy/language arts of the immersion language (i.e. French). Secondary immersion continuation programs are becoming more popular and are typically found as strands within middle and high schools. To be considered an immersion program at the middle and/or high school level, a minimum of two year-long content courses is typically required with instruction being completely in the immersion languages (Fortune & Tedick, 2008a). The two middle-level programs featured in this study represent both a one-way continuation model (Japanese) and also a two-way continuation model (Spanish).

It is important to note that the field of DLI education in the US has historically operated in a realm separate from the traditional world language field. Practitioners of immersion education are typically licenced in their content areas, such as elementary education or secondary social studies, and they are highly proficient speakers of the target language. To be considered an immersion program, at least 50% of the core academic content must be delivered in the immersion language (Fortune & Tedick, 2008a). Immersion teachers are responsible for delivering academic content instruction in a new language, and as such are beholden to state content standards rather than the World-Readiness Standards for Learning Languages (ACTFL, 2015), for which world language teachers are responsible.

The call for intercultural citizenship development in language education originates with recent significant publications from the American Council on the Teaching of Foreign Languages (ACTFL) (see ACTFL, 2017; Wagner et al., 2019). ACTFL's framework draws on Byram's intercultural communicative competence model (Byram, 1997, 2021), and is further distilled into a call for intercultural citizenship in language teaching (Byram, 2006; Wagner et al., 2019). While the use of intercultural can-do statements has been increasingly adopted by teachers in traditional world language teaching settings, immersion programs are not beholden to ACTFL standards and these programs are not explicitly encouraged to adopt intercultural learning goals. While research on the field of dual language and immersion education does not currently indicate use of the ACTFL intercultural can-do statements in these contexts, the present study aims to add to our understanding of how intercultural development can be further supported in these programs. However, Wagner et al.'s recent publication through ACTFL urges teachers in ALL subject areas to adopt the framework for intercultural citizenship education to help better prepare students for their future in a transnationally connected world (Wagner et al., 2019).

Intercultural competence in dual language and immersion education

Intercultural competence refers to the knowledge, attitudes and skills related to operating across cultures (Byram, 1997, 2021; Deardorff, 2006). Intercultural communicative competence (ICC) recognizes the significant role that language use plays in cross-cultural interactions. Byram's ICC describes how linguistic, sociolinguistic, discourse, strategic, sociocultural and social competencies support successful intercultural communication (Byram, 2021). These competencies should inform teaching practice, including instructional objectives and assessments (Byram, 1997; Byram *et al.*, 2013). Abbott (2019) describes the goal of intercultural citizenship as 'embarking on that journey toward global competence that allows students to see themselves as people who can make their way through unfamiliar territory as they experience other cultures and ways of thinking and doing—and do it with a growing sense of comfort and curiosity'. While immersion teachers focus first on academic content, there is significant opportunity for these programs to build global competencies in their students.

Fortune and Tedick (2008a) explain that language immersion teachers in the US ardently point to the benefits of these programs for building an appreciation for other cultures in language majority students. For Indigenous language immersion programs, the goal of revitalizing an endangered linguistic and cultural community is accompanied by the aim to instill a positive sense of native identity in learners (Fortune & Tedick, 2008b). These goals of appreciation for other cultures and a focus on fostering positive cultural identity development illustrate elements of intercultural development that can lay the foundation for intercultural citizenship development. Furthermore, because immersion teachers foster language competencies through their classroom practices, it seems likely that many of the goals of ICC are naturally being realized in this specialized educational context.

Meeting the needs of challenging historical and social contexts

For marginalized communities, the amplification of voices through the promotion of language and cultures can have a profound impact on individuals and society. TWI programs have the opportunity to disrupt systems of power and privilege, amplifying voices that have been silenced in the broader community. In young learners, we may see this in how students express their identity by making choices about the language they use in different situations (Feinauer & Howard, 2014: 266). Programs for the revitalization of Indigenous languages and cultures play an important role in making positive social change. Indigenous revitalization immersion (IRI) programs are designed to support both language and culture revitalization within Native or Aboriginal communities (Curtain & Dahlberg, 2016). In the US, Hawai'i has paved the way for other Indigenous languages as they have been working on revitalizing the Hawaiian language for more than 40 years. The goals of social justice education implore us to recognize injustice and work towards positive social change and the empowerment of those who have been marginalized.

Little attention has been paid to how immersion students develop critical stances on issues, recognizing power and privilege, or challenging social inequities. Fairclough (1992) notes that we should aim to transform language awareness activities to achieve this goal, but to do so we must 'adopt an explicit critical stance and make issues of equity central to classroom initiatives' (Fortune & Tedick, 2008b: 214). Intercultural citizenship, also called ICit, aims to engage students in critical cultural awareness, which includes an element of political engagement (Byram, 2021). Byram *et al.* (2013) note that the curriculum could be augmented to allow for more intercultural citizenship/ICC and critical awareness goals. They also make the case for teaching interdisciplinary intercultural citizenship (ICit), which lends itself to the kinds of instruction seen in DLI programs. Byram notes that teaching for ICit requires teaching that 'encourages and expects learners to challenge their own society, and this is a major responsibility' (Byram, 2021: 122). Furthermore, ICit is informed by the goals of education for democracy (also known as *Demokratie Lernen*), and the responsibility lies not only with language teachers but with educators across the subject areas (Byram, 2021: 122). Unlike traditional world language settings, immersion teachers are trained to teach academic content in many additional subject areas. Elementary teachers regularly teach units that are interdisciplinary in nature. One would expect that elementary immersion classrooms would afford many opportunities for interdisciplinary intercultural citizenship instruction. Immersion contexts have the potential to inform traditional world language teaching. Wagner *et al.* (2019) point to how content-based instruction (CBI) and the European content and language integrated learning (CLIL) models support IC development, which is endorsed by ACTFL as a research priority, and is an approach which has been shown to be effective for both language and content learning. The ICit framework implores teachers to prepare learners for 'active citizenship' and the ability to work effectively in transnational situations. These goals prepare learners for a more interconnected future wherein they can work and live in a global community. 'The goal is to support students' development of the attitudes, knowledge and skills that foster their critical cultural awareness and help them generate thoughtful plans of action, substantially supported by all subjects involved, to address a critical societal issue' (Wagner *et al.*, 2019: 49).

Context of the Study

Anchorage is the largest city in Alaska, with a population of roughly 350,000. Half Alaska's population lives in Anchorage. Anchorage School District (ASD) is a large urban school district serving approximately 45,000 students. Ethnically and linguistically diverse, minority students represent more than 50% of the student population. There are more than 100 home languages spoken by ASD students, with the top five being (following English and Spanish): Hmong, Samoan, Tagalog, Korean and Yup'ik (an Alaska Native language). ASD has been offering dual language immersion programs since 1989, starting with Japanese. Since then, programs have been added in Spanish (both one-way and two-way), Russian, German, Mandarin Chinese, Yup'ik and French. All these programs are K–12 with the exception of Mandarin, Yup'ik and French, which continue to grow and will eventually be K–12 as well.

For the purposes of this study, the researchers spent time observing and interviewing teachers in three immersion programs that spanned grades K–12. Our focus was on K–8 Japanese and K–3 Yup'ik immersion one-way programs, as well as grades 6–8 in the Spanish two-way program. The study aimed to investigate how programs and teachers enact education for intercultural citizenship through immersion pedagogies. While the programs studied did not explicitly name ICit as an educational goal, dual language and immersion programs aim to foster deeper cross-cultural understanding in students, often referred to as the 'third goal' of immersion (Curtain & Dahlberg, 2016). ICit provides educators with a helpful lens through which to examine how we foster cross-cultural skills and understandings. Even though these programs were not aiming to meet ICit learning goals, we anticipated that aspects of the ICit framework were occurring naturally within the immersion context. We wanted to investigate which traits of the ICit framework were being realized in these dual language and immersion contexts, as well as identify those that were not. The study looks to answer the following research questions:

(1) What do aspects of intercultural citizenship (ICit) look like in dual language and immersion classrooms?
(2) What challenges prevent immersion programs and teachers from pursuing the goals of intercultural citizenship in dual language and immersion programs?

We are interested in knowing which aspects of intercultural citizenship are most readily met in dual language and immersion programs. Which are less commonly observed, and why?

Methods and Data Sources

We employed an ethnographic case study design to look at how the ICit framework is enacted in dual language and immersion programs. Taking an ethnographic approach allows us to examine classroom practices related to ICC and the ICit framework, and it provides opportunities for teachers to explain their perspectives on how they teach for ICC and ICit. An ethnographic case study approach provides opportunity to recognize multiple perspectives and perceptions within a specific context (Cohen *et al.*, 2018). An ethnographic approach allows us to observe social behaviors within the context of immersion classrooms. Wolcott (1999: 68) reminds us that ethnography requires 'a strong descriptive element', and we set out to allow these immersion settings to show us how teachers and students engage in ICC and ICit, in the hope that we could describe and contextualize these practices and teachers' perspectives. This study was conducted by a pair of investigators who could approach the task of ethnographic inquiry from both outsider and insider perspectives (see Wolcott, 1999). Each of the three immersion programs constitutes a case. Non-participant observations were conducted in multiple classrooms in the fall of 2021, ranging from 20 minutes to more than an hour in each. All observations were video recorded to allow us to review the observations if needed. Some observations were undertaken by both researchers simultaneously, and at other times we worked separately to observe two different classrooms at the same time. Observational field notes were taken by the researchers, using an observation protocol organized by the features of ICC and ICit and the codes described in Table 3.2. During these observations, the researchers also made notes of questions they wanted to ask the teachers in the interview phase of data collection, in order to allow a richer description of the phenomena and for participant voices to be heard. Teachers who had been observed were invited to participate in individual or small group interviews. Interviews took place in the spring of the same academic year. While only a subset of invited teachers took part in interviews, the teachers who did so represented a variety of programs and grade levels (see Table 3.1).

Setting and Participants

This study was conducted within various dual language immersion programs in the Anchorage School District (ASD). Anchorage School District launched its first immersion program in Japanese in 1989 at Sand Lake Elementary. For the purpose of this study, we focused on K–8 settings and also selected three unique languages/programs, representing a diverse group: Spanish Two-Way (TWI) at Government

Table 3.1 Data sources: Classrooms and teachers

Program	Grades Observed	Teachers Interviewed
Japanese	4th–6th grade (Akari, Benio, Etsuko, Kay, Sakura) 7th grade (Yoko)	Kay, Sakura (Elementary) Yoko (Middle school)
Spanish	6th–8th grade (Yolanda, Socorro, Pilar)	6th–8th grade (Yolanda, Socorro, Pilar)
Yup'ik	1st–3rd (Cillaraq, Nancy, Linda, Sandra)	K–3 (Cillaraq, Linda, Sandra, Nancy)

Hill Elementary and Romig Middle School; Japanese DLI at Sand Lake Elementary and Mears Middle School; and Yup'ik, an Alaska Native language, a DLI program at College Gate Elementary.

Focusing on the K–8 setting, teachers were identified and invited to participate, based upon their years of experience in addition to selecting a diverse group of languages. It is helpful to note that, often in immersion programs in the US, teachers are sponsored on visas, limiting their time and longevity in programs. Our aim was to include teachers with more than just a year or two of experience in the program. Once these more experienced teachers were identified, the researchers invited them to participate in this study, which included at least one classroom observation, as well as an opportunity to participate in an individual or group interview via Zoom.

Data Analysis

Observational field notes were recorded in real time during the classroom observations, using the codes listed in Table 3.2. Interviews, which utilized questions gleaned from the observational data, were recorded via Zoom and later transcribed prior to analysis. The researchers then affirmed the assigned codes in the observational notes and coded the interviews both according to Byram's traits of ICC, as well as key characteristics of ICit (Wagner *et al.*, 2019). The codes used are listed and described in relation to central definitions of ICit in Table 3.2. Both researchers engaged in deductive coding of the interview and observational data. The researchers met to code the observational notes and interviews together. This allowed for ongoing discussion about the appropriate coding of each quote and observational note. We engaged in a process of reviewing our codes collaboratively, resolving discrepancies in our coding, and identifying particularly illustrative examples from our data set. This allowed us to see patterns in the behaviors of teachers and students, as well as in the perspectives of teachers, which are described in detail in our findings.

Findings

Japanese immersion

Anchorage's first language immersion program began in 1989 with Japanese at Sand Lake Elementary School. The program grew out of community interest as, at the time, many Japan Airlines pilots were based in Anchorage. Sand Lake is located close to the Ted Stevens Anchorage International Airport, so many Japanese children attended Sand Lake. Over time, this led to the establishment of ASD's first immersion program. Sand Lake is a K–6 elementary school, and the

Table 3.2 Data analysis codes

Thematic Codes	Related Core Components of ICit
Knowledge: Knowledge of social groups and their products and practices in one's own and in one's interlocutor's country or region, and of the general processes of societal and individual interaction. • Acquire new knowledge and understandings of the 3 Ps related to the topic/theme. • Discover for themselves the practices of people in other regions or contexts. • Reflection on one's own culture.	Acquiring knowledge and understanding about speakers of the language, and about learners themselves, in support of 'mutual gaze' (Byram *et al.*, 2013).
Attitudes: Curiosity and openness, readiness to suspend disbelief about other cultures and belief about one's own culture. • Readiness to suspend disbelief about other cultures. • Readiness to suspend belief about one's own culture.	Encouragement and planned development of attitudes of curiosity and critical questioning, related to critical cultural awareness (see below) and a concern for social justice (Byram *et al.*, 2013). Readiness to encourage a questioning attitude that recognizes the positive and negative in a social group's beliefs, values and behaviors when evaluated against humanistic standards (Wagner *et al.*, 2019).
Skills: • *Skills of interpreting and relating:* Ability to interpret a document or event from another culture, to explain it and relate it to documents or events from one's own culture. • *Skills of discovery and interaction:* Ability to acquire new knowledge of a culture and cultural practices, and ability to operate knowledge, attitudes and skills under the constraints of real-time communication and interaction.	Engagement in some kind of action, in the future, or in the here and now (Byram *et al.*, 2013).
Critical cultural awareness: Ability to evaluate perspectives, practices and products in one's own and other cultures and countries, both critically and on the basis of explicit criteria.	Identification and evaluation of values in documents and events in own and others' cultures, involving systematic and conscious reasoning; also interaction in intercultural exchanges drawing on knowledge, skills and attitudes to develop a reasoned response (Byram, 2021).
Action beyond the classroom • Learning activities that lead to engagement with people from outside the classroom. • Participate in community life outside the classroom by drawing on competences acquired within the classroom. • A concern about social justice.	Engagement with people from outside the classroom; taking decisions to participate in community life outside the classroom by drawing on competences acquired within the classroom (Byram *et al.*, 2013). A concern about social justice and a belief in the values of humanistic thought and action; a willingness to promote social action in the world and the creation of identification with others beyond the limits of national boundaries; may include involving students in decisions about their own learning (Wagner *et al.*, 2019).

program has a continuation strand at Mears Middle School and Dimond High School. In addition to the K–12 school setting, the program has additional support from *Tomo No Kai*, a non-profit parent group (similar to a PTA), which fundraises to enhance the overall program by funding Japanese interns to come for an academic year, living with Japanese immersion families, working in classrooms and providing after-school tutoring and cultural enrichment. *Tomo No Kai* also subsidizes costs for both Sand Lake and Mears students to participate in exchanges with their peers in Chitose, Japan. It also helps fund the culturally authentic high school Japanese Immersion Completion Ceremony (prior to high school graduation), where students give speeches in Japanese, talking about their Japanese immersion journey. At this prestigious ceremony, the local Japanese consulate speaks and provides gifts to all graduates. *Tomo No Kai* organizes several community events as well, such as the Fall Festival, the art auction (with art created by Japanese immersion students), and the annual cherry blossom festival. Furthermore, an internationally known taiko drumming group, *Tomodachi Daiko*, was born out of the Japanese immersion program some twenty years ago. Over the years, this group features students, teachers, parents and community members, all with the desire to share their love of Japanese culture through the art of taiko drumming.

Knowledge

Evidence of the knowledge domain of ICC in the Japanese program was plentiful at both the elementary and middle school levels. Students in the Japanese immersion program explored their own and others' identities as part of their state-mandated curriculum. In elementary grades, Kay reported having her students investigate where their ancestors came from, including if they have Indigenous heritage. Sakura described how she supported learning of both own and other cultural perspectives in her class:

> When I teach social studies I often use 'so you guys are, let's say, the people who came to Jamestown, and you guys are the Native American people'. I often assign the students a role, and there's a conflict there so what to do? Sometimes I ask the students [to play] roles to get at under-standing the content. (Sakura, interview)

This role-play activity allows Sakura's students to discover for themselves the perspectives and practices of people in a historical context. Another instructor, Benio, was inspired by the World-Readiness Standards (ACTFL) to augment his social studies curriculum by creating a more culturally focused unit on Japanese schools. He begins by presenting ideas about Japanese vs American schools. Students are surprised to learn about the lack of janitors in schools in Japan, and students taking off their shoes in schools. His students then write ideas about American schools, after getting examples from Japanese schools to inspire their work, comparing and contrasting perspectives (Benio, observation). Benio's students are engaged in analyzing perspectives that influence cultural practices.

At the middle school level, Yoko reflected on her intent to deepen knowledge of other cultures with her students. She shared that she wants to do more instruction about Japanese history, but 'since they are middle school kids I talk a lot about popular culture, fashion, food. I probably focus too much on the culture that is recent. That's because I want to engage them' (Yoko, interview). She describes a cultural unit she recently developed:

> have you heard of KunMari – Marie Kondo? I have done that project. I have them fold the stuff, folding is really Japanese. We fold things really neatly. I have them do it and then videotape it in Japanese. So it's pretty funny like 'here are my socks, and then I fold here'. (Yoko, interview)

Through these activities focused on popular culture, Yoko's students are able to reflect on the perspectives that inform contemporary cultural products and practices.

Students in the Japanese immersion program explored individual and societal interactions in terms of honorific language and politeness patterns, as well as expectations for students' roles in caring for the school. The teachers stressed how they instructed their students to behave in culturally appropriate ways when interacting with different interlocutors. Sakura shared: '... if I communicate with the students, I ask them, teach the students that this is a way to talk to teachers, this is the way to talk to peers, so like manners or respect, that's maybe one of the cultural aspects' (Sakura, interview). Benio, Sakura and Kay all shared how they talked to students about the roles that students play in their schools in Japan, caring for the building and community by participating in cleaning and serving lunch. Teachers were intentional in explaining how to observe and participate in these social practices of interaction and in explaining why it was important.

Attitudes

Elementary students are asked to suspend disbelief about Japanese culture when exploring Japanese schools as part of social studies. Sakura shared:

> I briefly talked about Japanese schools, how students clean the classroom by themselves and serve lunch themselves. 'Why do you think Japanese schools have them serve lunch, and why do they clean their classrooms?' Some students already knew, some students were surprised. (Sakura, interview)

Kay chimed in: 'they get shocked that students clean their own bathrooms too' (interview). During the observation of Benio's classroom, students were similarly engaged in suspending their disbelief about Japanese school practices. He began with a slideshow explaining how students remove their shoes when they enter the school, and how students clean the bathrooms – these examples were met with 'aahs' and also surprised reactions. Benio's students also laugh and make connections to their own cultural products and perspectives related to schooling, in particular calling out the presence of 'mystery meat' in the school cafeteria (observation).

Students at Mears Middle School have the opportunity to participate in a Japanese exchange program that has been in place for many years. This exchange occurs between both Sand Lake Elementary and Chitose Elementary in Chitose, Japan. Chitose is Anchorage's oldest Sister City, and the elementary exchange has been occurring for close to 25 years. Mears students attend a few different host middle schools and stay with host families. In both the elementary and middle school exchanges, ASD students visit Chitose and live with Japanese families for 1–2 weeks, and Chitose students visit Anchorage and live with American families, typically for a week. These exchanges occur every other year. Yoko shared:

> when they host Japanese students, they realize how shy the Japanese students are. They never open the fridge without asking... they don't really tell you what they want. The American students try to help and say 'It's ok, dude just open the fridge and take what you want'. (Yoko, interview)

US host students are able to observe their Japanese peers navigating new cultural experiences, and they suspend disbelief about Japanese culture in noticing the timid behavior of the guest students. Yoko further fosters attitudes of openness and curiosity by exposing her students to popular food brands in Japan:

> The project that kids really like is that I give them the website – like the Starbucks website or McDonald's, then they get on the website in Japanese and they find the menu that they would never find in the US. Like Starbucks, now we have matcha frappuccino that originated from Japan. But we have all kinds of crazy flavors like sweet potato flavor, so they're gonna find it and they're gonna write about it and they are gonna make the poster so Americans are gonna know what those stores sell. It's so funny to see them go 'Oh they have a Pikachu ice cream at Baskin Robbins!'. (Yoko, interview)

Through investigating new food products, Yoko's students are asked to suspend disbelief about Japanese culture, and to be open to different flavors and products. However, we did not see evidence of students taking the further step of using these contrasts to examine their own cultural products, practices and perspectives.

Skills

Immersion classrooms often reflect the cultural norms, beliefs and values of the communities of the languages in which they teach. We found many examples of classroom behavior expectations that were directly reflective of Japanese cultural norms, allowing students to engage in interactions that mimic those they would encounter in Japan. At the elementary level, we observed students standing and greeting their teachers, bowing and greeting each other, and sharing a traditional *itadakimasu* (the customary phrase used before eating) before starting their lunch (observations). These examples of etiquette illustrate the skills of discovery and interaction, students acquiring cultural knowledge, and interacting in real time. Sakura also shared how she '... often builds leadership skills for the students. And as the leader, you need to help everyone in your group. I did [this] when I was teaching in Japan, but I bring that here as well' (Sakura, interview). Sakura's students discover for themselves what leadership means in a Japanese context and engage in culturally appropriate interactions. Students also engage in skills of interpreting and relating. While teaching a lesson on the colonization of North America, Akari asked her students to imagine they were English colonist John White, and to imagine how and why he acted in the way that he did and what the impact was on the Indigenous community (Akari, observation). Benio also engaged his students in the skills of interpretation and relating by asking them to compare Japanese and American schools. By looking at images and artifacts from Japanese schools, students began to think about their own cultural frameworks, and prepared a video project that would allow the audience to relate to these cultural comparisons (Benio, observation).

Yoko worked to help her students engage in skills of discovery and interaction by asking them to participate in a Japanese homeroom environment. Yoko stressed the importance of group work and collectivist culture in her aim to create the feeling of a Japanese homeroom. While her US middle school students frequently changed classrooms throughout the day, she wanted them to develop significant bonds with their teacher and with each other. She reflected:

> That's because Japanese middle schools have a homeroom and they are together all day. So their community is pretty strong there [in Japan]. So I implemented this class system like 'Hey, we are working together', like the dancing and singing, I reward them for that. Because we are doing this together. So that's something I want to do more... even though they are going to be separated in other classes, when you come to my class *this* is the community, this is the homeroom. This is our immersion pride. (Yoko, interview)

Her students participated in unfamiliar cultural interactions, drawing on their knowledge, attitudes and skills to navigate and negotiate the Japanese homeroom.

Critical cultural awareness

We found limited evidence of teachers fostering critical cultural awareness in the Japanese immersion program. Yet we heard from teachers that this was an area in which they hoped to do more. One opportunity for students in the Japanese immersion elementary program to critically examine values across cultures was when studying US history. Sakura shared:

> ... I teach in Social Studies, and I usually teach different perspectives. For example, now students just finished the civil war. And like, the people who live in the south believe having slaves is part of their culture, but in the north they actually do not – they do not have plantations, they do not need to use slaves. But not always compared with the Japanese cultural perspectives. I'm sure in [higher grades] my colleague teaches WWII – I assume there's more ... they look from an American perspective and he may teach, 'This is a Japanese perspective on WWII'. (Sakura, interview)

The social studies curriculum affords elementary teachers the opportunity to encourage attitudes of curiosity as well as the practices of critical questioning. Teachers saw possibilities for engaging in more cross-cultural awareness building but, for some reason, this goal was not being realized.

Action beyond the classroom

The ICit framework emphasizes the importance of engaging with communities of language users outside the classroom, drawing on skills learned in the classroom. The Japanese immersion program benefits from having an international exchange program, providing opportunities for students to use their Japanese language skills to interact with Japanese peers. Teachers reported that the prospect of hosting Japanese students and going abroad themselves was motivating to students. Many of the learning opportunities in the Japanese immersion program prepared students for the international exchange that would allow students to engage with their Japanese peers. Sakura reflected:

> sometimes I get students who talk to me in a cultural way and I tell the student 'that's a way to talk to your friend, but not to a teacher'... sometimes in exchange years, particularly, I let them know that when you talk with adults, you need to think about the formality is different. (Sakura, interview)

Students also had opportunities to engage locally with other speakers of Japanese. For example, Sakura described the Japanese speech contest:

> not only for our school, but also the other 2 schools where students who took Japanese as an elective, and University of Alaska students, and even UAF (Fairbanks) Japanese learners, they get together and perform. And these events students have [other] opportunities like... there's a bake sale at the same time, or... calligraphy activities going on. So students have the opportunity to actually use their Japanese to communicate, not necessarily with [our school] students and teachers. We used to have a fall dinner... that kind of event is pretty open to the community, like Japanese people who just live in Anchorage may come to visit us. (Sakura, interview)

Kay also mentioned the taiko traditional drumming group as an opportunity for students to use their language and cultural skills beyond the school. Whether global or local, students in the Japanese program have chances to interact with peers, using their knowledge and skills gained in school to forge cross-cultural relationships.

While students in the Japanese immersion program benefit from ample opportunities to use their language and cultural knowledge to engage with peers locally and internationally, we did not find evidence of engagement with social justice initiatives. Examples of promotion of social action were not observed in the Japanese immersion program. We see this as an area for further development towards realizing the goals of the ICit framework.

Spanish immersion

The Anchorage School District has two different K–12 Spanish immersion programs: a one-way program, where the vast majority of students are English-speakers learning Spanish, and a two-way program, where half the student population is predominantly English-speaking and the other half are Spanish-speakers or heritage speakers of Spanish. The program highlighted in this chapter is the two-way immersion (TWI) program, which began in 1993 at Government Hill Elementary. At the time, Government Hill was considered a 'failing school'. In a predominantly Hispanic area with many monolingual Spanish students, several federal grants were written to establish a two-way Spanish/ English bilingual immersion program. Federal Title VII discretionary grants as well as federal FLAP (Foreign Language Assistance Program) grants were awarded and the program was established. The program continues at Romig Middle School for grades 7–8, and then at West Anchorage High School. To date this is the only two-way immersion program in Alaska, with an annual K–12 enrollment of close to 575 students. The teaching staff of this program represent Spain, Central and South America, as well as Native speakers of Spanish from the US. The middle school program has an ongoing partnership with a school in Puerto Rico, whereby ASD students typically visit every other year. Thus far, the students from Puerto Rico have yet to visit Anchorage.

Classrooms in this program include students with English and Spanish as their first languages, allowing for abundant interaction in both languages between peers. We observed and interviewed teachers working at the elementary and middle school levels of this program. This elementary school had a Spanish-speaking principal, which was unique among the schools studied here.

Knowledge

Because so many of the students in the Spanish program are Spanish heritage learners, many examples of their own culture learning were observed. Pilar's observed lesson focused on conquistadors and examined questions that included: Why is Latin America Catholic? and What does it mean to be a savior? Her colleague Yolanda described Pilar's approach as follows:

> the way that she's teaching these 10 students, it's so impressive because they're starting to talk to you in *español* which before they never did because it was all *inglés* … so now they're like, 'Oh, that's what that book was about', you know, because they're reading it and they're seeing it and they're starting to get that sense of ownership in that sense of pride. (Yolanda, interview)

At the same time, the examples above also represent development of knowledge of *other* cultures, as not all the students are heritage learners of Spanish. Regardless of cultural background, all learners in this classroom were acquiring new knowledge and understanding of cultural products, practices and perspectives related to the social studies curriculum. Furthermore, because of the diverse backgrounds of the teaching staff, students regularly encounter a variety of cultural perspectives as they participate in the program. Socorro explains:

> … if you speak to Senora X [sic] her perspective on democracy is going to be much different than it is for someone like me who grew up in Dominican Republic in a somewhat democratic country versus where she grew up in Cuba, so that's going to be a different perspective just right there. (Socorro, interview)

Students also made discoveries regarding cultural perspectives and practices by engaging with current primary source resources:

> What I like about the social studies course right now is that we have so much material that society in the world has given us, and it's worldwide

so our our issues are so worldwide that they come in Spanish, that they come in English, and it's all primary you know it is not it hasn't been translated, we can easily go to, you know, any website, all over the world, and all of it will be in *español* [in Spanish]. (Yolanda, interview)

In the Spanish program, many opportunities for exploring cultural similarities and differences were facilitated by the teaching of social studies content and were further fostered by teachers who were willing to draw on their own diverse cultural backgrounds to enhance the learning goals and materials.

Attitudes

We were surprised not to find evidence of students suspending disbelief about other cultures. We attribute this to the fact that we focused on grades 7 and above in a TWI context wherein students had been engaging in cross-cultural learning since Kindergarten. We also note that because the program is two-way immersion, all the learners constantly engage with their own and others' cultures in a seamless manner. However, we did find abundant evidence of suspension of belief around students' own culture, particularly in comments by teachers. Yolanda described how her Latinx students engaged in identity exploration, commenting:

… what I have experienced is students that want to know more… you know, 'What is it that you say that I am? You're saying that I'm from Mexico, what does that really mean? I was born and raised here, my grandparents are the ones that taught me *español* [sic] my grandparents or my great grandmother, and they've never even been to Mexico'. So, when we bring it to light in a classroom when we start showing it off… they become more curious, they want to know more. (Yolanda, interview)

Middle school teacher Pilar described how many of her students were born in Mexico and how she worked to foster a sense of pride. She tells them: 'Being bilingual is a superpower!' (Pilar, interview). She describes how students are watching current news, and 'they are getting rid of the stigma, they are being more open to other cultures and languages and heritage' (Pilar, interview). Pilar's work to dispel stereotypes and connect students with current events transnationally illustrates how she is fostering curiosity and openness towards cultural others.

Skills

Students engaged in the practice of interpreting and relating to authentic documents in Spanish, with Pilar reporting how she 'relies on primary sources, because it brings awareness' in her instruction (interview). Pilar also augments her social studies curriculum in ways that would not be possible in a non-immersion setting but that has significant benefits for the students' intercultural development. Unlike in the English-medium social studies class, Pilar's students read Columbus's diary in the original Spanish as part of this unit on *conquistadores*. She described how students also read a primary source document by the last Inca Emperor, Atahualpa, and:

> we discuss [the questions] 'Did he put the bible on his ear? When they gave him a bible, did he listen to it? Or did he throw it on the floor?'. Students analyze fake history vs. facts. They made it sound like he wasn't educated enough. And I asked the kids whether they agreed with that. So the [text] book sometimes portrays Indigenous people one way… there's a lot of culture and stigma, and how we perceive people when they are different. (Pilar, interview)

Pilar is intentional about supporting students' identification of ethnocentric perspectives in these documents and in the broader discussions around conquests in the Americas. She has students look specifically at contradictions in the interpretation of historical events, allowing them to deepen their understanding, all the while relying on their linguistic and cultural competencies. Students in this class have had practice in the skills of interpreting and relating. In our observation notes we wrote:

> Wow! Students reject some of these [flash] cards for being too simplistic. They require more context and not glossing over. This activity requires them to negotiate their collective understanding of these definitions – and they argue. They are riled up! They clearly want more accuracy, more nuance. (Pilar, observation)

In Yolanda's class, students were reading the book *Bajo Las Palmas Reales,* and the author Alma Flor Ada had come and worked with the teachers. Yolanda described:

> one of the beautiful parts about having the pleasure of meeting some of these authors in person, you know that the material is authentic, and it hasn't been, it has been translated from Spanish to English rather than English to Spanish. So you know that, that little saying that says 'Things get lost in translation' is very true, with many of the books that we have read in our literature class. (Yolanda, interview)

She described how students strengthened their ability to relate to the book by taking time to uncover cultural nuance in the story. She shared this example:

> Having the students be a part of authentic writing and culture, and… one of the lines was when she sat down and had *Cafecito con Leche*

with her grandmother. So, some of these kids that are Native speakers [but] they do know what a *Cafecito con Leche* is… okay this is what a *Cafecito* looks like and they're like 'Oh wait a minute. It's not the 20 ounce venti latte that my mom gets, it's actually, you know, a small little cup'. So you know those are the things [benefits] that, you know, having that privilege of getting these books that are authentic. It's huge, huge. (Yolanda, interview)

Students were guided through the text and urged to make a comparison with their own cultural frameworks. They delved deeper into the text by exploring the product and related practices of the *Cafecito* while working with this authentic text, in a way that is unique to the immersion setting.

Critical cultural awareness

Teachers in the Spanish immersion program prioritized the development of a critical attitude towards course content. Students engaged in analysis of conscious and systemic realization and investigated cultural beliefs and value systems. Pilar says: 'It's important to have tough conversations… even if you don't bring it up, the kids do. The kids are aware enough, and there's a culture [in my classroom] that they can express themselves' (Pilar, interview). She described how, during Black History Month, her middle school students researched an African American who was important to them and 'They brought a lot of examples, and talked about how they still have a long way to go' (Pilar, interview).

Similarly, Socorro engaged her elementary students in a critical analysis related to President Roosevelt, deepening the traditional history course content. She shared:

One of the things that he did was help Panama become independent from Colombia. That is not normally taught in sixth grade but I said, 'Okay, so do you guys realize that Panama was part of Colombia? Because the United States was interested in building and having control of the area, they helped Panama become independent so that they could control the canal for the next 100 years', and that was Roosevelt's doing. (Socorro, interview)

Socorro also found an opportunity to delve into an examination of freedom of political expression as a result of a comment she had made in class about former President Trump. She had shared with students that she found his politics divisive and discriminatory. She reported:

Well, one of my kiddos felt somewhat uncomfortable because of my comment and went home and told mom that he felt uncomfortable because they're [the student's family) so pro-Trump. I heard about it and I explained what I said, but then again, I explained that freedom of speech also gives me the liberty of saying what I think about any politician. I don't care which one it is. We made a comparison in other countries where that doesn't happen. If you talk about a politician or a president or whatever, your family disappears. I told them back in the 1930s, between the 1930s and 1960s, the Dominican Republic had a dictatorship, and I told them anecdotes of what my mom's friends went through at that time because they were not allowed to express their feelings about their president. (Socorro, interview)

This example illustrates how cultural values and beliefs can be explored in a meaningful and systemic way, fostering new realizations and the ability to critique events through a critical lens.

Action beyond the classroom

Spanish immersion students had the opportunity to use their language and intercultural skills outside the classroom environment, yet the kinds of engagement varied due to the age of the students. Socorro commented about the challenge of realizing the goal of participation in the larger community for elementary students:

I had one of my previous students a couple of years ago that got involved with writing to the politicians, and tried to have a law or something done, a petition signed for social justice and social support of the LGBTQ community. I do believe that they are very capable but the elementary [context] is somewhat limited by what we can do and teach in the sense of their understanding and how protected the kids might be. Once they get into middle and high school, then their minds are much more open to the social issues that are occurring in our country or different countries, but absolutely, there are opportunities for them to get involved socially. (Socorro, interview)

At the middle school level, Yolanda found numerous opportunities for her students to engage in community action, building on their ICC that had been carefully cultivated in the classroom. One opportunity her students have is to participate in a Model United Nations, which requires students to research a topic from a particular national perspective. Model UN allows students to engage with peers from other schools, and even students from the University of Alaska. Model UN requires students to take on the perspective of another nation, allowing students to engage in transnational negotiations with peers from diverse backgrounds, in pursuit of meaningful political or social change. Another significant example is the students' contributions to the local Spanish language newspaper *Sol de Media Noche* (*The Midnight Sun*). Yolanda shares:

We have written articles for this newspaper, as a class. We have a little student corner, and the kids all write a story… the newspaper [editor] comes in, tells us what type of story she's looking for for her next edition, and she picks one of our stories, and it gets published and the students need to write it and they need to translate it, which is huge because that way you know just shows a full circle completion of understanding. We've done topics as you know like school uniforms or school lunches, you know things that are relatable to them. It's a very unique opportunity that we have… to write for a newspaper that's shared with, you know, 300,000 people that live in Anchorage. So that's really neat, we've enjoyed that opportunity you know just to connect with our community. (Yolanda, interview)

When students write for a broader audience, they must utilize their intercultural communicative competence, drawing on linguistic, socio-cultural and discourse competencies. The topics that Yolanda highlights further illustrate a commitment to social justice issues that matter to students, and a commitments to share students' perspectives with a wider audience.

Another example of students concerning themselves with social justice included Pilar's comment about interactions outside of the classroom: 'In the cafeteria, the students are really close together, if someone isn't fair, they take action. They defend their classmates. There's a culture of brotherhood, the students are so close to each other' (Pilar, interview). Interest in engaging in the work of social justice was guided by teacher-led activities, such as newspaper writing and Model UN, but was also perpetuated by students themselves in unstructured social contexts. The Spanish immersion program yielded numerous examples of engagement beyond the classroom walls, as well as a concern for social justice. The many traits of the ICit framework were readily identified through a variety of exemplars across the Spanish program.

Yup'ik immersion

The Yup'ik (an Alaska Native language from southwestern Alaska) immersion program is one of Anchorage's newest programs, followed by French. Anchorage School District was awarded a grant from the US Department of Education, Office of Indian Education, to launch the program in the fall of 2018. An additional federal grant was awarded through September 2023, which will bring the program into grade 5. In the US in recent years there has been an emphasis on increasing the number of language programs to revitalize/support American Indian, Alaska Native and Native Hawaiian students. So, when the US Department of Education announced the Native American Language (NAL@ED) grants, Anchorage School District was eager to apply. In addition to English, Alaska has 20 other Alaska Native languages as official languages of the state, the most prevalent being Yup'ik. Yup'ik also happens to be the second most spoken Indigenous language in the US after Navajo. Still a growing program, at the time of data collection, the program consisted of grades K–3.

The school employs teachers who largely hail from rural villages with thriving communities of Yup'ik speakers. Because teachers are largely imported to Anchorage, the immersion school serves as a proxy village, providing cultural comfort and safety to teachers, as well as some students from remote Yup'ik villages. Walking into the Yup'ik immersion classrooms, we were greeted by posters and decorations portraying the Yup'ik language and cultural artifacts. Each classroom had large paper salmon filets hanging from the ceiling, and the alphabet posted above the whiteboard included images of culturally important items, including seals, sleds and knives. While the building housed both a mainstream English program as well as the Yup'ik program, it was clear that visual supports were intentionally placed to surround learners with language and culture.

Knowledge

In the Yup'ik program, the line between *own* and *other* cultures sometimes blurs. We often observed students being introduced to cultural practices, products and perspectives, and being guided to discovery. Yet whether this knowledge was new or familiar depended on the student's background. As in the Spanish program, this program had students who were heritage speakers of the language of instruction. While we saw some focus on how cultural practices, products and perspectives compared between Yup'ik and non-Yup'ik Alaskans, we did not find evidence of students of non-Yup'ik heritage being asked to reflect upon their own culture.

The classroom observations included multiple examples of students learning through singing. Singing for learning is both a cultural practice as well as a perspective on how knowledge is transferred. In the 1st grade classroom, students sang the alphabet song in Yup'ik but to a different melody than the English version. Written Yup'ik dates back to the 1950s, and the program in Anchorage has many books and print materials created in the 1950s and 1960s for the town of Bethel, Alaska. First graders were asked by their teacher to sing the alphabet song for each other. The teachers told us that singing and showing knowledge through performance is a cultural practice (Cillaraq, observation).

The teachers explained a naming ceremony that is held each year whereby all new students are given a Yup'ik name. This is an example of new cultural knowledge about students' *own* culture for some, and about *other* cultures for others. Cillaraq explained: 'we want those people that have passed on (died) to continue in these kids' lives. So we name these kids according to the people who have passed on' (Cillaraq, interview). Nancy chimed in: '...or who they remind us of. Like this year, there were a couple of kids in kindergarten. So I named one of the kids after my uncle because whatever Cillaraq had said about him reminded me of that' (Nancy, interview). We observed lessons on the state-mandated curriculum but with strong cultural connections, such as telling stories about Yup'ik traditions and making and eating fry bread with local berries made into jam. Nancy described how the science curriculum dealing with the lifecycle of salmon got particular attention, with additional information about cultural products, practices and perspectives related to this fish being shared with students: 'When I taught the salmon stuff, I used those [paper salmon filets] and showed them how they are fileted, and how they are cut, and how they are hung. And they've just been hanging ever since' (Nancy, interview).

Knowledge about individual and societal interactions was developed in subtle ways in the Yup'ik immersion setting. One example relates to the naming ceremony described above, in which learners realize that connections with deceased community members are intentionally maintained through remembering those individuals by passing along their names. Students also learn how daily life and interactions are different for Yup'ik peoples living in the city as compared to back in their villages. Nancy described how they work to help students understand these differences: 'And they, you know, start to see how we're different from how our lives are lived in the village versus the city. And just how family life may be for us, for like a Yup'ik family versus a non-Yup'ik family' (Nancy, interview). We found that the knowledge domain of the ICit framework in this program focused mainly on exposing students to cultural comparisons, and relatively little attention was paid to reflection upon one's own culture. The age of the students and the newness of this immersion program should be considered as we seek to understand how and why ICit might be realized differently within the Yup'ik context as compared to the others.

Attitudes

Students in Yup'ik immersion are constantly given opportunities to build their attitudes of curiosity and openness. Even for students who identify as Yup'ik, living in Anchorage does not expose them to language and traditions that they would experience in the villages. The line between one's own and other cultures is unclear, as students may identify as Yup'ik but may not yet know aspects of their own cultural heritage. The teachers shared examples of how they help their students to suspend disbelief about unfamiliar cultural products. Several poignant examples were related to food. We observed students making and eating fry bread. While Nancy explained that this wasn't the traditional way of making fry bread (they used pre-made dough), they had decided it was valuable for students to try it. This also gave them a chance to try the jam they had made from local berries. As Nancy began to hand out pieces of dough, having students smell and feel it, they began to say 'Aaaaaah' as they realized what they would be doing. Nancy sparked curiosity by allowing students to create something culturally unfamiliar (Nancy, observation).

Several teachers shared how they had brought in dead birds and fish to class and had shown students how the animals would be handled in traditional culture. Linda shared:

> I show them things like the fish, or the bird, and show them the insides. Show them pictures on the computer. And a lot of the kids, their first response is 'Eww'. And then I make a lesson note of that saying, 'No, you cannot do that. Even though it's "Eww" to you, it's not something you should blurt out. You show respect. You watch. You listen. You learn'. (Linda, interview)

Linda is purposeful in her work with students to help them suspend disbelief about a new cultural practice. Similarly, Sandra brought dried herring back from the village for her students to try:

> We were reading about Nelson area people making dry fish herring. And we studied that for quite some time because… a majority of food is herring they prepare in so many different ways. So after I asked permission, I brought in dried herring that my daughter had made last year, and I let them all taste. And I was really shocked that every one of them ate it because it's kind of smelly… But they all tasted it. Some wanted more. I think if you'll let them see and feel, they remember more of what they learned. (Sandra, interview)

Nancy chimed in 'think also that helps, you know, like because they see our food, they smell our food. And when we talk to them about how they're supposed to react or how they're not supposed to react, that helps with teaching them respect for others' (Nancy, interview). The Yup'ik teachers were intentional about helping their students to engage with new cultural products and practices by building their capacity for openness and curiosity.

Skills

Walking through the school, it was apparent that students were participating in a learning community that observed particular behavior expectations reflecting Yup'ik values. Students lined up quietly in the hallways and sat and listened intently to teachers telling them stories (observations). Nancy explained:

> when they first come to kindergarten, you know, Linda has the job of having them sit still and all that stuff. She does an amazing job doing that. And the specials [special subjects, ex. art] teachers always tell us how good our kids are compared to the other [non-immersion] classes… our kids tend to be quieter, more respectful because we really make sure to tell them, 'No, you're not supposed to do that'. (Nancy, interview)

Classroom observations also revealed that students' classroom routines also reflected a Yup'ik communication style in that students focus on listening and do not interrupt, as well as many instances of the use of choral response and singing to support learning.

The pedagogical approach used by teachers reflected traditional Yup'ik values and beliefs about learning, exposing students to new cultural practices and allowing them to interact with their teachers and peers in culturally appropriate ways. The teachers were intentional about their use of storytelling as a pedagogical practice. Nancy shared:

> with the younger grades because they can't sit for very long, they [the stories] have to be really short. When the pandemic started... we needed things like stories and songs recorded. And so Cook Inlet Tribal Council did some for us, and then Alice, and Linda, they did a whole bunch of stuff that they still use today. Not so much like the traditional storytelling, like you know, where you sit there and tell a story to the kids. I think as they get older in the program, we just build on that. And so they're able to, you know, sit longer, listen longer. (Nancy, interview)

Linda shared: 'we incorporate today's academic stuff with the storytelling that they used to do long ago... or I use the classroom rules to keep reminding the kids that one of the rules is to listen, to watch, so you can learn' (Linda, interview).

Examples of students using the skills of interpreting and relating included engagement with Yup'ik language materials such as oral stories, books and flashcards. Because Yup'ik has traditionally been a language relying on oral tradition, interpretation of 'authentic documents' does not occur in the way it does in the other immersion programs. Instead, teachers drew upon Indigenous knowledge through experiences and storytelling to bring rich, authentic cultural knowledge to their students. When asked about the use of authentic materials that would allow for interpretation and relating, Nancy shared:

> ... we bring in things that we have. We've brought in seal skins, other types of fur. I remember last year I brought in a couple of birds, and I cut those up right in front of the kids. You know, we tried to do as many things like that as possible to, you know, make the learning more relevant. (Nancy, interview)

Critical cultural awareness

Students in the Yup'ik program experience a curriculum that reflects cultural beliefs that differ from the mainstream. One example is the science curriculum, which teaches that there are six seasons in the year, rather than four (Linda, observation). Students learn about how people relate to their environment through a specific cultural lens, while still meeting the standards set by the state of Alaska. They had opportunities to notice and interpret cultural values reflected by the six Yup'ik seasons. Teachers are intentional about fostering attitudes of curiosity through the use of sensory experiences, such as in the aforementioned examples of using animal skins and furs, and sampling Yup'ik traditional foods. Nancy describes that students 'need to be able to feel things and smell them' in order to learn (Nancy, interview). Teachers supported students' understanding of differing value systems through stories and direct experiences with animals and foods. However, we did not see evidence of students interacting or mediating intercultural exchanges beyond interactions with peers in the classroom setting.

Action beyond the classroom

The Yup'ik immersion students make connections with Yup'ik community members primarily through the teachers in the school. Because the program is new, it does not have the same opportunities for students to participate in events and experiences outside the school. Nancy describes how community engagement with the program has already begun to grow:

> ... working here with the Yup'ik immersion program, it feels like our circle has gotten bigger. Not just because of the relationship I have with the teachers and stuff like that, you know. I feel like we're a community within a community in our school. Like I know all of the kids in the Yup'ik immersion program... They know I'm part of the program. We have lots of kids that are in the regular neighborhood program that, you know, they'll greet us in Yup'ik... or try to say Yup'ik words. And it's nice. I mean like when the first year, we had a few, and then now we have a bigger group, and it's more, I guess like we're more part of the College Gate community now. (Nancy, interview)

The Yup'ik program interviews and observations did not yield evidence of concern for social justice and only limited engagement in action outside the school community, specifically that some ethnically Yup'ik students return to their villages over the summer months.

Limitations Leading to ICit Opportunities

While immersion education naturally affords many opportunities for students to engage in meaningful ICit development that builds on students' ICC, we also discovered some traits of immersion settings that appear to limit implementation of the ICit framework. These limitations are simultaneously opportunities for immersion programs to adapt in ways that would allow for the goals of ICit to be more readily realized.

Some teachers, particularly in the Japanese program, reported feeling limited in the degree to which they could explore cultural and intercultural issues in their classrooms. They felt somewhat bound by the state-mandated curriculum and were unsure as to how much they could veer from the required learning goals to incorporate more culturally focused or critical learning goals. Sakura shared: 'if I try to teach all the curriculum, there's so much to teach with vocabulary and the content is sometimes too much. I want to teach them Japanese cultural things, but my focus tends to be "Ok let's finish social studies, or let's finish science"' (Sakura, interview). Yoko stated: 'I think the Anchorage school district is pretty open. If I want to add more cultural aspects to my Japanese language arts class I can. But the social studies [curriculum] kind of prevents me from having time to teach cultural aspects because I have to catch up with social studies' (Yoko, interview). Kay shared the sentiment: '... some people say why don't you teach Japanese history instead of US history...but the curriculum' (Kay, interview). However, teachers in the Spanish and Yup'ik programs did not note this as a limitation. Perhaps the balance between heritage learners of Spanish and Yup'ik within these programs naturally allowed for a feeling of empowerment to incorporate more culturally focused learning goals?

Infusing criticality is challenging for many teachers, who may feel unprepared or may question whether such an approach is appropriate or even welcome within the school or community context. When asked whether her teaching of social studies allowed for exploration of Japanese perspectives on historical events, including WWII, Yoko shared:

> Unfortunately I don't think so. When they are learning US history in Japanese they are pretty much focused on US history. And I do want to teach them more Japanese history. Some kids know a lot about Japanese history. And I do want to invite them to talk about it more, but unfortunately again we are too busy to talk about something else. (Yoko, interview)

She also noted a further challenge related to exploring particular topics from multiple perspectives: 'well the topic is sensitive, but I want to talk about World War II, you know, what happened in Japan' (Yoko, interview). Sakura shared that she believed her colleague in the upper grades was incorporating Japanese perspectives on WWII at that level. While the teachers and the school district seem to be supportive of delving into some critical issues, it is unclear to what extent that is happening. Furthermore, we note that issues related to Japanese perspectives on WWII are highly sensitive and pose challenges to teachers of Japanese (see Kubota, 2016). While there is certainly opportunity for more critical approaches in immersion teaching that would lead to stronger implementation of the ICit framework, we also recognize there are significant challenges and constraints.

Another limitation to note is the lack of opportunities for students to engage in social justice concerns and practice. Byram (2021: 123) states: 'Teachers encourage and sometimes require their learners to make judgements, as in "critical cultural awareness", and then, in a major change of purpose, to take action, to become involved in *political engagement*'. Because these immersion programs are part of the public schools and follow the state-mandated curriculum, these programs face the same challenges in engaging politically and in implementing social justice teaching that non-immersion schools face. Yet one would expect that the focus on languages and cultures might naturally lead to more avenues for social justice teaching. While the Spanish immersion program was found to be engaging with social justice topics, Japanese and Yup'ik were not. While numerous opportunities were available for students to interact with speakers of Japanese locally and transnationally, we noted a missed opportunity for concern for and engagement in social justice. The Yup'ik program is much newer, and their learners much younger, which could explain why teachers were not focusing on social justice. Instead, the curriculum in grades K–2 was largely focused on learning how to learn, developing literacy skills and math. Yet an opportunity to make connections between the science curriculum and how the climate impacts Yup'ik traditional life would be possible. Schools could seek out more structured ways to engage with and promote social justice within the school, or with the Yup'ik diaspora living in Anchorage. One Spanish teacher shared her thoughts on the role of age and engagement:

> elementary is somewhat limited by what we can do and teach in the sense of their understanding and how protected [by their parents] the kids might be. Once they get to middle and high school, then their minds are much more open to the social issues that are occurring in our country or different countries... there are opportunities to get involved socially. (Socorro, interview)

Infusing social justice education into these programs would allow for additional opportunities for 'active citizenship', further realizing the goals of ICit.

Another area for further ICit enactment is in the development of critical cultural awareness. Related to the aforementioned limitations related to critical approaches to instruction, Spanish teacher Socorro took the time to dig into why free speech, including political speech, was important. She helped students understand how differing experiences led to different kinds of appreciation for democracy and free speech by helping students compare and contrast between the Dominican Republic and the US. The Yup'ik teachers had similar opportunities to explore the origins of a food associated with Native peoples in the US – fry bread. But they did not delve into the fraught history of this seemingly culturally authentic product. The teachers even approximated the product by using store-bought Pillsbury dough. Nancy shared: 'you know, jam is not something that's traditionally made' (Nancy, interview).

But the teachers did not help students to understand and evaluate these food items as products of the Yup'ik people or, more importantly, *not* of the Yup'ik people. It is possible again that students in the Yup'ik program will be able to explore, analyze and evaluate cultural practices and events more thoroughly through the guidance of their teachers as they begin to explore more complex topics in later grades. Doing so would build students' capacities for critical cultural awareness. Socorro offered this insight related to early grades:

> I think that the switch mentally happens between second and third grade. By third grade, they're thinking a little bit different. By fourth grade, they start asking, 'Where are you from? Where did you grow up, Señora?' because I remember them in fourth grade asking me. (Socorro, interview)

Finally, we note further opportunity for the exploration of one's own cultural values and perspectives in all three immersion settings studied here. Teachers in these immersion settings were intentional about helping their students explore the cultural products, practices and perspectives of the cultures where the languages are spoken. However, they did not make intentional and explicit comparisons and connections to US or other cultures or engage readily in 'suspending belief' about their own culture. They did not engage in the same kinds of meaningful critique of the values and beliefs behind US cultural behaviors, documents or events that seemed to happen rather naturally in exploring other cultures. ICit requires learners to critique their own society, and facilitating this is 'a major responsibility' of teachers (Byram, 2021: 122). This is further complicated by the challenge of distinguishing between what constitutes one's own vs another's culture when groups are mixed in an Indigenous immersion program or a two-way immersion program. Yet all programs would benefit from more intentional, ongoing exploration of students' own cultural frameworks in order to move towards 'active citizenship' and the goals of ICit.

Discussion

The immersion programs studied here provide clear examples of the development of ICC in student grades K–8. We found abundant examples of teachers planning and delivering instruction that supported knowledge, attitudes and skills development that can lead to intercultural citizenship. We found several notable examples of ICC development and the ICit framework. When Pilar had her students engage with primary source documents (Columbus's diary and a primary source documenting how Atahualpa received a Bible), she engaged them in the process of interpreting Spanish-language documents within a social and political context and appreciating the conflicting interpretations of a historic event. She is intentional about tackling areas of misunderstanding and misinformation in this and other units of study. Similarly, Socorro's exploration of free speech as a cultural construct illustrates how intercultural skills can connect with subject area content. Teachers were interested in infusing cultural exploration and analysis into their teaching, even though there were time and curricular constraints that made it challenging to do so.

The programs met the goals of the ICit framework to different degrees and in different ways. The Spanish and Japanese programs were more established and included a variety of learning activities that allowed for meaningful engagement with speakers of those languages in the community and also through international exchange. Participation in community events, hosting students from abroad and writing for a local newspaper were all salient examples of this aspect of ICit. Furthermore, students drew on the intercultural and linguistic competencies developed in the classroom to participate in these opportunities. As the Yup'ik program grows, it may also develop these kinds of programs and partnerships that allow students to utilize their ICC beyond the school environment. It is clear that these kinds of initiatives require careful planning and ongoing attention to ensure successful implementation.

ICit incorporates a concern with social justice and urges action towards social change. We found that this trait of ICit was less prevalent in the immersion programs studied. While the Spanish program was engaging in social justice action locally and globally, we did not find similar instances in the Yup'ik or Japanese programs. This is an area worthy of further exploration, both in terms of understanding why they are not already happening, and what avenues would allow for more social action.

The findings of this study implore us to continue to consider the realities and potentials of ICit in immersion contexts, and particularly in relation to Indigenous language programs. It is also important to note that the use of a 'transnational' standard for evaluating the success of ICit may not apply to Indigenous language contexts. Furthermore, it is important to consider how our conceptualization of ICit may or may not reflect Indigenous (and other) worldviews related to knowledge, learning and criticality. Another challenge in conceptualizing ICit in the immersion context is the distinction between one's own and other cultures. We found that it was difficult to decipher this distinction in some of these immersion settings. Because the student population is fairly balanced between Indigenous and non-Indigenous students in the Yup'ik program, and because all their teachers are themselves members of the Yup'ik community, the curriculum is simultaneously examining their own and others' cultures. Similarly, the Spanish program is constantly teaching content that reflects and examines both Hispanic/ Latinx cultures and non-Hispanic/Latinx cultures. In the case of

Spanish, the program is a two-way immersion program, with a balance of students and teachers from both cultural and linguistic backgrounds. For students in two-way immersion, 'culture' is simultaneously one's own and another, making this distinction difficult to observe.

Age-related development can help illuminate our understanding of why one's own and other's cultures are so difficult to disentangle. Our findings support the conclusions reached by Feinauer and Howard (2014) that a developmental approach is needed to understand how intercultural competence is reached across the age range. They note the role of *ethnic* identity development in students. Pre-adolescence is a time when the saliency of one's ethnic identity is largely unexamined (Phinney, 1990, 1993). Elementary students in immersion programs will thus have little sense of membership to an ethnic group, as *achieved* ethnic identity doesn't occur until late adolescence. One would not expect elementary students to feel strong allegiance to one ethnic identity or another. Particularly in two-way immersion programs and in the Yup'ik program where the population is rather balanced between multiple ethnic groups, young learners work with diverse peers on a daily basis. Classrooms and schools are important contexts for identity development for children (Bronfenbrenner, 1979, 1992), and ethnic identity undergoes significant change and plays an important role in middle and late adolescence (Phinney, 1990). In highly diverse classrooms such as the ones studied here, students will learn about their ethnic and social group identity through these social learning experiences. Immersion students are likely developing an understanding of 'own' ethnic and cultural identity that incorporates values and beliefs from the various cultural frameworks represented by the teachers and peers in those classrooms. Thus, the IC development in immersion settings, particularly Indigenous and two-way immersion programs, will impact students' ethnic identity development. Further exploration of developing IC and ICit in elementary students in traditional world language classrooms has been done by Wagner *et al.* (2018). Primary grades students certainly are learning about cultures and thinking about their own positions in the world, and a developmentally informed perspective may explain why we did not see the same kinds of evidence of critical cultural awareness development and social justice action in those grades as we did in later grades.

Conclusion

The goals of immersion education are three-fold: to teach academic content, to develop high levels of language proficiency and to develop intercultural competence (Curtain & Dahlberg, 2016; Fortune & Tedick, 2008a). We embarked on this study to learn how language immersion settings meet the third goal: fostering intercultural competence, and how they go further and realize the goals of ICit education. Central to this goal is focused attention on developing critical stances, recognizing issues of power and privilege, and developing concern for social justice and taking action to challenge social inequities (Dagenais, 2008; Wagner *et al.*, 2019).

We discovered a multitude of examples supporting how many – but not all – aspects of ICC and ICit are inherently fostered in the three K–8 programs studied here. These strengths may or may not be limited to the programs of the Anchorage School District, and it is imperative that we look at more dual-language and TWI programs to investigate how widespread these best practices for ICit are. While immersion contexts are uniquely situated to provide plentiful opportunities for ICC and ICit development, these opportunities are not always realized due to a myriad of constraints. Teachers should be empowered to delve into cross-cultural exploration within the mandated curriculum. Existing state curricula do not always recognize the value of doing so, but the missed opportunity for ICit development comes at a cost: students are missing out on valuable skills that will prepare them for transnational engagement with wide-reaching benefits to the student and society. We should continue to investigate how younger students conceptualize and enact *culture* and to explore the feasibility of social action for elementary grades. Furthermore, as Indigenous language revitalization programs expand, we should explore how positive Native identities are fostered alongside ICit (see Fortune & Tedick, 2008b).

The findings of this study implore us to continue to engage students in 'active citizenship' beyond the classroom. Significant work is required in order to realize the goals of the ICit framework. Byram (2021) explains: 'There are ethical questions involved in this work which language teachers – and perhaps teachers of other subjects too – have not faced hitherto, and for which they have not been prepared in teacher education' (Byram, 2021: 123). While realizing that the aims of ICC may be readily realized in dual language and immersion settings, meeting the goals of education for democracy, social justice and critical cultural awareness appears to be more challenging and to require more intentional focus and support. While there is opportunity for further implementation of the ICit framework in the immersion programs studied here, there is also tremendous enactment of critical and action-oriented teaching that draws on the ICC that is inherently and intentionally developed in these programs.

References

Abbott, M.G. (2019) Foreword. In M. Wagner, F. Cardetti, F. and M. Byram (2019) *Teaching Intercultural Citizenship Across the Curriculum: The Role of Language Education* (pp. vii–ix). Alexandria, VA: American Council on the Teaching of Foreign Languages (ACTFL).

ACTFL (2015) *World-Readiness Standards for Language Learning.* Alexandria, VA: ACTFL (American Council on the Teaching of Foreign Languages) and NSFLP (National Standards in Foreign Language Education Project).

ACTFL (2017) NCSSFL-ACTFL can-do statements [Online]. See https://www.actfl.org/publications/guidelines-and-manuals/ncssfl-actfl-can-do-statements.

Bronfenbrenner, U. (1979) *The Ecology of Human Development: Experiments by Nature and Design*. Cambridge, MA: Harvard University Press.

Bronfenbrenner, U. (1992) Ecological systems theory. In R. Vasta (ed.) *Six Theories of Child Development: Revised Formulations and Current Issues* (pp. 187–249). London: Jessica Kingsley.

Byram, M. (1997) *Teaching and Assessing Intercultural Communicative Competence*. Clevedon: Multilingual Matters.

Byram, M. (2006) Developing a concept of intercultural citizenship. In G. Alred, M. Byram and M. Fleming (eds) *Education for Intercultural Citizenship: Concepts and Comparisons* (pp. 109–129). Clevedon: Multilingual Matters.

Byram, M. (2021) *Teaching and Assessing Intercultural Communicative Competence: Revisited* (2nd edn). Bristol: Multilingual Matters.

Byram, M., Perugini, D. and Wagner, M. (2013) The development of intercultural citizenship in the elementary school Spanish classroom. *Learning Languages* 18 (2), 16–31.

Cohen, L., Manion, L. and Morrison, K. (2018) *Research Methods in Education*. New York, NY: Routledge.

Curtain, H. and Dahlberg, C. (2016) *Languages and Learners: Making the Match: World Language Instruction in K–8 Classrooms and Beyond*. New York, NY: Pearson.

Dagenais, D. (2008) Developing a critical awareness of language diversity in immersion. In T.W. Fortune and D.J. Tedick (eds) *Pathways to Multilingualism: Evolving Perspectives on Immersion Education* (pp. 201–220). Clevedon: Multilingual Matters.

Deardorff, D. (2006) The identification and assessment of intercultural competence as a student outcome of internationalization at institutions of higher education in the United States. *Journal of Studies on International Education* 10 (3), 241–266.

Fairclough, N. (1992) *Critical Language Awareness*. New York, NY: Longman.

Feinauer, E. and Howard, E. (2014) Attending to the third goal: Cross-cultural competence and identity development in two-way immersion programs. *Journal of Immersion and Content-Based Language Education* 2 (2), 257–272.

Fortune, T.W. and Tedick, D.J. (eds) (2008a) *Pathways to Multilingualism: Evolving Perspectives on Immersion Education*. Clevedon: Multilingual Matters.

Fortune, T.W. and Tedick, D. (2008b) One-way, two-way and Indigenous immersion: A call for cross fertilization. In T. Fortune and D. Tedick (eds) *Pathways to Multilingualism: Evolving Perspectives on Immersion Education* (pp. 3–21). Clevedon: Multilingual Matters.

Howard, E.R., Lindholm-Leary, K.J., Rogers, D., Olague, N., Medina, J., Kennedy, B., Sugarman, J. and Christian, D. (2018) *Guiding Principles for Dual Language Education* (3rd edn). Washington, DC: Center for Applied Linguistics.

Johnson, R.K. and Swain, M. (1997) *Immersion Education: International Perspectives*. Cambridge: Cambridge University Press.

Kubota, R. (2016) Critical content-based instruction in the foreign language classroom: Critical issues for implementation. In L. Cammarata (ed.) *Content-Based Foreign Language Teaching* (pp. 192–211). New York: Routledge.

Met, M. and Lorenz, E. (1997) Lessons from US immersion programs: Two decades of experience. In R. Johnson and M. Swain (eds) *Immersion Education: International Perspectives*. Cambridge: Cambridge University Press.

Phinney, J. (1990) Ethnic identity in adolescents and adults: Review of research. *Psychological Bulletin* 108 (3), 499–514.

Phinney, J. (1993) A three-stage model of ethnic identity development in adolescence. In M. Bernal and G. Knight (eds) *Ethnic Identity: Formation and Transmission among Hispanics and Other Minorities* (pp. 61–70). Albany, NY: State University of New York Press.

Wagner, M., Conlon Perugini, D. and Byram, M. (eds) (2018) *Teaching Intercultural Competence Across the Age Range: From Theory to Practice*. Bristol: Multilingual Matters.

Wagner, M., Cardetti, F. and Byram, M. (2019) *Teaching Intercultural Citizenship Across the Curriculum: The Role of Language Education*. Alexandria, VA: American Council on the Teaching of Foreign Languages (ACTFL).

Wesely, P. (2012) Cross-cultural understanding in immersion students: A mixed methods study. *L2 Journal* 4 (2), 189–213. https://escholarship.org/uc/item/23v8615w.

Wolcott, H. (1999) *Ethnography: A Way of Seeing*. Walnut Creek, CA: Sage.

4 Intercultural Talk: Fostering Intercultural Citizenship in a Chinese Program

Kaishan Kong

Intercultural citizenship (ICit) emphasizes the importance of linking language learning with community engagement. As Byram and Wagner (2018: 141) noted, language education has an 'important role and responsibility in educating Intercultural Citizens ready to live and thrive in multilingual and multicultural societies, including their own'. This notion is extremely important and is needed on the current global stage torn by increasing discrimination, division and racism. Developed from the model of intercultural communicative competence (ICC) (Byram, 1997, 2008, 2014), ICit 'expands the theoretical visions and pedagogical applications' (Porto, 2019: 148), illuminating a new direction for language educators. Despite the growing interest and discussion, there is a need for research to unpack what ICit looks like in actual language teaching and learning.

This chapter examines an Intercultural Talk (IT) project conducted in a college-level Chinese language program, analyzes the integration of ACTFL World-Readiness Standards and ICit in lesson planning, and discovers that students developed intercultural citizenship in several areas. The most salient results are identified in the students' explicit willingness, interest and curiosity to communicate with people from diverse cultures, their increased knowledge and skills in the intercultural communication process, their expanded knowledge and their ability to change perspectives. Students grew knowledge through making comparisons, contrasts and connections between their culture and other cultures, and some facilitated their own learning by actively connecting their daily observations with the IT talks with their partners. This study revealed that ICit goals were achievable through interactive pedagogy and offered suggestions for educators and researchers with similar interests.

Literature Review

Intercultural citizenship and language education

Intercultural citizenship (ICit) is not a new concept in language education, and it is often discussed in conjunction with intercultural communicative competence (ICC). When Byram (1997) enriched his original Intercultural Competence (IC) model by combining a layer of language competencies (linguistic, sociolinguistic and discourse), it was a transformative change in the field, enlightening language educators with a natural and fundamental bidirectional connection between language and culture: one direction being language learning as a tool to communicate with people from other cultures, and the other direction being interculturally competent to apply the language appropriately and effectively. In other words, the ICC framework broadened and deepened the implication of language education by reminding us that language education serves more than instrumental purposes. Learning languages is much more meaningful than having a tool to communicate for study, employment and tourism: rather, students embody knowledge, skills and attitudes towards people from varied linguistic and cultural backgrounds.

Built on the foundation of ICC, ICit takes a step further by highlighting the educational purpose and humanistic purpose of language learning (Wagner *et al.*, 2019). As Williams (2017) aptly stated:

> Learning a language is never merely a matter of acquiring verbal skills in order to conduct business; it can also involve a reaching out to other people that requires a form of cultural decentering that can often have moral and civic dimensions. (Williams, 2017: 59)

Language educators and learners are social human beings first and foremost; thus, our lives are inevitably impacted by global issues and their consequences, such as environment, developmental sustainability, humanitarian crises and democracy. The increased global interdependence 'brings a new urgency to come together to recognize and solve problems', which is 'both a practical/instrumental matter and part of our life as social human beings' (Wagner *et al.*, 2019: 11). Therefore, the educational and humanistic purposes do not contradict or negate the instrumental purpose of language teaching and learning: rather, they complement and enrich the profound mission of language education.

In this sense, ICit is more than a change of pedagogical approach: rather, a change of educational philosophy. Language education for ICit expects and requires teachers to embed citizenship aims in teaching, connecting the in-class language learning with the community and a wider world, inspiring students to engage in civic or social action at various levels, and contributing to the development of individuals and democratic societies (Byram, 2008, 2014; Bram & Wagner, 2018;

Byram *et al.*, 2017; Larsen-Freeman, 2018; Palpacuer Lee *et al.*, 2018). This perspective change propels both teachers' and students' critical cultural awareness to acknowledge cultural diversity, evaluate the impact of individual behaviors and cultures in the global system, decenter one's own culture and analyze relationships between cultures, embrace social justice actions and actively participate in the world as global citizens.

Intercultural citizenship: Definition and characteristics

This chapter adopts the definition of ICit from Wagner *et al.* (2019):

> being active in one's community—local or beyond the local—and using one's linguistic and intercultural competences to realize and enrich discussions, relationships, and activities with people of varied linguistic and cultural backgrounds. (Wagner *et al.*, 2019: xv)

This definition unfolds four significant characteristics of ICit. Firstly, it retains the quintessential connection between language and intercultural competence, asserting the unfathomable role of language education to prepare students with proficiency, curiosity and openness to endeavor in intercultural communication.

Secondly, it transcends learning beyond school walls and national borders. While traditional citizenship education aims to develop good citizens within a national perspective, ICit extends the parameters of a community; instead, 'students are encouraged to look beyond the limits of their own countries and to think about their relationships with others in other countries or with others in their own communities' (Wagner *et al.*, 2019: 24). This concept is not only important but also necessary in the current world with its unprecedented ideological divide and political volatility. The call for building 'local or beyond the local' relationships takes on humanistic and relational perspectives to interpret the role of language education in constructing an interdependent world and mediating conflicts in a culturally ethnorelative way. Bennett (2004) coined the term 'ethnorelativism' to underscore 'the experience of one's own beliefs and behaviors as just one organization of reality among many viable possibilities' (2004: 62). Ethnorelativism indicates an opposition to ethnocentrism, which sees one's own culture as central to reality.

Thirdly, ICit promotes critical reflection in both teachers and students. According to the definition above, in order to 'realize and enrich discussions, relationships, and activities' across cultures (Wagner *et al.*, 2019: xv), students need to have the awareness and competence to 'decenter' their own cultures during intercultural interactions (Porto, 2019; Williams, 2017). This process engages students in considerable self-reflection, confronting their own monolingual biases (Larsen-Freeman,

2018) and 'distancing' themselves from their own cultures to 'question the ordinary, the known and the accepted' (Lomicka, 2009: 1228). Such self-reflection is equally critical for teachers, who need to invest time and efforts to reflect on their cultural positionality and to review their curriculum design to truly construct a community-engaged classroom culture. Practicing deep and critical reflection cultivates Intercultural Humility (IH) (Lynch *et al.*, 2016), acknowledging one's own limitations and demonstrating curiosity and openness to learn from other cultures.

Last but not least, a distinct characteristic of ICit is amplifying students' active participation in civic and social duties. In particular, students demonstrate 'a concern about social justice and a belief in the values of humanistic thought and action' and 'a willingness to promote social action in the world' (Wagner *et al.*, 2019: 24). To achieve this active participation, students need to be equipped with intercultural knowledge, skills and attitudes; more importantly, students are linguistically and culturally prepared to embody a questioning attitude to challenge injustice, a critical lens to evaluate systems, and a willingness to do advocacy work. The relationship between ICit and ICC is vibrant, in that ICit is a step further in fostering students' critical cultural awareness, which is a central dimension in Byram's ICC framework (1997).

Intercultural citizenship and the 5 Cs of ACTFL

For language educators in the US, the principal guidance in world language education is the World-Readiness Standards for Learning Languages offered by the American Council on the Teaching of Foreign Languages (ACTFL), also known as the 5 Cs:

> The five 'C' goal areas (Communication, Cultures, Connections, Comparisons, and Communities) stress the application of learning a language beyond the instructional setting. The goal is to prepare learners to apply the skills and understandings measured by the Standards, to bring a global competence to their future careers and experiences. (ACTFL, 2015: 2)

To facilitate teachers' integration and application of the five C goals in actual teaching, the National Council of State Supervisors for Languages (NCSSFL) and ACTFL translated these goals into more specific and detailed NCSSFL-ACTFL Can-Do Statements for Intercultural Communication (2017). These statements offered a more feasible roadmap to scaffold teachers' curriculum design and instruction in two aspects. Firstly, these statements defined culture in terms of 3 Ps, namely perspectives (the beliefs and values of a group), practices (what people do in this culture) and products (tangible and intangible results in relation to the other two Ps). As many teachers may be concerned that culture is an overwhelmingly broad and abstract concept, this multilayered definition guides teachers to approach culture with flexibility. Secondly, these statements linked cultural learning with three modes of communication: interpretive, interpersonal and presentational. These Can-Do Statements define intercultural communicative competence as 'the ability to interact effectively and appropriately with people from other language and cultural backgrounds' (ACTFL, 2017).

The ACTFL guidance (including the 5 Cs and the Can-Do statements) closely aligns with the tenets of ICit in that they both address the application of language learning beyond the instructional setting and national borders, aim to nurture students' intentional goal-setting and self-reflection around language and culture, prepare students with the knowledge and skills to conduct effective and appropriate intercultural communication, and encourage students to connect global competence with their life experiences and their future careers.

Intercultural citizenship and virtual exchange

Language instructors and teacher educators have explored numerous ways to connect in-class learning with the community. Some popular practices include inviting guest speakers to the class to share authentic experiences (e.g. Albirini, 2009; Kong, 2018a; Lee, 2012; Shenk, 2014), taking students on field trips or study abroad programs (e.g. Diao & Trentman, 2021; Plutino, 2016; Soong *et al.*, 2018), community service projects (e.g. Chan *et al.*, 2021; Kong, 2018b; Palpacuer Lee *et al.*, 2018; Wu, 2018), and pairing students with native speakers for tandem learning projects (e.g. Christensen & Kong, 2022; Kong, 2021, 2022; O'Dowd, 2020; O'Rourke, 2007).

There is immense value in creating in-person communication between language learners and the community, but such interactional opportunities are sometimes limited or disrupted by various challenges, such as the logistic challenges of bringing in guest speakers, students' affordability to study abroad, a lack of native speakers in the community, or a global pandemic as we have recently experienced. The rapid development of technology and the internet helped to solve such problems and greatly increased convenience and accessibility for such connections to happen. Virtual exchange, also known as telecollaboration (Belz, 2003), internet-mediated intercultural foreign language education (Belz & Thorne, 2006), Computer-Mediated Communication (CMC), Online Language Learning (OLL), and technology-mediated tasks, has become an influential and transformative contribution towards intercultural learning and foreign language education (Arnold, 2007). Virtual exchange 'involves engaging classes in online intercultural collaboration projects with international partners as an integrated part of their educational programmes' (O'Dowd, 2020: 477). This pedagogy enhances students' language development (Blake, 2011; Kong, 2022; Lee, 2008; Oskoz, 2009; Sotillo, 2000; Yanguas, 2010), as it offers 'a platform where interlocutors employ language resources and communicative strategies to express ideas, to make clarifications' (Kong, 2022: 96). More importantly, virtual exchange nurtures intercultural learning, as Schenker (2012: 450) called it 'a useful tool for enabling students to develop intercultural competence'.

Many studies have examined the positive impact of virtual exchange on students' intercultural competences (e.g. Belz, 2003; Liaw, 2006; Luo & Gao, 2022; O'Dowd, 2020; Schenker, 2012). Some studies discovered that the sociocultural element of virtual exchange could foster intercultural competence, empathetic exchanges, and integrative motivation towards language and cultural learning (González-Lloret, 2020; Kong, 2022; O'Dowd, 2020); others shed light on students' reflexivity and reflection through a virtual exchange (Christensen & Kong, 2022; O'Dowd, 2012). For example, in Freiermuth and Huang's (2021) study, where five Taiwanese students and six Japanese students participated in a virtual cultural exchange project, the authors concluded that telecollaborative video activities developed students' intercultural competences 'via increased verbosity, the application of polite language, and of the utmost importance, by building interpersonal relationships' (Freiermuth & Huang, 2021: 186). Their conclusion echoes the definition of ICit (Wagner *et al.*, 2019) to foster relationships beyond national borders. Further, Luo and Gao (2022) engaged Chinese and American students in an innovative telecollaboration project by sharing songs in Chinese and English. Their results implied that activities that integrate language and arts through virtual exchange were conducive to intercultural learning, evident in a growing interest in cultural exchange and in the ability to change perspective. In addition, Wagner *et al.*'s (2019) book offered detailed class task examples to inspire more interdisciplinary projects to promote intercultural citizenship. In particular, they reported a transatlantic middle school project on the global water crisis, where students adopted virtual exchange as a platform to investigate the various aspects of the problem and collaboratively seek various solutions. These empirical studies presented a wealth of insights on the value of virtual exchange in teaching for ICit.

The Aims of the Current Project

The last literature review section aims to explain the meaning of ICit, unpack its significant characteristics, underscore its prominence in language education, and present its manifestation through empirical studies. Recent publications in the field have signaled an increased effort to bring ICit to the center of language education. For instance, in a special issue of *Language Teaching Research* journal, Porto *et al.* (2018: 485) made this purpose unequivocal, which was to 'bring the theory of intercultural citizenship education to readers' attention and to offer teachers and researchers working with this or similar concepts the opportunity to make their work known in a context of a coherent presentation of theory and practice'. However, there are two areas that need to be addressed and improved. (1) There is a scarcity of understanding among teachers regarding how to infuse ICit concepts in curriculum design, instruction and assessment (Byram, 2014; Byram *et al.*, 2017). More empirical studies are needed in order to document, present and analyze teachers' practices in reality, including what they do, how they do it, the contextual circumstances and teachers' reflections. (2) Examples of virtual exchange in teaching ICit are particularly scarce in less commonly taught languages such as Chinese (Chun, 2014; Luo & Yang, 2018; Luo & Gao, 2022). Existing literature exemplifies studies in Spanish (Yulita, 2018); EFL (Fang & Baker, 2018; Huh & Suh, 2018); German (Wagner *et al.*, 2019) as well as teacher education preparing teachers for multilingual and multicultural classrooms (Krulatz *et al.*, 2018; Sharkey, 2018). The field would benefit from research on a wider range of language representation in order to unfold a fuller picture of ICit as a theory and pedagogy.

Against this backdrop, this current project reports on a Chinese–American Intercultural Talk (IT) project, where 21 college students participated in semester-long weekly virtual discussions on a variety of topics to explore cultural knowledge as well as practice their target language. This chapter reports on the project design and delivery, as well as the results gathered from various data sets. The study attempts to identify the evidence of ICit from this virtual exchange project, and to explore effective ways to embed ICit in language education. More specifically, this study seeks answers to the following two research questions:

(1) How did the students on both sides of the partnership perceive the Intercultural Talk project?
(2) In what way(s) did the Intercultural Talk project foster intercultural citizenship among the students?

Methods

The Intercultural Talk project: Context and aims

The Intercultural Talk (IT) project was a semester-long tandem learning situated in a college-level Chinese language program in the US. I was the instructor of this program, teaching Beginning Chinese and Intermediate Chinese classes. The purpose of this IT project was to create opportunities for students of Chinese as a Foreign Language (CFL) to interact with their international peers from Chinese-speaking regions, including mainland China, Taiwan, Malaysia and Hong Kong. The international peers reported upon in this chapter were all from mainland China, so they will be referred to as Chinese students henceforward.

Distinguished from traditional tandem learning with a focus on language practice, this IT project was designed with two principles. Firstly, similar to Porto's (2019) design, the IT project under discussion had linguistic, intercultural and citizenship aims, with a stress on the development of cultural knowledge, skills, critical cultural awareness and community engagement. More specifically, the IT project aimed to develop students' ability to:

- appreciate linguistic diversity within China;
- develop language awareness and vocabulary related to the topic;
- engage in intercultural dialogue using the target language;
- demonstrate a willingness and ability to engage in intercultural dialogue with others;
- listen to other viewpoints with respect, even if these viewpoints disagree with theirs;
- develop values such as respect, mutual understanding, social awareness and openness, and social and civic responsibility; and
- engage in local and global communities.

Secondly, this IT project aimed to offer mutual and equitable benefits for both CFL students and Chinese students. Although the project occurred in a CFL class, I was mindful to avoid 'instrumental, utilitarian and uncritical orientations' (Porto, 2019: 150) that would tokenize the international peers and consequently only benefit CFL students. Hence, I intentionally designed activities with the purpose of eliciting each student's cultural experience and knowledge, and activities that allowed the dyads to practice their respective target language (Chinese for the CFL students and English for the Chinese students).

Participants and procedures

The data for this study were collected in 2021, when in-person classes were disrupted by COVID-19. As a result, students conducted these intercultural exchange activities online. As shown in Table 4.1, the participants in this current study included 21 students (five CFL students in Beginning Chinese class, eight CFL students from Intermediate Chinese class and eight Chinese students who were international students

Table 4.1 Participants in the IT project (all names are pseudonyms)

CFL in the Beginning Chinese class	CFL in the Intermediate Chinese class	Chinese Students Volunteers
Kay	Chris	Wang
Reed	Ann	Zhou
Iris	Kate	Zhang
Liam	Norah	Cai
Helen	Jen	Deng
x	Zoe	Yan
x	Nina	Zhao
x	Mark	Chen

on campus). The students in the Beginning Chinese class were at novice low level and those in the Intermediate Chinese class were at novice mid to novice high. For the CFL students, this project was part of the instructional activities and accounted for 20% of the final grade. Relevant assignments included participation in weekly meetings, weekly reports and a final reflection paper.

All eight Chinese students volunteered to participate in this program and used this opportunity to fulfill a 30-hour service-learning requirement by the university. Many of them envisioned this to be a valuable opportunity to make friends with local community members, practice their English and gain more knowledge about American culture, as reported in their application statement. They needed to finish weekly reflective reports and a final reflection paper to receive the service-learning credit. Each Chinese student was paired up with one CFL beginning student and one CFL intermediate student. In other words, each international student had two partners and had two IT meetings each week. Due to the uneven number of students enrolled in the Beginning Chinese and Intermediate Chinese classes, three international students (Yan, Zhao, Chen) only had one partner.

Each Chinese class covered five chapters during the semester, and each chapter lasted two weeks. The IT project lasted 11 weeks: during the first week students met to get to know each other without specific tasks, while the remaining 10 weeks were devoted to these five chapters and relevant activities. Activities included interview, presentation, role play and story writing. Although activities might vary between Beginning Chinese class and Intermediate Chinese class, all the activities required students to *communicate* in their target language and involved *cultural comparisons* and *connections* as in the ACTFL 5 Cs. Table 4.2 shows the chapter themes and their relevant cultural topics.

Table 4.2 Topics discussed in the IT project

Beginning Chinese	Intermediate Chinese
Theme: Making appointments • classroom culture • social media use among young people	Theme: Dating • dating culture on campus • marriage and match-making
Theme: Studying Chinese • school culture and student workload • bragging about academic achievements	Theme: Renting a residential place • housing culture • pet culture
Theme: School life • college entrance exam • birthday celebrations	Theme: Sports • sports culture • people's attitudes towards sports
Theme: Shopping • shopping and bargaining • payment and customer service	Theme: Travel • urban lifestyle • summer plans
Theme: Transportation • transportation in different cultures • showing appreciation and taboos	Theme: Airport farewell • travel culture • family activities

The weekly IT project involved three steps, as shown in Figure 4.1.

In Step One, I assigned the topic of the week and delivered a worksheet for the CFL students to prepare. The worksheet listed the activities they were to conduct in the IT session, so it was like a preview for the students. As a tool for scaffolding, the worksheet also included some sample questions and useful phrases to be used in communication breakdowns. The types of activities varied for

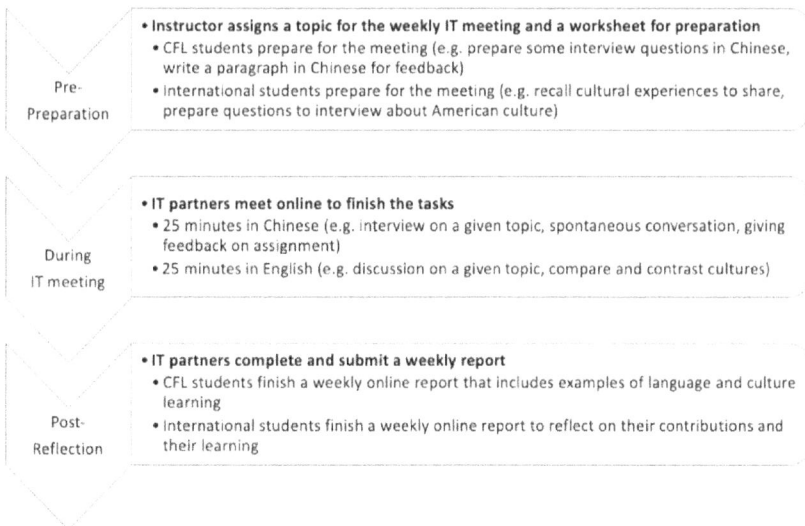

Pre-Preparation
• Instructor assigns a topic for the weekly IT meeting and a worksheet for preparation
  • CFL students prepare for the meeting (e.g. prepare some interview questions in Chinese, write a paragraph in Chinese for feedback)
  • International students prepare for the meeting (e.g. recall cultural experiences to share, prepare questions to interview about American culture)

During IT meeting
• IT partners meet online to finish the tasks
  • 25 minutes in Chinese (e.g. interview on a given topic, spontaneous conversation, giving feedback on assignment)
  • 25 minutes in English (e.g. discussion on a given topic, compare and contrast cultures)

Post-Reflection
• IT partners complete and submit a weekly report
  • CFL students finish a weekly online report that includes examples of language and culture learning
  • International students finish a weekly online report to reflect on their contributions and their learning

Figure 4.1 The flowchart of weekly IT meetings

the Beginning Class and the Intermediate Class due to their different language proficiency level and the theme of the week, but they all included language exchange and cultural comparison activities. The worksheet was also shared with the international students so they were aware of the topic under discussion.

Step Two was when students met online at a mutually agreed time to complete the tasks on the worksheet. They were required to meet for at least 50 minutes and they divided their time equally to speak Chinese and English. They were allowed to talk for more than 50 minutes if they liked.

Step Three required both dyads to submit a weekly report online. The CFL students were required to report specific examples of language gains and cultural learning. For instance, they had to share what their IT partner had helped them with regarding language expressions, and what corrections and suggestions were given. For the Chinese international students, because their English proficiency was much higher than the CFL students' Chinese proficiency they were more motivated to develop cultural knowledge: therefore, the weekly report engaged them to share more profound cultural learning instead of their English language improvement.

Data collection and analysis

As shown in Table 4.3, I collected four types of qualitative data for analysis, including students' weekly reports, final reflection papers, end-of-semester interviews with the Chinese students, and recorded IT meetings. Each dyad was required to submit five recorded IT meetings during the semester. Not all students were able to submit all the homework due to busy schedules, mental health issues and technical failures to record videos.

The data were analyzed with attention being given to the central concepts and characteristics of ICit. To provide evidence for these concepts, I adopted Byram's (2000) intercultural competence assessment model to identify specific and nuanced dimensions: knowledge of one's own and the interlocutor's culture, curiosity and interest in intercultural exchange, knowledge of and skills in intercultural communication, ability to change perspective, critical reflection on one's own cultures and community engagement.

The data analysis process was continuous through the three stages in a deductive and inductive way (Bingham & Witkowsky, 2021). In the

Table 4.3 Types of research data

Weekly reports	Final reflection papers	End-of-semester interviews	Recorded IT meetings
244	17	5 hours	26 hours

first stage, after each week's reports were submitted I read through the reports and highlighted key phrases and ideas frequently mentioned by the students. On a weekly basis, I created annotations and memos to record my interpretations of the data of the week. Based on these memos, I deducted possible themes related to the concepts of ICit for that particular week. In the second stage, at the end of the semester when all data were collected, I read and analyzed all memos and I began coding, meaning categorizing segments of data and assigned codes (Charmaz, 2006). These codes helped me organize and develop my understanding of the interaction between dyads. The last stage was developing themes in relation to ICit. Inductive analysis was employed to help me identify patterns and generate themes across dyads, data sets and topics.

Findings

Research Question 1: How did the students on both sides of the partnership perceive the Intercultural Talk project?

All CFL students and Chinese students in the IT project indicated a very positive perception of this virtual exchange. Some high-frequency words across responses included: 'definitely enjoyed', 'very/really helpful', 'felt comfortable', 'pushed me forward', and 'took risks'. Several general comments were identified across the students: relationship building, developing cultural knowledge, feeling safe to make mistakes, and feeling more confident.

For the CFL students, their response reflected their primary identity in this project: language learner. They all addressed the impact of this project on their language improvement and its subsequent ramification of their confidence in intercultural communication. Examples fell into three categories: (1) learning authentic language use such as vocabulary and slang; (2) receiving constructive feedback from partners; and (3) helping them realize their strengths and weaknesses, so they could learn from their own mistakes.

The CFL students also underscored two favorite aspects of the project design. One aspect was the strategic progression of the activities, which helped to lower their anxiety and prepared them well for language application. In many worksheets, especially at the beginning of the semester when students were getting used to the IT tasks, I provided several interview questions as an example to help them get started, and then they were asked to raise their own questions. CFL students welcomed this design, calling it 'a good foundation to build on' (Kate, final report), 'a basis for us to stand on and have us adventure out and create new things' (Nina, final report), 'useful guidance to further discussion' (Liam, final report), 'reminders of vocabulary and sentence structures to make open talk more comfortable' (Kay, final report), and 'a way to lower the risks for us in the beginning as we adjust to the situation' (Zoe, final report). Chris said she enjoyed reading the question examples because she could practice the grammar structure before creating her own (Chris, final report).

After these interview question examples, CFL students had to create their own interview questions as well as follow-up questions. CFL students found this step beneficial. Iris said, 'This developmental design pushed me to forward my language development. Having to create my own questions made me practice various sentence structures and vocabulary' (Iris, final report). Reed echoed that this expectation to create their own questions 'pushed us to develop our own language', which led to him 'feeling more comfortable speaking this new language' (Reed, final report). Similarly, Mark shared that 'Creating my own questions allows me to think outside of the box. For example, during the L15D2 IT talk, I asked three follow up questions that I came up with on the spot. This taught me to respond spontaneously to a conversation' (Mark, final report).

Kate wrote:

> I think this design helps because it requires me to stop and think about how I can get information across and speak in a proper way that my partner will understand. So, I put much more thought into developing my language, to make sure that I was developing it in a way that both him and I would understand. This made things like grammar and sentence structure very important to me, as I had to figure out how to use them properly, making comparisons with previously created questions. (Kate, final report)

As shown in Kate's response above, this interview activity design was effective in two ways: in allowing the students to compare their language application with examples provided and by motivating them to consider how to create questions in a culturally appropriate way.

The other aspect of the exchange applauded by the CFL students was that of retaining a stable partnership with the same partner so they were able to deepen their relationship. Norah's comment reflected a shared sentiment among the participants, as she wrote: 'I really enjoyed that we got to have the same partner every time because I was actually able to get to know her so it was much easier speaking to her in Chinese' (Norah, final report). Because they had the same partner throughout the semester, CFL students appreciated the opportunity to know their partner better, enabling them to open up and feel comfortable making mistakes as their partner already knew them, and avoiding the same awkward get-to-know-you moment every week.

By contrast, for the Chinese students, because many of them already spoke fluent English, their attention was more focused on content exchange rather than language improvement, although they sometimes reported learning some new phrases in weekly reports. The Chinese students' positive perception of the project focused on three aspects.

(1) The IT project was an opportunity to explore nuanced American cultures through partners' experiences. Students felt that the open-ended task design pushed them to ask questions they were truly interested in, so they could 'learn and understand American culture better' (Chen, final report), 'discover nuances and diversity within the US' (Yan, final interview) and 'learn more authentic American culture' (Wang, final report). Zhang echoed:

> I have studied in the United States for a year, and to be honest, I do not have much in-depth communication with local Americans. In this project, the weekly video with two American friends and the communication at the request of the teacher let me know a lot of things, which I did not know in the United States. (Zhang, final report)

(2) The IT project was an opportunity to share Chinese culture and to enhance their pride in being Chinese. Yan called it a chance to 'express myself and share my own culture positively to my American partners in the process' (Yan, final report). Chen called this an opportunity 'to show my pride about my own culture' (Chen, final report).

(3) The IT project developed their confidence in using English in intercultural communication. Many attributed such confidence to their partners' patience and encouragement. For instance, Deng said: 'This project gave me a lot of confidence, allowing me to confidently introduce the culture of my country to people from other countries, and at the same time not feel timid because I am a non-native speaker. Both students are very friendly and don't care about my English level' (Deng, final report). Cai gave a similar response, highlighting that her partners were 'always patient and willing to hear my explanations' (Cai, final report).

Moreover, similar to the CFL students' responses, the Chinese students also emphasized the positive result of having stable partners so they could develop true friendships. In the final interview with the Chinese students, I asked them to use a phrase or a sentence to summarize this experience, and they could use Chinese or English. Their responses were predominantly about friendships. For instance, Zhou felt that those weekly meetings were getting together with friends, saying, '很值得，不再是一个任务，是每个星期有个朋友和你一起，很开心 [It was worthwhile. It was no longer a task, but a weekly hangout with friends. I was really happy]' (Zhou, final interview). Zhang called his two partners '两个真正的好朋友 [two truly good friends]', and Chen used the Chinese phrase '相见恨晚 [wishing they had known each other earlier]' to describe her wish to have known the partners earlier.

Research Question 2: In what way(s) did the Intercultural Talk project foster intercultural citizenship among the students?

This research question aims to identify key concepts and characteristics of ICit demonstrated by the participants during the 11 IT meetings. As discussed in the earlier data analysis section of this chapter, I employed the dimensions in Byram's (2000) intercultural competence assessment model to analyze the data sets and the following aspects emerged: (1) knowledge of one's own and the interlocutor's culture; (2) curiosity and interest in intercultural exchange; (3) knowledge of and skills in intercultural communication; (4) ability to change perspective; (5) critical reflection on one's own cultures; and (6) community engagement. Table 4.4 illustrates the types of evidence and examples revealed from the data, providing a general overview of what each element of ICit looked like in the dataset. All participants in the project shared examples on knowledge growth, skill development and increased willingness to learn about others, while only four participants' data were related to perspective change, critical reflection and community engagement. In other words, data displayed a significantly larger number of examples in the first three types of intercultural competencies than in the next three types. Due to the limited space of this chapter, only a few examples are presented for discussion in this section.

Knowledge of one's own and the interlocutor's culture

There was abundant evidence to show that students expanded their knowledge of the interlocutor's culture as well as their own culture through the IT project. For the CFL students, their cultural knowledge spans food, education, sports and holiday celebrations. Many of them were excited to learn about Chinese 广场舞 [square dance], an exercise routine similar to the line dance in the US culture but much more prevalent in China. Many CFL students called this topic their favorite one, as Nina wrote about her Chinese partner: 'After dinner she and her family go to town, same as every family and square dance. I think this was the most memorable topic because I thought it was so cool how everyone knew the dance' (Nina, weekly report #7). Many of them were simply thrilled to learn about their partner's Chinese family members and daily routine.

For the Chinese students, although some mentioned the same topics as the CFL students, their cultural knowledge was more obviously extensive on nuances and complexity. Many students addressed these topics in their final report and final interview: familial influence on romantic relationships, Hmong culture within the US, gun rights and crime rates, and societal divide on the LGBTQ topic. For instance, Zhao talked about her discussion with her IT partner Nina about safety issues in the US. Having heard considerable news about gun crimes brought her

Table 4.4 Examples of ICit development

	Intercultural competence types	Data example
1	Knowledge of one's own and the interlocutor's culture	'We shared the sports culture. Sports are of great significance for Americans. They can enter middle schools, universities, and even get a job by virtue of their excellent physical ability. But in my culture, physical education does not seem to be that important. We pay more attention to knowledge acquired courses because good knowledge acquired courses results can help you enter a good middle school and university.' (Cai, final report)
2	Curiosity and interest in intercultural exchange	'I think the double-happiness character is pretty cool. It's almost like each character represents one person in the marriage, and when they come together, they become more happy. I think I want to incorporate it into my wedding somehow. And I want to learn more.' (Chris, weekly report #3)
3	Knowledge of and skills in intercultural communication	'I know how to gently point out the other party's mistakes without damaging the confidence of others. When I was studying in China, it was very straightforward for others to point out my mistakes. However, I found that in the process of communicating with my partners, even if I was not fluent in English or even made mistakes, my partners would gently point out my mistakes and constantly encourage me. So I think I should do the same when I point out her Chinese mistakes.' (Wang, final report)
4	Ability to change perspective	'Knowing more about the local humanistic culture will help me develop friendship with my American classmates in the future, so that I can view and understand things in life in a better American way.' (Wang, final report)
5	Critical reflection on one's own cultures	'It's a chance for me to "fact check" what I already know to what it actually is in real life. For example, a lot of what I know about China is based on TV dramas, which is not the most credible source. Some American news reports about China are biased and full of stereotypes. But I love the talking and the safe space it creates to just learn, especially because I always get along with my partner.' (Zoe, final report)
6	Community engagement	'Take me for example, when I was in high school, I still didn't know how it would cause girls to become pregnant. My parents will not talk about this topic with me, and I have no other way to learn. I think sex education in China is very scarce and we need a way to understand it and do something about it. We should do more to educate the youth.' (Cai, final report)

anxiety while studying in the US, but her partner Nina gave her a more balanced view of gun rights and helped her understand that not everyone has a gun in the US. Nina also offered some safety tips to Zhao.

The difference in knowledge expansion between the CFL students and the Chinese students could be explained by the various amount of time these students had spent in their target culture. Many CFL students were exposed to the Chinese culture for the first time through their Chinese classes on campus; to them, some general cultural knowledge was already a new concept. On the contrary, the Chinese students had already been exposed to western cultures for at least 10 years before coming to the US and their interest was discovering more profound and sophisticated knowledge.

According to Byram (2000), knowledge about one's own culture and others' cultures for intercultural communication involves both knowing facts and knowing how to engage others in conversation. Data also offered evidence that students gained knowledge on how to engage others in conversations more effectively. For instance, Cai said that she learned 'how to talk with people from different cultures and how to share own culture' by providing a variety of examples (Cai, final report); Mark considered 'listening with an interest and then asking relevant follow-up questions' as an effective strategy to engage his partner. Chris effectively engaged her partner by finding similarities in their life; for instance, once she and her partner realized that they both had a boyfriend, they were immediately bonded and often laughed together.

Curiosity and interest in intercultural exchange

Multiple data sources unfolded that the students from both sides demonstrated extraordinary interest in this IT project and intercultural exchange in general. From the recorded IT videos, it was noticeable that the students were slightly nervous, reserved and timid during the first meeting when they were getting to know each other; however, the following videos clearly showed that they were becoming more comfortable with each other. As a result, they were more open to expressing their curiosity and interest. Cai used three Chinese words to capture the process, as she wrote: 'I want to use 紧张 [nervous], 适应 [adapt], 享受 [enjoy] to summarize my experience' (Cai, final report). There were a number of examples indicative of such comfort level and openness to learning from each other. For instance, Zhou wrote in her final report, '完成任务后，我和Ann会讨论一些彼此感兴趣的话题，比如疫情，中美神话故事还有喜欢的音乐，电影等等 [After our worksheet tasks, Ann and I would discuss topics of our mutual interest, such as the pandemic, Chinese and American mythology stories, music and movies]' (Zhou, final report). Further, in Zhou's final interview, she talked about her curiosity again and said she felt 'magical' when she and her partner Ann could share stories across the Pacific Ocean. These moments made her want to continue the virtual exchange and learn more.

Similarly, the CFL students also reported enhanced curiosity through various examples and moments. Iris wrote: 'we have a relationship beyond classmates; we are friends and will help each other learn more'

(Iris, final report); Liam said his favorite moment of this IT project was connecting with his partner on Instagram so they could continue to discuss topics beyond the class; Reed said his favorite moment was introducing his children to his IT partner Zhang and asked his children to greet Zhang in Chinese, which was also Zhang's highlight in this project. It is worth mentioning that the IT project inspired several CFL students to build further connections with China, including applying to study abroad in China (Iris, Mark), participating in a Chinese speech contest (Zoe, Ann, Norah, Kate), and planning to teach English in China upon graduation (Chris).

It was discernable that the curiosity and interest were greatly stimulated by the constructive synergy between partners. All the students attributed their positive experience and continuous interest to their partners' patience, empathy, sincerity, curiosity about their culture, respect, raising good questions and friendliness. For instance, Yan was impressed by her partner's own experience as an LGBTQ member, and the partner invited her to ask any questions she might have. Such candid sharing greatly stimulated Yan's curiosity about this marginalized community within the US.

Knowledge of and skills in intercultural communication

Both ICC and ICit underscore the importance of a knowledge of the general process of individual interaction and skills of interpreting, relating, discovery and interaction (Wagner & Byram, 2017). In particular, this knowledge and skill set entails the ability to resolve misunderstandings resulting from a lack of awareness of the viewpoints of other cultures, and discover new aspects of culture (Byram, 2000). A close analysis of the data divulged some examples to indicate that the IT project fostered such knowledge and skills among the students.

Both the CFL students and Chinese students demonstrated their knowledge growth and skill development through the IT project. For instance, some stated that this project allowed them to realize the importance of being patient and empathetic in intercultural communication (Deng, Yan, Wang); some noted the importance of recognizing commonalities and individualities between cultures (Deng, Mark, Jen); and some learned to meet their partners' cultural knowledge level to have a more relevant and effective conversation (Yan, Chris). Liam said this IT project compelled him to 'figure out how to navigate conversations' so he would not embarrass himself or unintentionally insult others in future intercultural interactions. Kate's quote about trying to figure out how to use grammar and sentences properly and making comparisons with previously created questions also exemplifies skills of interaction, drawing on knowledge learned in class to operate in real time.

Observing and adopting culturally appropriate practices were significant strategies for effective communication. For instance, Yan was very mindful not only to observe but also to adopt her partner's practices to make their communication more natural. She noticed that her partner Zoe often liked to have greetings and small talk at the beginning of their IT meetings; instead of going directly to the tasks, she adopted these practices and their conversation became more relaxed and natural. Additionally, Yan noticed that her partner was very supportive and encouraging in their conversation, which reminded her to remain in the same manner when giving corrective feedback on her partner's Chinese language. She realized the importance of empathy in language and culture learning. Such a notice-adopt practice was mutual in this dyad. Likewise, Yan's partner Zoe also gave similar examples. Noticing Yan's efforts in adapting to her cultural practices, Zoe also took a more direct approach to ask for clarification and was more attentive to observing her partners' verbal and nonverbal communication. Zoe said: 'It also made me better at reading my partner and being able to communicate with her more effectively' (Zoe, final report). In this dyad, Yan and Zoe were observant, attentive and adaptive in their communication; both reached the middle ground and achieved effective communication through a vigorous dynamic.

Ability to change perspective

The evidence of perspective change was implicit in the data. In other words, students rarely openly stated that their views changed, but the way they described their cultural understanding demonstrated their ability to change perspective. Especially when the Chinese students asked in-depth questions, their understandings of US culture became more complex, which was indicative of perspective change. For instance, Cai was firstly surprised to hear that introducing boyfriends or girlfriends to the family was a common practice in the US even if the romantic relationship had just started, because, by comparison, meeting parents would be a serious matter in Chinese culture; nonetheless, she explained that 'it may be related to our cultural attitudes. Americans are very open while the Chinese are very restrained. I learned to be open and understanding towards their way' (Cai, final report). Although Cai's cultural comparison here might be oversimplified, it nonetheless did reveal her willingness and ability to explore reasons to support a view change. The same reaction was found in Wang's data, who considered her partner Chris's cultural experience 'authentic American culture' and 'local humanistic culture' that helped her 'view and understand things in life in a better American way' (Wang, final report).

Perspective change was also found in CFL students. On the same topic of marriage and romantic relationships, Nina learned from her partner Zhao that many Chinese women were expected to do all the housework, that arranged marriage was not uncommon and that married couples would live with their parents. While Nina said, 'It amazes me how two people living on the same planet, and we have such different views and opinions on things' (Nina, weekly report #3), she did learn to understand from the Chinese people's perspective, as she later explained that her partner helped her understand that Chinese parents' involvement in marriage was out of good intention, hoping their children would have a companion in life. Living with parents and sometimes even grandparents was a reflection of the filial piety in traditional Chinese culture.

Sometimes, talking about daily cultural practices could also foster perspective change. Take Ann for example: she was perplexed about why Chinese people often drink hot water even in the summer, but, through her IT meetings with Zhou, she was also challenged by Zhou's confusion as to why Americans like to drink cold water even in the winter. The mutual perplexity pushed them both to look at each other's perspectives. Ann later learned that the Chinese habit of drinking hot water could be accounted for by Chinese medical beliefs in balancing the chi inside the body. She shared another example about women's choice of marriage. She had held an impression that women over 30 years old and unmarried would be frowned upon in China, but the IT exchange with her partner helped to dismantle this overly-sweeping stereotype. Although such a conservative view exists in China, as it does elsewhere in the world, her partner helped her understand that Chinese women were playing an increasingly independent and important role in China. Ann reflected: 'Despite our cultural differences, it is interesting to me that the same social phenomena of women putting off marriage in two highly developed countries has occurred' (Ann, weekly report #3). She said the IT exchange helped her 'become more open-minded and aware of others' (Ann, weekly report #3).

Critical reflection on one's own culture and other cultures

The evidence for this aspect was less abundant and less overt than the previously reported aspects. Instead of using direct and critical rhetoric to analyze their own culture and other cultures, students conveyed and demonstrated a degree of critical view by admitting some disadvantages of a culture, and by conveying a questioning attitude. For instance, when Yan talked about romantic relationships with her partner, their conversation expanded to the cultural acceptance of gay marriage. Although Yan knew that her home culture (Chinese culture) was less open and less accepting of gay marriage than US culture, yet she did not know that China has such strict rules about child adoption that the adopter's gender, income, marital status and sexual orientation would be considered. Gay people are not allowed to adopt children in China. She said, 'it was an eye-opening experience for my own culture, 重新认识自己的文化 [to get to know my own culture again]' (Yan, final interview). This newly revealed knowledge pushed her to examine her own culture through a more critical lens. She began to question the inequity for those who were not able to adopt children because of their gender identity and sexual orientation.

In a similar light, another Chinese student, Cai, admitted that the relatively conservative cultural beliefs in China prohibited her openness and comfort level in talking about sexual relationships. When her partner Norah talked about resources for support in US universities, such as mental health counseling and contraceptive advice, Cai was embarrassed about this topic because sex education was never mentioned by her parents or her school. In her final interview, Cai said she noticed 'the difference in sex education between the two countries'. She felt that Chinese culture could and should be more open to talk about sex education without making people feel shy or shameful.

CFL students' critical view of one's culture and other cultures was even more scant in the data. I was able to identify only two examples. One was Zoe asking her partner Yan many questions about Chinese daily life to compare with her information received from American TV and media. She acknowledged that US media could present prejudiced descriptions of China for a political agenda, and that US TV shows depicting Asians could be stereotypical; therefore, she raised many questions to her partner Yan and their conversation developed deeper to include cultural appropriation. The other example was Ann's conversation about COVID-19 with her partner Zhou, when Ann reflected critically that COVID-19 was used as a political weapon in the US to divide society and achieve some politicians' hidden agenda at the cost of public health. In these two examples, both Zoe and Ann demonstrated a degree of critical cultural awareness to suspend belief about one's own culture (Byram, 1997).

The insufficient evidence of critical view from both groups of students could be explained in relation to their limited prior knowledge of the target culture and cultural background. As mentioned earlier in this chapter, many CFL students were introduced to Chinese culture for the first time; they were overjoyed by simply learning new things about the culture and might not have formed a critical view yet. As for the Chinese students, the traditional values, including harmony and respect for others, coupled with their developing English proficiency, might have restricted their demonstration of a critical view.

Community engagement

Community engagement in ICit refers to students' participation in civic and social duties. In manifestation of community engagement in ICit, students may engage their critical thinking skills and collaborate with others in solving problems in the community (Byram et al., 2017; Porto, 2019), and students may devote themselves to community-based service-learning projects (Jackson, 2014; Palpacuer Lee *et al.*, 2018). Unfortunately, the results in this study reveal little evidence that students were actually solving problems.

However, community engagement did manifest itself in other ways in this study. Wagner *et al.* (2019) gave four scenarios where students exhibited active participation in community, including taking their language or target language out into the community to do something with it, interaction 'with their real or imagined communities, local or transnational', and engagement 'in conversations about current challenges/topics in society' (Wagner *et al.*, 2019: 6). In resonance with these results, this study identified two examples.

One example was from a CFL student, Ann, in the Intermediate Chinese class. Ann and her partner discussed COVID-19 and both countries' (China and the US) handling of the situation. This was not a required discussion topic but their endeavor reflected their concern about current challenges in society. They compared both governments' policies, citizens' responses and the ramifications on society. Ann called it 'one memorable exchange' with her partner, as she noted, 'because it was such a relevant and global issue that I thought our discussion was really mind-opening' (Ann, final report). After her IT meeting, Ann wrote a short essay in Chinese and asked me for feedback. Her essay talked about COVID in the US in relation to political divide, selfishness, American values and the importance of public health. It was the time when she was preparing for the state Chinese speech contest, so she wanted to share this piece with a wider audience. It is worth noting that most of the speeches in this state-level Chinese speech contest included familiar everyday topics such as family, hobbies and travels. The fact that Ann took on this social topic was an exceptional example of her willingness to fulfil her civic duty as she wanted to elevate public awareness of this social issue.

The other example was from a Chinese student, Zhang, who planned to bring his knowledge, skills and attitudes from this intercultural exchange to his future career. In his final interview, Zhang happily shared the news that he had already passed all qualification tests to become a civil servant in the Immigration Office in China. He said: 'In my future job, I will deal with foreigners. Now I have my own tolerance for different cultures, and I gradually learned how to get along with people with completely different cultures. I think this project is very helpful to me now and in the future' (Zhang, final report). This example reflected Zhang's intention to take the skills out to the community and do something with them.

Discussion

This study has reported that students perceived the virtual exchange project in a positive light and that their feedback proved the effectiveness of a thoughtful project design that was based on the ACTFL 5 Cs and

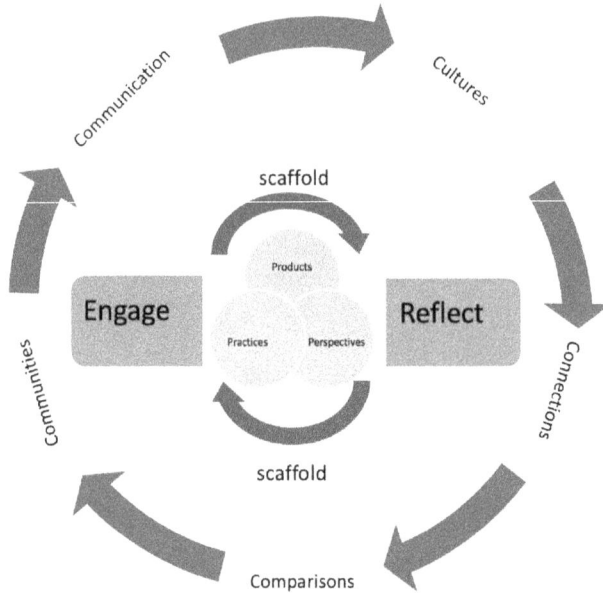

Figure 4.2 The design of the IT project

inspired by the elements of ICit. Figure 4.2 illustrates the intention of the project design and can be described as comprising three layers. Firstly, the outer layer reflects the overarching guidance of this project. The 5 Cs serve as a reminder in the design that the IT project needed to provide ample opportunities for students to make connections and comparisons in many spheres within cultures. Secondly, the middle layer stresses a balance between the students' role and the instructor's role in this project design. To give prominence to students' participation, activities were designed in an engaging way and topics were relatable. On the other hand, my role as an instructor was 'to periodically check in with them about challenges', and to offer corresponding strategies (Wagner *et al.*, 2019: 109) as well as a scaffold to support students' smooth communication. As students' responses in the findings section showed, offering some sample interview questions served as effective scaffolding to stimulate students' metalinguistic awareness; in other words, students had examples to guide their question formation. Especially for beginning learners, they could compare their sentences and my samples, and consider how to make understandable sentences and talk in a proper way so that their intercultural communication would be culturally appropriate and effective, fitting the definition of intercultural communicative competence. Last but not least, the inner layer addresses the principal approach to complicating an understanding of culture. Students were introduced to ACTFL's interpretation of culture and learned to unpack culture from various angles. Multiple examples in the findings section, especially when addressing students' change of perspective, were a depiction of them utilizing cultural values (perspectives) to interpret cultural phenomena (products and practices).

This design model fits in the definition of what Byram and Wagner (2018: 149) would call 'a more holistic approach', using relevant content to students' lives and to society to foster critical thinking skills, and helping students 'understand the utility of language education in their lives beyond classroom walls' through collaboration. It was evident that they interacted beyond classroom walls, and Zhang's plan to apply the skills in his future career as an immigration officer was a further testimony of intercultural citizenship.

Corroborating the results in existing studies on virtual exchange (Jiang *et al.*, 2014; Jin, 2018; Luo & Gao, 2022; Luo & Yang, 2018; Porto, 2019), this study also discovered that virtual exchange increased students' intercultural citizenship, as reflected through students' expanded knowledge of cultures, through their curiosity in learning beyond school walls and national borders, and through integrating knowledge and skills to maneuver intercultural communication process, profound reflection and community engagement. Echoing Luo and Gao's (2022: 21) study on a Chinese–American song-sharing project, where they concluded that virtual exchange is a 'promising pedagogical tool for teaching culture in Chinese language classrooms', CFL students in the current project were overwhelmingly appreciative of the cultural knowledge shared by their IT partners; they asked good questions in the target language and demonstrated a genuine interest, which catalyzed further discussion. By comparison, Chinese students exhibited abilities to elicit nuances in cultural knowledge to problematize their stereotypes. Regardless of the different amounts of prior knowledge of the target culture, partners were able to build on that foundation and strive to learn more, because they had what scholars would call Intellectual Humility (IH) (Whitcomb *et al.*, 2017). IH refers to individuals owning their intellectual limitations, weaknesses and mistakes, which in turn fosters an open mindset to dissenting views. IH was evident here in that all students were very open to learning from each other and then reflected on their learning. The trusting relationship and optimal rapport between partners made them feel comfortable about admitting their limitations and learning from each other. Gradually their reflection along the process also advanced their cultural decentering, meaning that they distanced themselves from their own culture to 'question the ordinary, the known and the accepted' (Lomicka, 2009: 1228).

The findings of this study also illuminate opportunities for future research. An essential element in ICit is students' community engagement, referring to students' active participation in civic and social duties. Based on the data presented in this study, some may argue that students' intercultural citizenship is on the periphery, mainly exhibited through enriched discussion, sharing cultural knowledge in an appropriate and effective way, and students' reflection; that there was little evidence to reflect students' concrete actions to solve community problems or students' fulfilment of civic duties. In other words, the results could be interpreted as little more than superficial pen-pal projects without profound criticality.

It is worth noting that the students' language proficiency limited the extent of critical discussion. Although they were able to speak both languages (Chinese, English) in the IT sessions, their language proficiency was not high enough to discuss complicated topics in depth. In the meanwhile, Barnett (1997) reminded us that criticality is a complex concept and a developmental process. Barnett unpacked criticality at four levels: (1) learning to be critical; (2) applying critical skills to knowledge, own selves and the world; (3) changing perspective and challenging the accepted status quo; and (4) subversive action to make a radical change. These four levels represent progression and development in deepening criticality. There were moments in this study to show students' emerging criticality at the first three levels. There were many reflections from amongst the students' data to show that they observed, listened, made cultural comparisons and used cultural values to explain cultural practices, which documented their exploration of critical skills to evaluate a cultural aspect. When Zoe raised the topic of cultural appropriation displayed through American TV shows and wanted to have a fact-check of her own knowledge through TV, she was applying critical skills to understand the world and herself through a critical lens. In addition, from Cai's critique of sex education in China and calling for more openness towards this sensitive topic, to Ann's critical speech about the American public's reaction to COVID-19 in relation to cultural values, they were exemplary in rejecting the status quo and instead calling for a change, resonating the second and the third level of criticality. I can imagine that, if the IT project continued and the exchange tasks were more project-based and involved deliverable civic actions, students could advance to the fourth level of criticality, and engage in community actions for radical change.

An unexpected yet fascinating discovery was Chinese students' unanimous and strong expression of their cultural pride in this project. The Chinese students repeatedly stressed the importance of presenting to the world a real China and its positive developments, dismantling some of America's outdated stereotypes and reducing prejudice. The Chinese students' reaction could be explained by the social and political tension at the time when the IT project occurred. The spring of 2021 witnessed increased anti-Asian violence caused by a combination of COVID-19 conspiracy theories, political tension in the US–China relationship, and societal divide within the US. Chinese students were so emotionally impacted, and some even distraught, that the IT project offered them an opportunity to voice their views and to make a change. This discovery needs to be interpreted with caution because there is a fine line between pride in one's culture and nationalism. It was not clear whether the Chinese students in this study were feeling proud to stand up for their home culture or feeling nationalistic, nor was this study's goal to examine that; however, the repetition of showing the positive sides of China was conspicuous. It will be a meaningful direction for future research.

Conclusion

This study reports on the results of a Chinese–American online virtual exchange project where students practiced the target language and exchanged cultural knowledge. This study joins the findings from previous research to further support the imperative value of intercultural virtual exchange in nurturing students' openness, curiosity and interest in other cultures. Although the students in the present IT project came from different linguistic and cultural backgrounds, their rapport with each other beyond the language classroom, their enriched conversations and genuine interest in learning with and learning from each other, were reflections of the definition of intercultural citizenship. It was evident that their knowledge growth transcended national borders and that their ability to interpret knowledge in the context of cultural values reflected an ethnorelative lens in intercultural communication. These findings highlight the importance of an engaging, interactive, culture-based and ACTFL-informed pedagogical design.

The college setting in this current study also sheds light on the importance of implementing ICit and researching ICit at the college level. As much ICit research is conducted in the K–12 context, this study expands the landscape and displays the potential for college instructors to teach and research ICit. Since college students from a variety of academic majors may gather in one language classroom, it is conducive for them to draw upon diverse disciplinary knowledge to enrich discussion and create community engagement plans. More importantly, the findings in this study illuminate that, when instructors offer equal learning opportunities for partners in intercultural learning, both partners can benefit and develop ICit. It is an effective way to avoid 'instrumental, utilitarian and uncritical orientations' (Porto, 2019: 150) that would tokenize the international students.

However, the limitations of this study also illuminated considerations for pedagogy and future research. Firstly, the total number of participants was relatively small, and due to mental stress and technical challenges during COVID-19, not every student submitted all the assignments. Future studies could examine a larger population and include more extensive data. Secondly, the lack of evidence of students' concrete actions in civic/social duties lessened the connection to the core principle of ICit. Future projects could consider emphasizing students' action plans, and assigning extensive collaborative projects that would require students to solve problems and address social issues explicitly. Finally, future research could also investigate Chinese students' emotions and cultural identity in intercultural exchange. This would be a particularly stimulating topic to explore in light of the current tension between China and the US.

In conclusion, the findings of this study show that intercultural virtual exchange is promising in connecting students with communities beyond the classroom walls, through conducting intercultural dialogue, enhancing critical cultural awareness and addressing critical topics in the community. It is strongly recommended that Chinese language educators judiciously adopt this pedagogy, giving careful intention and attention to preparing students and providing scaffolding during the process. More empirical studies in this line of research are needed to present a fuller picture of virtual exchange and ICit to inform teaching.

References

ACTFL (2015) World-readiness standards for learning languages. See https://www.actfl.org/sites/default/files/publications/standards/World-ReadinessStandardsforLearningLanguages.pdf (Accessed July 2022.)

ACTFL (2017) NCSSFL-ACTFL Can-do statements for intercultural communication. https://www.actfl.org/publications/guidelines-and-manuals/ncssfl-actfl-can-do-statements (Accessed July 2022.)

Albirini, A. (2009) Using technology, literature and guest speakers to raise the cultural awareness of Arabic language learners. *The International Journal of Language Society and Culture* 28, 1–15.

Arnold, N. (2007) Technology-mediated learning 10 years later: Emphasizing pedagogical or utilitarian applications? *Foreign Language Annals* 40 (1), 161–181. See https://doi.org/10.1111/j.1944-9720.2007.tb02859.x.

Barnett, R. (1997) *Higher Education: A Critical Business*. Buckingham: Society for Research into Higher Education and the Open University Press.

Belz, J.A. (2003) Linguistic perspectives on the development of intercultural communicative competence in telecollaboration. *Language Learning and Technology* 7 (2), 68–117.

Belz, J.A. and Thorne, S.L. (eds) (2006) *Internet-Mediated Intercultural Foreign Language Education*. Boston, MA: Thomson Heinle.

Bennett, M.J. (2004) Becoming interculturally competent. In J. Wurzel (ed.) *Toward Multiculturalism: A Reader in Multicultural Education* (2nd edn, pp. 62–77). Newton, MA: Intercultural Resource Corporation.

Bingham, A.J. and Witkowsky, P. (2021) Deductive and inductive approaches to qualitative data analysis. In C. Vanover, P. Mihas and J. Saldana (eds) *Analyzing and Interpreting Qualitative Research: After the Interview* (pp. 133–148). Thousand Oaks, CA: Sage Publications.

Blake, R. (2011) Current trends in online language learning. *Annual Review of Applied Linguistics* 31, 19–35.

Byram, M. (1997) *Teaching and Assessing Intercultural Communicative Competence*. Clevedon: Multilingual Matters.

Byram, M. (2000) Assessing intercultural competence in language teaching. *Sprogforum* 18 (6), 8–13.

Byram, M. (2008) *From Foreign Language Education to Education for Intercultural Citizenship: Essays and Reflections*. Clevedon: Multilingual Matters.

Byram, M. (2014) Twenty-five years on – from cultural studies to intercultural citizenship. *Language, Culture and Curriculum* 27 (3), 209–225. See https://doi.org/10.1080/07908318.2014.974329.

Byram, M. and Wagner, M. (2018) Making a difference: Language teaching for intercultural and international dialogue. *Foreign Language Annals* 51 (1), 140–151. See https://doi.org/10.1111/flan.12319.

Byram, M., Golubeva, I., Han, H. and Wagner, M. (eds) (2017) *From Principles to Practice in Education for Intercultural Citizenship*. Bristol: Multilingual Matters.

Chan, S.C.F., Ngai, G., Yau, J.H., Chan, S.C.F., Ngai, G., Yau, J.H. and Kwan, K.P. (2021) Impact of international service-learning on students' global citizenship and intercultural effectiveness development. *International Journal of Research on Service-Learning and Community Engagement* 9 (1), 1–12.

Charmaz, K. (2006) *Constructing Grounded Theory: A Practical Guide through Qualitative Analysis*. London: Sage.

Christensen, A. and Kong, K. (2022) Flipgrid classroom conversations: International virtual pen pal exchange. *MinneTESOL Journal*. https://minnetesoljournal.org/current-issue/peer-reviewed-article/flipgrid-classroom-conversations-international-virtual-pen-pal-exchange/ (Accessed 9 July 2022).

Chun, D.M. (2014) Editor's introduction. In D.M. Chun (ed.) *Cultura-Inspired Intercultural Exchanges: Focus on Asian and Pacific Languages* (pp. xi–xx). Honolulu: University of Hawaii, National Foreign Language Resource Center.

Diao, W. and Trentman, E. (eds) (2021) *Language Learning in Study Abroad: The Multilingual Turn*. Bristol: Multilingual Matters.

Fang, F. and Baker, W. (2018) 'A more inclusive mind towards the world': English language teaching and study abroad in China from intercultural citizenship and English as a lingua franca perspective. *Language Teaching Research* 22 (5), 608–624. See https://doi.org/10.1177/1362168817718574.

Freiermuth, M.R. and Huang, H.-C. (2021) Zooming across cultures: Can a telecollaborative video exchange between language learning partners further the development of intercultural competences? *Foreign Language Annals* 54 (1), 185–206. See https://doi.org/10.1111/flan.12504.

González-Lloret, M. (2020) Collaborative tasks for online language teaching. *Foreign Language Annals* 53 (2), 260–269.

Huh, S. and Suh, Y.M. (2018) Preparing elementary readers to be critical intercultural citizens through literacy education. *Language Teaching Research* 22 (5), 532–551. See https://doi.org/10.1177/1362168817718575.

Jackson, J. (2014) Global citizenship and intercultural (communicative) competence. In J. Jackson (ed.) *Introducing Language and Intercultural Communication* (pp. 297–323). London: Routledge.

Jiang, S., Wang, H. and Tschudi, S. (2014) Intercultural learning on the web: Reflections on practice. In D.M. Chun (ed.) *Cultura-Inspired Intercultural Exchanges: Focus on Asian and Pacific Languages* (pp. 121–137). Honolulu: University of Hawaii, National Foreign Language Resource Center.

Jin, L. (2018) Digital affordances on WeChat: Learning Chinese as a second language. *Computer Assisted Language Learning* 31 (1–2), 27–52. See https://doi.org/10.1080/09588221.2017.1376687.

Kong, K. (2018a) Different voices: Guest speakers as pedagogy in a culture class. In E. Jean-Francois (ed.) *Transnational Perspectives on Innovation in Teaching and Learning Technologies* (pp. 262–284). Leiden: Brill.

Kong, K. (2018b) Learning Chinese: Connections and comparisons in study abroad. In D. M. Velliaris (ed.) *Study Abroad Contexts for Enhanced Foreign Language Learning* (pp. 44–69). Hershey, PA: IGI Global.

Kong, K. (2021) Engaging native speakers in language scaffolding in a Chinese classroom. *Second Language Research & Practice* 2 (1), 41–64.

Kong, K. (2022) 'Zoom' in and speak out: Virtual exchange in language learning. In S. Hilliker (ed.) *Second Language Teaching and Learning through Virtual Exchange* (pp. 97–114). Berlin: De Gruyter Mouton.

Krulatz, A., Steen-Olsen, T. and Torgersen, E. (2018) Towards critical cultural and linguistic awareness in language classrooms in Norway: Fostering respect for diversity through identity texts. *Language Teaching Research* 22 (5), 552–569. See https://doi.org/10.1177/1362168817718572.

Larsen-Freeman, D. (2018) Looking ahead: Future directions in, and future research into, second language acquisition. *Foreign Language Annals* 51 (1), 55–72.

Lee, K.Y. (2012) Teaching intercultural English learning/teaching in world Englishes: Some classroom activities in South Korea. *English Teaching: Practice and Critique* 11 (4), 190–205.

Lee, L. (2008) Focus-on-form through collaborative scaffolding in expert-to-novice online interaction. *Language Learning and Technology* 12 (3), 53–72.

Liaw, M. (2006) E-learning and the development of intercultural competence. *Language Learning and Technology* 10 (3), 49–64.

Lomicka, L. (2009) An intercultural approach to teaching and learning French. *The French Review* 82 (6), 1227–1243.

Luo, H. and Yang, C. (2018) Twenty years of telecollaborative practice: Implications for teaching Chinese as a foreign language. *Computer Assisted Language Learning* 31 (5–6), 546–571. See https://doi.org/10.1080/09588221.2017.1420083.

Luo, H. and Gao, P. (2022) Intercultural learning through Chinese–American telecollaboration: Results of a song sharing project. *Computer Assisted Language Learning*. See https://doi.org/10.1080/09588221.2022.2026405.

Lynch, M.P., Johnson, C.R., Sheff, N. and Gunn, H. (2016) Intellectual humility in public discourse. *IHPD Literature Review*. https://humilityandconviction.uconn.edu/wp-content/uploads/sites/1877/2016/09/IHPD-Literature-Reviewrevised.pdf

O'Dowd, R. (2012) Intercultural communicative competence through telecollaboration. In J. Jackson (ed.) *The Routledge Handbook of Language and Intercultural Communication* (pp. 342–358). London: Routledge.

O'Dowd, R. (2020) A transnational model of virtual exchange for global citizenship education. *Language Teaching* 53 (4), 477–490. See https://doi.org/10.1017/S0261444819000077.

O'Rourke, B. (2007) Models of telecollaboration (1): eTandem. In R. O'Dowd (ed.) *Online Intercultural Exchange: An Introduction for Foreign Language Teachers* (pp. 41–61). Clevedon: Multilingual Matters.

Oskoz, A. (2009) Learners' feedback in online chats: What does it reveal about students' learning? *CALICO Journal* 27 (1), 48–68.

Palpacuer Lee, C., Hutchison Curtis, J. and Curran, M.E. (2018) Stories of engagement: Pre-service language teachers negotiate intercultural citizenship in a community-based English language program. *Language Teaching Research* 22 (5), 590–607. See https://doi.org/10.1177/1362168817718578.

Plutino, A. (2016) Anything can happen out there: A holistic approach to field trips. In C. Goria, O. Speicher and S. Stollhans (eds) *Innovative Language Teaching and Learning at University: Enhancing Participation and Collaboration* (pp. 113–120). Dublin: Research-publishing.net.

Porto, M. (2019) Affordances, complexities, and challenges of intercultural citizenship for foreign language teachers. *Foreign Language Annals* 52 (1), 141–164. See https://doi.org/10.1111/flan.12375.

Porto, M., Houghton, S.A. and Byram, M. (2018) Intercultural citizenship in the (foreign) language classroom. *Language Teaching Research* 22 (5), 484–498. See https://doi.org/10.1177/1362168817718580.

Schenker, T. (2012) Intercultural competence and cultural learning through telecollaboration. *CALICO Journal* 29 (3), 449–470. See https://doi.org/10.11139/cj.29.3.449-470.

Sharkey, J. (2018) The promising potential role of intercultural citizenship in preparing mainstream teachers for im/migrant populations. *Language Teaching Research* 22 (5), 570–589. See https://doi.org/10.1177/1362168817718577.

Shenk, E.M. (2014) Teaching sociolinguistic variation in the intermediate language classroom: Voseo in Latin America. *Hispania* 97 (3), 368–381.

Soong, H., Caldwell, D. and Restall, G. (2018) Teaching Chinese language for Asia literacy: Chinese teachers' experiences teaching Australian students. In H. Soong and N. Cominos (eds) *Asia Literacy in a Global World* (pp. 145–163). Singapore: Springer.

Sotillo, S.M. (2000) Discourse functions and syntactic complexity in synchronous and asynchronous communication. *Language Learning and Technology* 4 (1), 77–110.

Wagner, M. and Byram, M. (2017) Intercultural citizenship. In Y.Y. Kim and K.L. McKay-Semmler (eds) *The International Encyclopedia of Intercultural Communication* (pp. 1–6). Hoboken, NJ: Wiley.

Wagner, M., Cardetti, F. and Byram, M. (2019) *Teaching Intercultural Citizenship across the Curriculum: The Role of Language Education.* Alexandria, VA: ACTFL.

Whitcomb, D., Battaly, H., Baehr, J. and Howard-Snyder, D. (2017) Intellectual humility: Owning our limitations. *Philosophy and Phenomenological Research* 94 (3), 509–539.

Williams, K. (2017) Language learning: Its moral and civic remit. *Pedagogy, Culture and Society* 25 (1), 59–71. See https://doi. org/10.1080/14681366.2016.1216463.

Wu, C.H. (2018) Intercultural citizenship through participation in an international service-learning program: A case study from Taiwan. *Language Teaching Research* 22 (5), 517–531. See https://doi.org/10.1177/1362168817718573.

Yanguas, Í. (2010) Oral computer-mediated interaction between L2 learners: It's about time! *Language Learning and Technology* 14 (3), 72–93.

Yulita, L. (2018) Competences for democratic culture: An empirical study of an intercultural citizenship project in language pedagogy. *Language Teaching Research* 22 (5), 499–516. See https://doi.org/10.1177/1362168817718579.

5 Study Abroad in Teacher Education: Fostering Intercultural Citizenship

Allison J. Spenader and Adriana L. Medina

Introduction

As local and global challenges become more complex, it becomes evident that solutions to world challenges will require communication among individuals across the globe. International communication will require the development of skills as part of an internationalized curriculum that is not currently in place universally across K–12 education. Medina and Kiefel (2021) note that curriculum 'internationalization can include the transformation of coursework and activities to include readings, assignments, learning outcomes, and instructional methods that infuse global knowledge and awareness and intercultural competence' (Medina & Kiefel, 2021: 63). While higher education has heeded the call to internationalize the curriculum (Knight, 2003; Longview Foundation for Education in World Affairs and International Understanding, 2008), K–12 contexts, outside the context of World Languages education, have not mobilized at the same pace.

In the US, teacher preparation works to ensure that teachers will be able to work in settings that are racially, culturally and linguistically diverse. Effective teachers employ culturally responsive and sustaining teaching practices (Ladson-Billings, 1995; Paris, 2012) to meet the needs of their K–12 students and prepare them to engage with peers locally and globally. One way that teacher education programs work toward this aim is by offering study abroad opportunities. Study abroad is seen as an opportunity for pre-service teachers to enhance their intercultural skills and knowledge about the world, which can prepare them to be culturally responsive. Study abroad experiences are known to positively impact teacher quality, and it is believed that teachers with global competencies will be better equipped to teach about multicultural issues (Longview Foundation for Education in World Affairs and International Understanding, 2008). In addition to a focus on intercultural competence, global competencies and cultural responsiveness, all of which involve a specialized set of beliefs, knowledge and skills (Deardorff, 2006; Ladson-Billings, 1995), there has been a more recent focus on intercultural citizenship (Byram, 2006; Byram *et al.*, 2017). Intercultural citizenship (ICit) furthers pre-existing conceptualizations of intercultural competence by adding a dimension of action for social change. If the aim is to foster ICit in K–12 students so that they can be better future citizens of the world and work towards solving world issues, then a precursor is to foster intercultural competence in preservice teachers. This study explores how study abroad fostered requisite intercultural competence for the enactment of intercultural citizenship in preservice teachers.

Review of the Literature

While the processes and outcomes of Intercultural Competence (IC) development in undergraduate students through study abroad have been widely described, less is known about IC development and the impact of study abroad on teachers specifically. Furthermore, little is known about how teachers' IC informs their enactment of pedagogical practices in support of intercultural growth for their own students. This begs the question, What aspects of IC developed in study abroad do teachers bring forward to their work with students, leading to a praxis of teaching for intercultural citizenship?

The need for intercultural citizenship education

The Council of Europe and the American Council on the Teaching of Foreign Languages (ACTFL) have both incorporated goals for intercultural learning through knowledge, skills and attitudes development in their guidance for educators (ACTFL, 2017; Council of Europe, 2018). Historically, most of the work around intercultural learning in K–12 US contexts has taken place within world languages education. Approaches for incorporating intercultural learning goals have been adopted by language teachers in the US and are reflected in NCSSFL-ACTFL Can-Do Statements for Intercultural Communication, added in 2017 (ACTFL, 2017). A focus on evaluating cultural products, practices and perspectives (what ACTFL calls the 3 Ps) is central to developing critical cultural awareness. Although this approach is common in world language classrooms in the US, it should be infused in all areas of the curriculum to maximize the impact for intercultural growth. There has been a call to internationalize teacher education in a meaningful way in order to meet the needs of 21st-century learners (Longview Foundation for Education in World Affairs and International Understanding, 2008). National boundaries no longer separate individuals, and everyone must work towards improving transnational communication. The goal of intercultural citizenship education is to prepare students to participate effectively in intercultural settings locally as well as globally (Wagner *et al.*, 2019). Intercultural citizenship fosters learners' knowledge, skills and attitudes related to intercultural communicative competence (Byram, 2006), and action towards social change, known as 'active citizenship' (Byram *et al.*, 2017).

The ICit framework 'encompasses concern with social justice, with a questioning attitude to what learners experience in their local, national and international environment, and a concern to make changes for the better' (Wagner *et al.*, 2019: 9–10). ICit espouses the idea that 'citizenship' can be more than just nationality: it 'should equally involve learners in engagement and action, at an international level as well as at a local, regional or national level' (Byram, 2006: 127). It 'postulates that learners can, in addition to learning active citizenship in their own country, acquire the knowledge and skills necessary to act in a community which is multicultural and international, and comprises more than one set of cultural values, beliefs and behaviors' (Wagner & Byram, 2017: 3).

The ICit framework shares the values and goals promoted by educators for social justice and anti-bias education in world language classrooms (see Glynn *et al.*, 2018; Nieto, 2010; Osborn, 2006). Anti-bias education is a social justice approach to teaching wherein teachers work to help learners develop 'comfort with differences and awareness of unfairness and bias while explicitly teaching children about the complexity and nuances of human diversity' (Beneke & Park, 2019: 55–56; see also Derman-Sparks & Edwards, 2010; Kuh *et al.*, 2016). Today's classrooms need to support learners in their critical cultural awareness development and provide opportunities to engage in 'active citizenship' in social justice and human rights initiatives within and beyond the classroom setting (Byram *et al.*, 2017; Wagner *et al.*, 2019). Teachers enacting ICit facilitate interactions between learners and the communities in which they live and operate, whether those are real or imagined, local to them or international (Wagner *et al.*, 2019).

While multilingualism has long been the goal of educators, regrettably only a minority of US teachers and learners become multilingual as a result of their formal education. Even when working in one's own language, notions of cultural relativity may hinder one's ability to communicate and interact beyond one's own nation states and culture groups (Byram, 2006). Teachers and their students need to gain the requisite intercultural understandings and skills to participate in the global society effectively and with sensitivity, with or without proficiency in multiple languages. It is important to remember that the ICit framework derives from Byram's intercultural communicative competence (ICC) model (Byram 1997, 2021). ICC's focus is on preparing learners to be 'intercultural speakers' of the language they are learning, but its reach now extends to a wider variety of learning settings (Wagner & Byram, 2017). All teachers, not just those teaching world languages, can incorporate students' cultural backgrounds into their instruction and encourage multiple perspectives in all subjects, leading to intercultural learning for everybody (Wagner & Byram, 2017).

Preparing teachers for intercultural citizenship education

It is imperative that we work to prepare globally competent teachers, requiring IC to be a central focus in teacher preparation (Marx & Moss, 2011). For teachers to enact ICit they should possess intercultural competence themselves. Teachers who can operate effectively and with sensitivity in culturally dynamic settings, who approach their work with a questioning attitude, and who care about issues of social justice are poised better to meet the social, emotional and academic needs of their students and to help them engage in active citizenship.

Teacher education programs aim to prepare educators who can implement culturally responsive pedagogies to meet the needs of their diverse student populations. Culturally responsive pedagogies acknowledge the diverse backgrounds of students and work towards more equitable education (Ladson-Billings, 1995). In addition, we need to ensure that students are not required to assimilate to a euro-centric framework, a practice known as culturally sustaining pedagogy (Paris, 2012). Central to cultural relevance is the need for teachers to hold complex views around diversity and to be aware of the impact of sociopolitical factors on their students (Ladson-Billings, 2006). More recently, the addition of intercultural communicative competence (ICC) has been proposed as an important addition to the framework of culturally sustaining pedagogies (Allen *et al.*, 2020). In many teacher education programs, study abroad programs provide an opportunity for pre-service teachers to enhance their intercultural skills and knowledge about the world. Traditionally, world language teacher preparation has relied on study abroad to provide candidates with cultural knowledge and language proficiency growth. In 2019/20, foreign language/international studies majors made up 7.8% of all post-secondary study abroad participants (Institute of International Education, 2021a). Increasingly, teachers in a variety of licensure areas have benefited from the intercultural learning that study abroad affords. Study abroad experiences can positively impact teachers' global competencies, preparing them to teach about multicultural issues (Longview Foundation for Education in World Affairs and International Understanding, 2008). Additionally, study abroad may lead to teachers being more open-minded about approaches to schooling (Shively &

Misco, 2015) and may lead to changes in how teachers interact and communicate with their students (Savva, 2017). Teachers exposed to academic content in other countries may move towards incorporating more global literature into their teaching, i.e. literature 'set in a global context outside the readers' own global location' (Short *et al.*, 2016: 5). It follows that study abroad can provide experiences that develop IC in teachers, which can positively impact their capacity to enact the ICit framework.

The ICit framework has moved the goals of preparing interculturally sensitive and competent teachers who can enact pedagogies for relevant social change, it has moved them squarely into the classrooms of *all* subject areas (Wagner *et al.*, 2019). Teacher preparation programs must work actively to develop candidates' intercultural knowledge, skills and attitudes so that teachers can themselves engage in the work of active citizenship in support of social justice and advocacy for marginalized students and families, and also facilitate intercultural citizenship development in their K–12 classrooms.

Study abroad in teacher preparation

In the US, teacher preparation works to ensure that teachers will be able to work effectively in multicultural settings. Teachers must be trained to consider critically their curriculum and their pedagogical approach and they must be mindful of issues of bias and oppression in schools. Study abroad is seen as an opportunity for pre-service teachers to enhance their intercultural skills, attitudes and knowledge about the world, which can prepare them to be culturally responsive and sustaining. Research has established how carefully structured interventions can have a profound impact on IC development during a sojourn (Vande Berg *et al.*, 2012). Despite strong evidence supporting the value of study abroad for the development of IC, particularly semester-long programs (Engle & Engle, 2003, 2012; Lou & Bosely, 2012; Spenader & Retka, 2015), relatively few students in teacher preparation programs participate in these experiences. Of all US students who studied abroad at the post-secondary level in 2019/20, only 2.4% of those students were in the field of teacher education (Institute of International Education, 2021a). Furthermore, there is a trend across all majors towards short-term programs. The most commonly reported purpose for short-term (1–4 weeks) study abroad programs for pre-service teachers was to develop intercultural competence and to work with diverse students. Tied for second place were developing language and language pedagogy skills, and gaining teaching experience (Morley *et al.*, 2019).

Compared to other majors, teacher education students have more rigid programmatic requirements due to licensure rules and accreditation (Morley *et al.*, 2019). This means that spending a semester abroad is relatively less feasible for teacher education students compared to other undergraduate students. Morley *et al.* (2019) also note that, as a result, pre-service teachers often participate in short-term programs that involve some sort of volunteering or service-learning aspect. These kinds of programs can be fraught with ethical problems due to the dynamics created when well-meaning but 'privileged' volunteers provide 'service' in poorer communities (Morley *et al.*, 2019). Taranath (2019) reminds us: 'without conscientious and frequent discussion about the dynamics of history, identity, and systems of power embedded in any partnership – global or domestic – partnerships run the risk of concealing the inequitable dynamics at play while prematurely celebrating and romanticizing reciprocity' (Taranath, 2019: 129). Participants in service-oriented short-term programs can inadvertently perpetuate stereotypes about populations they work with and can adopt the identity of being a privileged 'savior' (see Onyenekwu *et al.*, 2017, as cited in Morley *et al.*, 2019: 7). Finally, Morley *et al.* (2019) point out how the majority of these programs are located in wealthy western countries in the Global North, and that relatively few candidates participate in programs in the Global South. In order to maximize the impact of study abroad for the development of intercultural sensitivity and competence, there is a need for longer-term programs in a wider variety of cultural contexts.

While there is general agreement that study abroad supports the development of valuable language and intercultural skills for teachers, the specific benefits of such programs as they pertain to teachers' praxis is less well studied. This study investigates how study abroad as part of teacher preparation leads to intercultural development in teachers. It also aims to show how teachers practice education for ICit and to trace those skills and practices back to their study abroad experience.

Frameworks

Within the field of IC development, there exist several theoretical and conceptual frameworks. A brief overview of pertinent and related frameworks is offered as they served to inform this study and were used as lenses through which to interpret the data.

Intercultural communicative competence (ICC)

Byram's model of intercultural communicative competence (ICC) (Byram, 1997, 2021) provides a perspective informed by the important role of language in IC and is the framework upon which ICit has been conceptualized. Byram's model provides educators with a prescriptive model for designing instruction that includes intercultural objectives and requires students to attend to the importance of critical cultural awareness. A focus on evaluating cultural products, practices and perspectives is central to developing critical cultural awareness. ICC includes domains of *knowledge, attitudes of curiosity and openness,* and skills. Byram's ICC divides skills into those of interpreting events or artifacts and relating them to one's own culture, and those of discovery and operating one's IC in real-time communication and interaction. Furthermore, importantly, the ICC model recognizes the role of language, with attention paid to linguistic, sociolinguistic, discourse, strategic, sociocultural and social competencies (Byram, 2021; Wagner & Byram, 2017).

American Association of Colleges and Universities (AAC&U)

The AAC&U Value Rubric for intercultural knowledge and competence (AAC&U, 2008) provides an overarching framework through which to conceptualize IC. Heavily informed by the work of Deardorff (2006) and by Bennett's (1993) developmental model of intercultural sensitivity, this framework outlines broad conceptual components of IC: Knowledge (including both cultural self-awareness and awareness of other cultural frameworks or worldviews), Skills of Empathy and Communication, and Attitudes, which encompasses Curiosity and Openness. Deardorff (2011) describes the skills domain as including listening, observation, evaluation, analysis, interpretation and relating. The AAC&U (2008) focuses on verbal and non-verbal communication skills. Attitudes are related to respecting and valuing cultures, tolerating ambiguity, and a willingness to initiate and develop relationships with members of different cultural groups (AAC&U, 2008; Deardorff, 2011). The AAC&U Value Rubric is widely used by institutions of higher education as a tool to inform their efforts to internationalize college campuses, and to improve IC learning outcomes among their students.

Developmental Model of Intercultural Sensitivity (DMIS)

Bennett's (1993) Developmental Model of Intercultural Sensitivity provides detailed descriptions of each stage of IC along a developmental continuum ranging from ethnocentric to ethnorelative orientations. Within each stage of development, the DMIS model includes descriptions of cognitive, affective and behavioral traits associated with that stage. In the DMIS, and as one becomes more ethnorelative, one seeks out additional knowledge and adapts to cultural differences (Bennett, 1993, 2012; Hammer, 2016). The DMIS provides the theoretical basis for the related instrument, the *Intercultural Development Inventory* (IDI) (Hammer Holdings Inc., 2022), which has been shown to be a valid and reliable measure of IC development and has been widely used both for development and for research purposes (Hammer, 2011; Hammer *et al.*, 2003; Terzuolo, 2018; Vande Berg *et al.*, 2012).

Congruencies between the three aforementioned models of IC illustrate the strength of agreement in the field around traits of the concept. Conceptually, the knowledge domain includes the awareness of one's own and other cultures (called the cognitive domain in Bennett's DMIS). The skills (or behavioral in the DMIS) domain encompasses behaviors of adapting and relating to others and exercising empathy, communication, as well as use of language in Byram's ICC model. The attitudes domain (called the affective domain in Bennett's DMIS) includes interest, mindfulness and curiosity about cultures, and open-mindedness. Additionally, informing this study is Byram's critical cultural awareness element of intercultural competence (2006).

Methodology

Research questions

The overarching research question was: What is the impact of study abroad on preparing future teachers to enact education for intercultural citizenship? Specifically, how does study abroad impact pre-service teachers' intercultural knowledge, skills and beliefs in support of intercultural citizenship education? Further, this study aimed to explore which traits of intercultural citizenship the participants are incorporating into their teaching as a result of study abroad.

Participants and setting

The sampling method was purposive in that only graduates who had participated in the study abroad programs offered to students of teacher education preparation programs at the authors' institutions between 2007 and 2018 were invited to participate in the study. One institution is a public university in the southeastern part of the US, which recommends 100–110 teachers each year, on average, for licensure. While the university offers many study abroad programs, three faculty-led study abroad programs out of the college of education are designed specifically for pre-service elementary teachers and are offered every other year.

The other institution is a private liberal arts college in the Midwest, which offers 16 semester-long study abroad programs (11 of which are faculty led) that are open to teacher education students but which are not specifically designed for pre-service teachers. These programs were designed to meet intercultural learning goals that were part of the general education curriculum requirements for the institution. This college recommends approximately 50–60 candidates for elementary and secondary licensure each year.

Forty-one respondents were asked to self-identify their gender and race. This resulted in 32 participants identifying as female (78%), eight identifying as male (19.5%), and one self-identifying as non-binary (2.5%). With regards to race, 38 identified as white or Caucasian (93%), one as southeast Asian (2%), one as biracial (2%) and one as African-American (2%).

Questionnaire

Data for this study were collected via a questionnaire. A questionnaire was developed in order to ascertain traits of intercultural development that resulted from study abroad and which impact teacher praxis in support of ICit. The questionnaire had 60 questions focused on demographics (gender, teaching position, study abroad program and year, etc.), how study abroad influenced one's personal and professional life, examples of intercultural knowledge, skills and beliefs development, the influence of language and culture, and the overall impact of having studied abroad. A mix of multiple-choice and open-ended prompts wase used to obtain more nuanced and detailed examples of how study abroad impacted participants' intercultural and professional development, including their current teaching practices. The questionnaire was branched according to whether participants had stayed in teacher education or not; thus, not all questions were answered by all participants.

Data collection methods/procedures

Through social media (Facebook messenger) and via email, 190 graduates of these two teacher education programs who had participated in semester-long study abroad between 2007 and 2018 were invited to participate in the study. Of these, 41 individuals agreed and responded to the questionnaire (21.5%).

The link to the SurveyShare questionnaires was sent electronically to interested participants, and included an informed consent statement requiring response. Participants were initially recruited during October 2019 via social media, and reminders were sent via email during June 2020 and again via email during October 2020.

Data analysis

Prior to the analysis, data were screened for valid entries and missing data. The questionnaire data were aggregated. Descriptive statistics and frequency counts were calculated. Open-ended question responses were qualitatively analyzed line by line using a constant comparison method (Strauss & Corbin, 1998). NVivo 12 (QSR International, 2019) was used to facilitate data organization and management, and a codebook was kept detailing the coding process completed collaboratively by both authors. As previously mentioned, there were several theoretical and conceptual frameworks underlying this study that influenced the data analysis and interpretation of the findings. Additionally, both authors are qualified administrators of the *Intercultural Development Inventory* (Hammer Holdings Inc., 2022). Thus, major codes reflected the widely recognized knowledge, skills and attitudes domains evident in the three IC frameworks described previously. These frameworks serve as lenses through which evidence of ICC and ICit development can be identified. Additional codes emerged through the process of data analysis. Some codes remained as originally conceived while others were subsumed into the major codes to which they most closely aligned. Together, the authors resolved discrepancies, discerned patterns, and defined themes, which were grouped into categories across the intercultural competence domains of knowledge, skills, attitudes and critical awareness.

Results

Results based on the questionnaires are provided for the participants' teaching experience and the study abroad programs as well as for each domain – knowledge, skills, attitudes, critical self-awareness – and for intercultural citizenship. Quantitative responses to the questionnaire revealed strong agreement with statements pertaining to the value of study abroad for the development of intercultural knowledge, skills and attitudes. Qualitative data illustrate how this development occurred. Upon analysis, themes emerged and were categorized under the appropriate domain. Where applicable, any associated IC model traits are noted in the description of the domains and codes. The domains and codes are discussed shortly. Where applicable, direct quotations from respondents are provided. To reflect that the findings represent the entire sample, the study abroad program and the year appear in parenthesis after each quotation. When data emerged in one domain that was strongly representational of one particular study abroad program (e.g. Chile, 2012), the participant identification number was included to illustrate that examples were not all from the same participant.

Participant teaching experience

With regards to teaching, 78% of the respondents were currently teaching; 71% of the respondents were teaching in the US and 7% were teaching in either Colombia, Sweden or the Philippines. Most respondents indicated they were teaching full time (76%). Of those not teaching full time, three planned to return to the classroom (7%), one was in educational administration (2%) and one was completing a master's program (2%). Unfortunately, five respondents did not plan to return to the classroom (12%). The majority of the respondents (66%) had 4+ years in the teaching profession and 15% self-identified as novice teachers in their first three years in the teaching profession. With regards to grade level, 2% indicated they were teaching at the pre-K/early childhood level, 32% were teaching at the elementary school level, 24% at the middle school level, 17% at the secondary level, 2% at post-secondary level, 2% at K–12 and 19.5% of the respondents indicated they were no longer in the classroom or in the field of education. Aside from the elementary teachers, who taught all elementary subjects, one respondent taught music, two taught science, four taught math, five taught English/Language Arts, and six taught social studies. Additionally, six respondents taught a world language and four taught English as a Second Language.

Study abroad locations

As can be seen in Table 5.1, 15 of the respondents (37%) had studied abroad in countries economically categorized as the Global South. The majority of the respondents (26; 63.3%) studied abroad in countries economically categorized as the Global North. Fourteen respondents

Table 5.1 Program locations and specifics

	Faculty-Led Locations	Offered at Both Institutions	Teacher Education Focused	Language Required	Number of Respondents (N = 41)	Percentage of Respondents*
Global North	Australia				5	12.2%
	Austria			X	1	2.4%
	France			X	1	2.4%
	Germany	X	X		4	9.8%
	Ireland				3	7.3%
	Italy & Greece (split time)				6	14.6%
	Japan			X	0	0%
	Spain	X		X	3	7.3%
	United Kingdom				3	7.3%
Global South	Chile			X	9	22%
	China				1	2.4%
	Guatemala			X	0	0%
	India				2	4.8%
	South Africa	X	X		3	7.3%

Note: * = may not total 100% due to rounding.

(34%) participated in programs that had a language prerequisite/ requirement. This study's data align with national data as per the Open Doors Report indicating that in 2019/20 more than half of all US students who studied abroad did so in Europe (57%), with the leading destinations being the UK, Italy and Spain, while Asia hosted 9.1%, Latin America 13.4%, Oceania 7.1% and Africa 3.3% (Institute of International Education, 2021b).

Knowledge domain

The knowledge domain encompasses learning about one's own culture, learning about other cultures, developing cultural worldview frameworks, fostering an appreciation for the complexity of other cultures, and gaining knowledge about the processes of intercultural communication. Developing understandings around one's own and other cultures is a foundational element of intercultural development. As can be seen in Table 5.2, quantitative responses to questionnaire items relating to these two types of knowledge development indicate very strong support for the role of study abroad in this domain. The majority of the respondents agreed or strongly agreed that study abroad positively influenced their awareness of their own and other cultures.

Qualitative analysis of open-ended questionnaire items yielded four codes under the domain of knowledge: culture learning, cultural self-awareness, further language learning and further content learning (see Table 5.3).

Culture learning

Participants expressed how the study abroad experience influenced their culture learning. Culture, the knowledge and values shared by a group of people, is often compared to an iceberg, with visible and invisible aspects. The visible products and practices of culture are informed by underlying perspectives, beliefs and values. One participant

Table 5.2 Quantitative results of knowledge questionnaire items

Item	Strongly Disagree/Disagree	Undecided	Agree/Strongly Agree
My college study abroad experience has had a positive influence on my awareness of other cultural values and beliefs.	2%	0%	98%
My college study abroad experience has had a positive influence on my awareness of my own culture.	2%	2%	95%

Note: percentages may not total 100% due to rounding.

Table 5.3 Knowledge domain codes and descriptions

Major Domain	Codes (frequency)	Description
Knowledge	Culture learning* (34)	Awareness of culture as a concept, learning about other cultures (AAC&U)
	Cultural self-awareness (31)	Recognizes own cultural rules and biases (AAC&U), also DMIS polarization-reversal stage wherein an individual is overly critical towards their own culture and assumes superiority of other culture(s) (Bennett)
	Further language learning* (20)	Study abroad leads to additional language learning. This is contrasted with further language use or skill; it refers to the value related to 'knowing' a language or learning more of a language.
	Further content learning* (5)	Inspired by study abroad to pursue knowledge in other subjects; focus on 'study' in study abroad.

Note: *denotes grounded codes emerging from the data set.

indicated that 'Studying abroad has helped [them] to understand the complexities of culture' (India 2011). Another participant wrote: 'It helped me seek to understand the nuances of culture beyond surface level things people can see' (Chile 2012). One participant described how cultural learning is transferable, and that studying in one context has value for other cultural or language groups: 'I studied abroad in Germany, and many of the families at my school come from a Hispanic background. So I've had to learn more about their culture in order to improve interactions with them' (Germany 2007).

Cultural self-awareness

Respondents shared how valuable it was to leave their home culture to learn more about it from the vantage point of another culture. One participant put it this way: 'Being immersed in other cultures really makes you think about your own culture' (Rome/Greece 2013). Several participants indicated that cultural self-awareness was facilitated by the contrast offered by being in another culture. One participant commented: 'Being able to experience a different culture firsthand and compare and contrast it to our own culture was eye opening and a valuable experience' (Germany 2007).

Living abroad provided pre-service teachers with the opportunity to reflect on their own culture by noticing and analyzing familiar products, practices and perspectives. The value of viewing one's own culture from the outside was expressed this way: 'I think the best way to learn about the environment you grew up in, is to leave it. To see how our family and society shaped us is best seen from afar. Therefore, I learned so much about how others see the world and how they see us' (Chile 2011). Another participant reflected: 'I often find myself analyzing my own culture and environment. I find it fascinating what types of things people take for granted, the odd things people do in their day-to-day lives, and the underlying assumptions that drive everything' (Austria 2012).

Participants noticed the connections between their behaviors and the underlying beliefs and values that informed those practices. Here a student reflects on lifestyle and energy consumption:

> I really learned about my own culture when visiting Ireland. Here, we are go-go-go all the time; we are constantly moving and not taking time to appreciate what is around us... when living in Ireland, we lived very simplistically. We stretched food and made it last longer than I ever would here, we conserved electricity, and we walked everything [sic]. (Galway 2013)

Further language learning and further content learning

Not all respondents participated in a study abroad program with a language requirement. For those who did, they often indicated that, through study abroad, 'one can become truly fluent and confident in the language' (Chile 2010). Another indicated that they 'learned most of [their] conversational Spanish while being there, which extremely helped [them] in various teaching situations [they] have been in since' (Chile 2011). Some participants 'did not learn the language [while they] studied abroad beyond a few short phrases, but [they did later] living in Greece' (Galway 2010). Others, upon returning from abroad, 'have since started to self-teach' themselves a language (Rome/Greece 2015). And one participant discovered they 'have a love for foreign languages' (France 2011).

While some participants furthered their language learning, others felt the value of study abroad was that they could further their content learning. One participant indicated that during study abroad they 'fell in love with [their] social studies major even more' (Rome/Greece 2013). Another participant valued learning in-situ: 'Learning historical theology in the actual location was the most significant draw for me' (Rome/Greece 2015).

Attitude domain

The attitude domain of intercultural competence involves interest, curiosity and beliefs around cultures, and an open-minded stance towards cultural difference. As can be seen in Table 5.4, quantitative responses to questionnaire items relating to this type of knowledge

Table 5.4 Quantitative results of attitude domain

Item	Strongly Disagree/Disagree	Undecided	Strongly Agree/Agree
I am interested in learning about the cultural beliefs and values of the people I work with.	5%	0%	95%

Table 5.5 Attitude domain codes and descriptions

Major Domain	Codes (frequency)	Description
Attitudes	Open-mindedness (41)	General open-minded attitude towards culture groups; suspension of judgment (AAC&U)
	Curiosity about culture (26)	Curiosity about culture as a general concept and about specific cultures; a desire to engage with other culture groups (AAC&U, Bennett)

development indicate very strong support for the role of study abroad in this domain. The majority of the respondents agreed or strongly agreed that study abroad had a positive effect on their interest in learning about the beliefs and values of their co-workers (see Table 5.4).

Qualitative analysis of open-ended questionnaire items yielded numerous mentions of the two major codes under the domain of attitude: open-mindedness and curiosity about culture (see Table 5.5). Examples of these attitude codes reflected traits described in numerous models of intercultural development.

Open-mindedness

As evidenced by the frequency of this code, many participants expressed that study abroad 'broadened their worldview' (Austria 2012), 'widened [their] perspective of the world' (London 2012) and, as a result, their 'perception of the world has changed' (Germany 2013). An important element of the open-mindedness code is the suspension of judgment, and the respect for and valuing of other cultures, which the quote below illustrates:

> After talking to so many people from so many different backgrounds and experiencing other cultures, I was able to see the world and others in a new way. I was able to see that my way of life isn't the only way of life, and just because something is different, it's not bad or wrong. (Germany 2013)

Likewise, another participant described how they became 'more apt to understand before making judgements or decisions' (Chile 2012, participant 17). Another participant indicated study abroad allowed them 'to become a more global thinker'. They added: 'It makes me think about how other people live and view events on a day-to-day basis versus just viewing it from a US citizen viewpoint' (Chile 2012, participant 25).

Curiosity about culture

According to the DMIS, non-evaluative curiosity about, and an interest in, cultural difference are evidence of movement towards ethnorelativism: acceptance stage (Hammer, 2016). One participant noted: 'In many ways my college study abroad experience ignited a love for learning more about the world' (Chile 2012). Another expressed that they are '... naturally curious and genuinely interested to learn more about the various cultures, values, beliefs, and languages of others that [they] come in contact with through [their] coworkers, students, and families' (Australia 2011). They described how they 'feel comfortable and confident when meeting people from different backgrounds and teaching students from different backgrounds'. Another participant described having a 'personal yearning for learning about other parts of the world' (Spain 2013). The development of attitudes of curiosity and open-mindedness are foundational and they impact all other domains of IC development (Deardorff, 2011).

Critical cultural awareness domain

According to Byram (1997), intercultural competence includes the domain of critical cultural awareness. This is the ability to critically evaluate perspectives, practices and products not just in one's own culture but also in other cultures and countries. While this aspect of IC was most famously advanced by Byram's ICC model, it relates to AAC&U's Cultural Worldview framework through its recognition of the complexity of social, historical and political influence on how one navigates cultural difference. Furthermore, Bennett's DMIS describes the most advanced stages of ethnorelative orientations as paying attention to how power can and should be exercised in culturally sensitive ways (Hammer, 2016). From the data in this study, 17 examples of critical cultural awareness were identified (Table 5.6).

Table 5.6 Critical cultural awareness domain code and description

Major Domain/Code (frequency)	Description
Critical cultural awareness (17)	Critically evaluate products, practices and perspectives in own and other cultures (Byram). Cultural worldview frameworks (AAC&U)

This code, in particular, highlighted examples of the participants' own development of critical cultural awareness, and their efforts to help their students become more critically aware. Consider how four different participants in the same program explained their own critical awareness development in relation to their classroom practices. One noted: 'I don't want my students to ever think there is only one right side or story to history (Chile 2012, participant 17). Another described how 'study abroad has still influenced how [they are] teaching history at [their] school as [they] know to be aware of indigenous cultures and make sure to teach from multiple perspectives instead of just one biased perspective' (Chile 2012, participant 35). Yet another stated: 'I have exposed myself to languages of indigenous communities, such as Quechua and Ojibwe. I worked at a Hmong charter school where a Hmong heritage program opened my eyes to the importance of language as a facet of identity. This all started with my college study abroad experience.' (Chile 2012, participant 17). And finally, one shared that they '...encourage students to look at events not only from our perspective but from all of the stakeholders' perspectives' (Chile 2012, participant 25). While this particular program in 2012 appears to have profoundly influenced participants' development of critical cultural awareness, it is clear that well-designed study abroad programs have the potential to develop this domain in meaningful ways.

Skills domain

Skills are conceived of as behaviors that draw on knowledge and attitudes. The skills domain represents the actions and applications of interculturality. Several survey items asked participants to reflect on how study abroad impacted their engagement with people of diverse backgrounds, including in the classroom setting. Broad agreement with statements regarding the belief that the participants are more effective in their work with students due to study abroad were found. However, as items became more specific to changes in teaching behaviors, the responses had less universal agreement: for example, the final item in Table 5.7, which refers to classroom management.

Several items in the survey asked participants about specific behaviors in teaching that might be influenced by IC development in study abroad. Participants reported employing diverse communication techniques to meet the needs of their students and learners' families to some extent. For most participants, these kinds of accommodations were happening more often than not (Table 5.8).

Responses to open-ended items indicated that the skills domain comprised the largest number of total mentions among all domains. General intercultural skills is explored first, followed by the powerful code that emerged from the data:- intercultural teaching skills.

Table 5.7 Results of skills items: General

Item	Strongly Disagree/Disagree	Undecided	Strongly Agree/Agree
My college study abroad experience has had a positive influence on my engagement with people of different cultural backgrounds.	2%	5%	93%
My college study abroad experience has had a positive influence on my engagement with people of diverse linguistic backgrounds.	4%	10%	86%
I believe I am more effective in teaching students who are from a different cultural background than me because of my study abroad experiences.	6%	24%	70%
Because of my study abroad experience, I work to actively promote intercultural understanding among the students in my classroom.	0%	18%	82%
Based on my study abroad experience, I utilize classroom management techniques (e. g. collaborative learning, discipline, grouping) that are supportive of the different cultural backgrounds of my students.	18%	18%	65%

Note: percentages may not total 100% due to rounding.

Table 5.8 Results of skills items: Teaching behaviors

Items	Always/Often	Sometimes	Rarely or Never
Based on your study abroad experience, to what extent do you modify the language you use with students to accommodate the needs of your students (either in English or by using another language)?	55%	38%	18%
Based on your study abroad experience, to what extent do you modulate or adapt your communication style (pictures, body language, directness, telling vs asking, realia, manipulatives, graphic organizers) as a way to work more effectively with diverse students?	62%	35%	3%
Based on your study abroad experience, to what extent are you willing to make modifications to assignments or assessments (for example, changing due dates) as a means of meeting the needs of your students?	67%	29%	3%
Based on your study abroad experience, to what extent do you modulate or adapt your communication style (face to face vs phone, use of body language, directness, telling vs asking) as a way to work more effectively with diverse parents and family members?	56%	32%	12%

Note: percentages may not total 100% due to rounding.

Table 5.9 Skills domain codes and descriptions

Major Domain	Codes (frequency)	Description
Skills	Language use (46)	Linguistic, sociolinguistic and discourse competencies (Byram, Paige, 1993)
	Communication (30)	Cultural accommodation theory (Giles *et al.*, 1973); skills of discovery and interaction (Byram); communication style (AAC&U, Bennett)
	Behavior change (25)	Changing one's behavior, adapting, decision-making, being patient and flexible (Bennett)
	Empathy (14)	Empathy in general terms and in terms of working with students and families; the ability to take perspectives from other worldviews (AAC&U)

Language use

Of particular significance was that the use of languages other than English was coded 46 times (Table 5.9), making it the most prevalent skill within the general skills domain. While only 10 of the participants were language (world language or ESL) teachers, the use of additional language skills emerged as one of the strongest codes in the skills domain. This indicates that linguistic (including sociolinguistic and discourse) competencies were developed as part of study abroad. Participants reported that while language learning was often a struggle, it was a valuable experience that helped contribute to deeper cultural learning and building empathy:

> Learning and interacting in a second language was a fun yet humbling experience which helped me realize that I could still effectively communicate without those language skills being perfect – the important thing was to try and just know that mistakes and misunderstandings will happen. (Austria 2012)

One participant emphasized the linguistic benefits of study abroad for language teachers because it provides 'deeper insight into the Chilean culture and the Spanish language' (Chile 2015). Another Spanish teacher noted how their language was used to support English Language Learners as well: 'I also work with ELL students that are mainly Hispanic. I tend to do some of my instruction in Spanish and some in English' (Chile 2012, participant 25). Participants described using language for personal enjoyment, to improve their job prospects in the field of education, and for instructional purposes. Teachers not only teach the languages they learned, they also use their language skills to support language minority students through instruction and through advocacy. One participant noted: 'these students spoke only Spanish…

and their indigenous village languages… so [they] continued using Spanish to try to communicate with these students and their families' (Chile 2012, participant 17). Our data showed strong support for the use of language both within study abroad and, later, as part of their professional practice as teachers.

Communication

Evidence of changes to communication styles and strategies focused on adapting to and accommodating the needs of students and their families. Giles *et al.* (1973) described cultural accommodation theory as instances whereby one person attempts to communicate using the recipient's preferred communication style, which leads to better comprehension and reception of the message. A participant who was working as a teacher in Colombia described how she and other North Americans 'struggle with the amount of talking and what it looks like to listen' and she noted how in 'such a collectivist culture, [she's] had to learn the benefit of collaborative work' (Chile 2011, participant 27). Her comment illustrates how her adaptation of communication style was informed by her awareness of deeply held cultural values of collectivism. She also reported: 'Adapting to their form of communication is very helpful in order to get them to know you're all on the same team', further illustrating her commitment to communicating effectively with the families of her students. Indeed, many participants reported adapting their communication strategies to try to accommodate their interlocutors. A participant described how they 'try to neutralize [their] experiences when [they] talk to parents and family members – especially during conferences. It's a time to learn about them…' (Chile 2010). One participant noted that they 'do not have any issues adjusting and adapting [their] style to meet the preferred communication styles of the diverse parents and families in [their] classroom' (Australia 2011). Other participants made mention of their 'awareness of non-verbal communication in various cultures' (Chile 2012), use of phone calls rather than email in order to 'communicate tone and clarify any confusion' (Spain 2012), and accommodating preferences for 'feedback that is very direct and to-the-point' (Chile 2011, participant 32).

Behavior change

Adaptations in behavior were split evenly between general changes to behavior, increased patience in cross-cultural situations and flexibility. One participant described general behavior adaptation in these terms: 'aspects of my life are different from others but instead of thinking their way is wrong, I wish to listen and possibly try it' (Germany 2018). Another shared: 'Living in a Latinx culture allowed me to understand

and be comfortable with customs when conducting home visits and in turn make families more comfortable' (Chile 2012). Several participants noted how they 'have more patience for families that are new to the country and for students who are adjusting to a new school and culture' (Rome/Greece 2010). With regards to flexibility, one noted: 'I am comfortable when students want to approach a task or situation in a different way than I would' (Spain 2012). Another reflected: 'Moving to another country implies a lot of autonomy, flexibility and setting aside your expectations to learn about the new ways around you' (Chile 2011).

Empathy

The empathy domain illustrates how participants gained the ability to imagine another person's experience and take on their perspective. One participant wrote: 'While I think I have always been a pretty compassionate person, my study abroad experience helps remind me to have compassion for the people I work with' (Spain 2012). Another mentioned: 'I have empathy for my students... in my willingness to work with them and try to understand and relate to what they may be going through' (Germany 2018). Study abroad gives pre-service teachers the chance to experience first hand what it feels like to be a cultural or linguistic outsider. One participant explained: 'I can empathize with people who feel like they don't belong or they don't understand right away because I was that person' (Chile 2015). Another participant elaborated on the profound impact that study abroad can have on teacher education:

> Experiencing other cultures first hand, being the foreigner, problem solving, creating relationships, ALL of that you will bring back to your classroom. Teachers are BETTER because of the empathy they learn abroad. These future educators are the future classroom influencers. If their life can be changed in 6 months, imagine the impact they'll have during their teaching career to countless students and so forth. The domino effect is astounding. (Chile 2011)

Intercultural teaching skills (ITS)

The most prevalent code in the skills domain was the grounded code of intercultural teaching skills (ITS). This code centered on ensuring meaningful engagement between students, the related code of helping learners develop ICC in support of real-time communication and interaction, as well as drawing upon study abroad experiences to inform culturally responsive and sustaining teaching practices.

Intercultural teaching skills involves being mindful about classroom interactions, and facilitating purposeful engagement between learners, as well as engagement with the community. One participant described the attention they paid to purposeful groupings in class as follows: 'Collaborative learning and classroom discussions are important to me. I make a conscious effort to use BOTH heterogenous and homogenous groupings at different times to help students feel comfortable, supported, and included' (Australia 2011). Another participant said: 'I provide an environment for students to do a lot of collaborative learning... Students are also allowed to work with others on most assignments. I find that their peers can explain things better sometimes and the interaction with each other makes the language more realistic' (Spain 2012). Another participant shared: 'I can make cultural connections in a community with strong German roots, and I can relate with families who are living in a new place speaking a new language' (Austria 2012). The importance of focusing on engagement in the classroom can be aptly summed up in this quote: 'I read something once that said you can work and work and work to change the culture of your classroom – from assignments, to environment, to rules, etc. – but if you don't connect with students, you simply won't be successful. Relationships are the first priority' (Galway 2013).

Participants using ITS worked to support ICC development in students to build capacities for real-time interactions. In particular, the relational aspect of ICC was found to be similar to the preceding code of engagement with others. One participant shared: 'We need to treat everyone with respect. We talk about that a lot in my classroom' (London 2012). Another participant described building language capacities in the classroom as a way of helping students interpret culture and prepare them to interact with speakers of different varieties of Spanish: 'I like introducing unique words and phrases [in] Chilean Spanish as a model of the richness of the language, which invites my dominant Spanish speakers to be comfortable in their variations and slang. I intend to create an environment where language and its variances are adored and valued' (Chile 2012, participant 31). Finally, one participant described how study abroad facilitated their own growth in interpreting cultural events and relating them to one's own culture:

> The most important part of study abroad that a teacher can gain from their program is not the linguistic or culture information gains, but the concept to view situations from the viewpoint of people of other walks of life or cultures. This allows a person to become a better teacher because it allows you to see where others are coming from, how they see certain events, and it allows you to tailor learning to their abilities/interests. (Chile 2012, participant 25)

Participants saw strong links between their study abroad experience and culturally relevant and culturally sustaining practices in their classrooms. Participants work to 'relate the curriculum to [their] students' background knowledge' (Rome/Greece 2013) and incorporate 'activities that relate more to student experiences' (India 2016). A participant described using 'community-created objectives and understandings to guide [their] teaching and respond to the students as they are' (Chile 2012, participant 31). Another participant described her thinking about students' ability to relate to her teaching, sharing that:

> Because of their cultural background and past experiences, they may not have the same background knowledge or they may not interpret certain lessons in the same manner. [She was] also more aware of the inequities that certain students of minority groups experience, and [she tries] to be very cognizant of that in [her] teaching. (Chile 2012, participant 17)

In addition to the general ITS code, three distinct types of intercultural teaching skills were identified: internationalization of the curriculum; advocating for students and families; and social justice and anti-bias education. Just as most participants reported employing communication and assignment/assessment modifications as a result of studying abroad (see Table 5.10), their responses to open-ended prompts indicated strong support for the adaptation and modification of the curriculum, advocating for students and effective engagement with families, and educating for social justice. Strong support for the ICit framework was evident in the general ITS code, wherein the

Table 5.10 Intercultural teaching skills codes and descriptions

Major Domain	Codes (frequency)	Description
Skills	Intercultural teaching skills* (ITS: 63)	Drawing on study abroad experiences to inform practices, engaging with others, and building ICC to interact, interpret and relate (Byram), and culturally responsive and sustaining pedagogy (Ladson-Billings, Paris)
	Strand 1: Internationalizing the curriculum (56)	Making and adapting curriculum, globalizing the curriculum, global literature, sharing study abroad experiences with students
	Strand 2: Student advocate* (21)	Advocating for students and their families, related to recognition and exercise of power in culturally appropriate ways (Bennett, Hammer); teachers as change agents
	Strand 3: Social justice and anti-bias education (8)	Facilitate interactions between learners and the communities in which they live and operate, concerns for social justice, concern to make changes for the better (Wagner, Cardetti, Byram); action domain of Social Justice Standards (Teaching for Tolerance, Glynn et al.), anti-racist and anti-bias education.

Note: *denotes grounded codes emerging from the data set.

employment of culturally responsive and culturally sustaining practices reflected the goals of ICit, as well as teachers' intentionality around connecting their students with individuals from cultural backgrounds different from their own, and the intentional building of ICC to support skills of communication and interaction. Strand 1 aligned with the ICit framework through connecting students with individuals from diverse cultural backgrounds either directly or through the use of global literature. Due to the focus on social justice and anti-bias education in the quotes coded as ITS Strand 3, this code in the data aligned closely with the framework of intercultural citizenship (ICit).

Internationalizing the curriculum

The first strand of ITS was found to be closely related to culturally responsive and culturally sustaining pedagogies but it focused specifically on the content of the curriculum as impacted by study abroad. This concept included changes to the curriculum that reflect intercultural sensitivity, and connecting students with other cultures in intentional ways. Many participants mention globalizing their curriculum due to the rich cultural experiences they had in study abroad. Study abroad raised their awareness of the complexities of cultural perspectives and caused them to create or adapt a curriculum in intercultural ways. For example, one participant reported: 'I teach a culture course to 7th graders at my school and my time abroad has been extremely valuable in sharing and explaining different cultural nuances' (Chile 2012, participant 25). Another participant described sharing 'cultural and linguistic experiences with [their] students in [their] social studies classes and with others [they] meet that are able to give people a new or different perspective on things' (Chile 2012, participant 17). Study abroad also led participants to talk to their students about the value of study abroad. An example of this code was the following quote:

> I talk about my time abroad on almost a daily basis in my classroom as a Spanish teacher... I still think that going abroad is one of the best ways to learn a new language and learn about a new culture. I stress this to my students as well. I tell them that if you find yourself being closed minded you should travel and then your mind will most certainly be more open. (Chile 2012)

Evidence of internationalizing the curriculum included examples of the use of global literature, adapting and creating the curriculum, informed by the study abroad experience, and sharing experiences from study abroad with students in ways that helped students connect with people from other cultural backgrounds in new ways. The ICit framework similarly stresses the importance of connecting students with diverse peers locally and globally, and facilitating critical cultural awareness which can occur through internationalizing the curriculum. Participants often indicated that they shared their study abroad experiences with their K–12 students as well as created a curriculum or made changes to the existing curriculum, and included global literature based on knowledge gained during study abroad. One participant wrote: 'When applicable I bring in examples from other cultures. For example, teaching percent. We have a conversation about tipping in different countries and what it can mean' (Australia 2016). Another participant wrote: 'I have the opportunity to bring global or multicultural perspectives into my curriculum through choice of literature' (Galway 2013). Participants saw strong links between their study abroad experience and culturally sustaining practices in their classrooms. Closely related to culturally responsive teaching (CRT) are examples of curriculum change as a result of study abroad, which in the coding process were referred to as internationalizing the curriculum. This concept includes changes to the curriculum that reflect intercultural sensitivity, connecting students with other cultures in intentional ways. Many participants reported drawing on their study abroad experiences to globalize their curriculum. Studying abroad raised their awareness of the complexities of cultural perspectives and caused them to create or adapt the curriculum in intercultural ways, and to talk to their students about the value of study abroad.

Student advocate

Participants expressed how they served as advocates for their K–12 students and their families. One participant wrote: 'I strive to advocate for students of all backgrounds and to teach this skill to my students' (Chile 2012). In addition to advocating generally for students, another participant indicated that they advocate specifically for diverse students and for exceptionalities. For example:

> Specifically for my students who speak more than one language, I advocate for them to be tested in environments that may be different, but still show their proficiency/abilities to succeed. For example, if a native Spanish-speaker does poorly on a written test, I will ask for their answers verbally so they can prove to me what they truly know. (Chile 2015)

Another participant shared: 'I continue to engage with my own whiteness and try to advocate using my power to open up spaces for different voices' (Chile 2010).

Social justice and anti-bias education

Evidence of social justice and anti-bias education emerged and was directly traced to the study abroad experience. ICit urges the practice of social justice education as a way to facilitate the active citizenship component of the framework. Participants gained deeper understandings from study abroad that allowed them to enact social justice education. For example, one participant wrote: 'I have a much better understanding of structural racism and the challenge of upward mobility in our society' (South Africa 2012). Another participant wrote:

> I do think that because of studying abroad, I am more open to modifying assignments for students who are not necessarily on an IEP [Individualized Education Plan] or 504 plan [education plan for students with disabilities]... I think knowing about how diverse some home environments are from studying abroad (and from other experiences) has made me think this way more. (Chile 2012, participant 17)

As a result of studying abroad, participants became mindful of systemic injustices, as illustrated by this quote: 'Learning about the Mapuche in Chile really opened my eyes to systematic racism...' (Chile 2010).

Value of study abroad for teacher education

Data emerged indicating there is value in including study abroad opportunities in teacher education. While this code did not fit the other categories in terms of being directly related to intercultural competence development and intercultural citizenship enactment, it emerged as relevant with 20 instances. These mentions illustrate the importance that pre-service teachers attach to the role of study abroad in teacher preparation. One reported that study abroad 'helps college students better understand the culture of the host country as well as their own culture. This is crucial to begin to understand the cultures of their students' (Chile 2011). Another noted how these programs help pre-service teachers develop 'open-mindedness, flexibility, compassion, patience, and a sense of constant learning. Not only are these skills helpful for teachers, but they are skills our students need to learn as well' (Spain 2012). Another shared:

> More than anything, it helps you connect with students. People I interacted with on my trip are from diverse backgrounds, and that's exactly what it's like in a classroom. By having these experiences, I was better prepared for the students I was teaching. (Galway 2013)

Limitations

The data were limited to two institutions and can only be generalized to a certain extent. It was beyond the scope of the study to assess the intercultural development of the participants or to gather evidence of their teaching practices. Data were based on self-reporting. Study abroad provides a significant opportunity for critical cultural awareness development, yet it should be noted that one program in particular – Chile 2012 – accounted for most of the qualitative examples in this domain (N = 9). The fact that one program represented the bulk of the evidence with regards to critical cultural awareness is a reminder that not all programs are created equal, and that faculty and administrators should be mindful of how study abroad can develop critical cultural awareness in all settings. Further research is needed to ascertain how critical cultural awareness can be intentionally developed during study abroad as part of teacher education. It was beyond the scope of this study to go deeper into case studies and conduct cross-tabulations to determine if responses were due to other demographic factors (e.g. years teaching, other experiences abroad). Thus, future research studies should explore the relationships among these factors, especially as to how they relate to the finding of intercultural teaching skills (ITS) and the development of intercultural citizenship (ICit). It should be noted there is a need for closer investigation into how teachers use the ICit framework in their teaching, and the role that study abroad plays in informing their use of ICit. The participants in this study were not teaching before they studied abroad, so it is unclear if some of the ICit practices they described are a direct result of study abroad experiences or of in-service professional development. Future research could explore if in-service professional development can be a source for intercultural competence development in preparation for enacting the ICit framework.

Discussion

This research explored how study abroad impacts pre-service teachers' intercultural knowledge, skills and beliefs in support of intercultural citizenship. The findings illustrate which elements of the ICit framework participants report using in the classroom, and how those were informed by the study abroad experience. The results of this study, which examined more than a decade's worth of teacher education study abroad programs, confirm previous work in IC development in study abroad. Participants' responses overwhelmingly indicated that they were gaining IC as a result of their study abroad programs and that the programs were facilitating IC growth in their classrooms. Study abroad positively impacts teachers' global competencies and their readiness to teach about multicultural issues (Longview Foundation for Education in World Affairs and International Understanding, 2008). Our data support previous findings that study abroad results in teachers being more open minded about teaching approaches (Shively & Misco, 2015), and that study abroad can impact teachers' abilities to interact and communicate effectively with students (Savva, 2017). Furthermore, this study found that both programs designed for pre-service teachers and those designed for a broader audience were able to facilitate meaningful IC growth that positively impacted teaching practices. Importantly, all the programs studied here were led by a faculty member on-site who was focused on IC development. This supports and aligns with the literature on the value of faculty-led study abroad programs (Medina *et al.*, 2015; Pilonieta *et al.*, 2017). This study adds to the field in that it identifies additional skills and behaviors used by teachers that reflect IC development gained as a result of participation in study abroad. Participants drew on study abroad experiences to inform practices, promote intercultural understanding, modify verbal and non-verbal communication, and modify assignments and assessments to meet diverse student needs. One area where the findings of this study were less in agreement with the research on the benefits of study abroad was on classroom management practices. It seems that this area could benefit from a targeted research focus since the data in this study did not indicate classroom management was being significantly impacted by study abroad. With the guidance of faculty, study abroad has the potential to help teachers expand their classroom management repertoire in culturally sensitive ways.

Study abroad is highly impactful for developing critical cultural awareness. Participants reported that study abroad had positively and significantly developed their ability to reflect critically on cultures. Participants shared examples of their own deepened understandings of historic and systemic inequities, as well as how these realizations informed their own teaching practice. It should be noted that the strongest examples in the data set came from one program – Chile 2012. This illustrates both the potential for developing this awareness but also that not all programs are taking advantage of that opportunity to the same extent. The strength of the examples from the program in Chile and others supports calls for pre-service teacher study abroad to expand beyond Europe and the Global North.

Importantly, strong evidence was found, from both the quantitative and qualitative data analysis, for the development of intercultural teaching skills (ITS) encompassing specific pedagogical practices that support ICit implementation in classrooms. Three subtypes, or strands, of ITS further illustrated the ways in which teachers operationalize their IC, and illustrated both traits of ICit that teachers enact, as well as areas in which teachers fall short of meeting the goals of the framework.

Strand 1, internationalizing the curriculum, was an important way to build critical cultural awareness and engage in culturally relevant and sustaining pedagogies. Internationalizing the curriculum also gave students opportunities to engage with resources from diverse communities, such as using global literature. Pre-service teachers would benefit from instruction on how to internationalize their future teaching curriculum. There is further potential to incorporate activities that put students into meaningful interactions with people outside their home communities.

Strand 2, student advocate, relates less directly to the ICit framework yet it is important nonetheless. Findings indicated participants' inclinations toward student advocacy. Advocating for students and their families is itself an action that supports the goals of social justice and it draws directly on the language skills and cultural perspective gained during study abroad. Guided instruction on how to advocate professionally for diverse students could be an outcome of the study abroad experience. Yet, to advocate for diverse students, requires that teachers develop appropriate communication styles. When pre-service teachers are taught intercultural communication competence and practice using it while abroad, they can add to their culturally sustaining pedagogy (Allen *et al.*, 2020).

Strong support was found for teachers drawing on their study abroad experiences to teach for social justice, including commitment to anti-racist and anti-bias education (Strand 3). This promotion of social action and concern for justice reflects the ICit framework. Study abroad provided the experience of feeling 'othered', which led to deeper understanding around systemic discrimination and privilege. Participants noted a link between their language abilities and being empowered to engage effectively with families and students from diverse backgrounds. While study abroad prepared pre-service teachers to engage in social justice education, there was not ample evidence that teachers were having their students participate in social justice action.

The ICit framework stresses the importance of engagement with communities for meaningful purposes. However, evidence of teachers connecting their students with peers outside the classroom was not found, nor were there any data indicating that students were using ICC acquired in the classroom to make decisions or to participate in community life beyond the classroom. Rather, participants' enactment of ICit centered on fostering IC development in students, supporting critical cultural awareness, and questioning attitudes around social and cultural groups' beliefs, values and behaviors. Participants were engaged in social action themselves (e.g. advocacy) but there were no examples of promoting social action in their students.

Study abroad programs provide significant opportunity for pre-service teachers to develop the requisite skills needed to enact the ICit framework in their future classrooms. While the benefits are clear, it is a challenge for many pre-service teachers to participate in study abroad. Teacher preparation programs are largely full of licensure requirements, leaving scant time to add more to the curriculum for an on-campus course much less for a study abroad program. Furthermore, programs should be carefully designed to meet the needs of pre-service teachers if the field is serious about enacting ICit. Education-focused faculty-led study abroad programs should aim for long-term experiences and should expand beyond the Global North. Additionally, more opportunities for faculty-led guided reflection and explicit instruction on how to integrate aspects of the study abroad experience into teaching practices such as ITS and planning for development of ICit in students should be provided. Faculty-led programs are vital for helping pre-service teachers integrate into their teaching practices what they have learned while abroad. Their students, in turn, will become active global citizens who can work effectively across cultures in their future personal and professional lives.

References

AAC&U (American Association of Colleges & University) (2008) VALUE rubrics – Intercultural knowledge and competence. https://www.aacu.org/value/rubrics/inter-cultural-knowledge (Accessed 7 June 2022).

ACTFL (2017) NCSSFL-ACTFL Can-do statements for intercultural communication. See https://www.actfl.org/publications/guidelines-and-manuals/ncssfl-actfl-can-do-statements.

Allen, J., Medina, A.L. and Starker-Glass, T. (2020) CSP v1.2: A continuation of the conversation on culturally sustaining pedagogy [Paper presentation]. American Educational Research Association (AERA) Annual Meeting, 17–21 April, San Francisco, California. (Conference canceled due to COVID19).

Beneke, M., Park, C. and Taitingfong, J. (2019) An inclusive, anti-bias framework for teaching and learning about race with young children. *Young Exceptional Children* 22 (2), 74–86.

Bennett, M. (1993) Towards ethnorelativism: A developmental model of intercultural sensitivity. In R.M. Paige (ed.) *Education for the Intercultural Experience. Second Edition* (pp. 21–71). Yarmouth, ME: Intercultural Press.

Bennett, M. (2012) Paradigmatic assumptions and a developmental approach to inter-cultural learning. In M. Vande Berg, R.M. Paige and K. Lou (eds) *Student Learning Abroad: What Our Students Are Learning, What They're Not, and What We Can Do About It* (pp. 90–114). Sterling, VA: Stylus Publishing.

Byram, M. (1997) *Teaching and Assessing Intercultural Communicative Competence.* Clevedon: Multilingual Matters.

Byram, M. (2006) Developing a concept of intercultural citizenship. In G. Alred, M. Byram and M. Fleming (eds) *Education for Intercultural Citizenship: Concepts and Comparisons* (pp. 109–129). Clevedon: Multilingual Matters.

Byram, M. (2021) *Teaching and Assessing Intercultural Communicative Competence: Revisited.* Bristol: Multilingual Matters.

Byram, M., Golubeva, I., Han, H. and Wagner, M. (eds) (2017) *From Principles to Practice in Education for Intercultural Citizenship.* Bristol: Multilingual Matters.

Council of Europe (2018) *Companion Volume to the Common European Framework of Reference for Languages.* Strasbourg: Council of Europe. Available at www.coe.int/en/web/common-european-framework-reference-languages (Accessed 1 July 2022).

Deardorff, D. (2006) The identification and assessment of intercultural competence as a student outcome of internationalization at institutions of higher education in the United States. *Journal of Studies on International Education* 10 (3), 241–266.

Deardorff, D. (2011) Assessing intercultural competence. *New Directions for Institutional Research* 149 (Special Issue), 65–79.

Derman-Sparks, L. and Edwards, J. (2010) *Anti-Bias Education for Young Children and Ourselves.* Washington, DC: National Association for the Education of Young Children. Retrieved from https://www.jstor.org/stable/10.2307/ycyoungchildren.71.1.58 (Accessed 7 June 2022).

Engle, L. and Engle, J. (2003) Study abroad levels: Toward a classification of program types. *Frontiers: The Interdisciplinary Journal of Study Abroad* 9 (1), 1–20.

Engle L. and Engle, J. (2012) Beyond immersion: The American University Center of Provence experiment in holistic intervention. In M. Vande Berg, R.M. Paige and K. Lou (eds) *Student Learning Abroad: What Our Students Are Learning, What They're Not, and What We Can Do About It* (pp. 284–307). Sterling, VA: Stylus Publishing.

Giles, H., Taylor, D.M. and Dourhis, R. (1973) Towards a theory of interpersonal accommodation through language: Some Canadian data. *Language in Society* 2 (2), 177–192.

Glynn, C., Wesely, P. and Wassell, B. (2018) *Words and Actions: Teaching Languages Through the Lens of Social Justice* (2nd edn). Alexandria, VA: ACTFL.

Hammer, M.R. (2011) Additional cross-cultural validity testing of the Intercultural Development Inventory. *International Journal of Intercultural Relations* 35 (4), 474–487.

Hammer, M. (2016) *Intercultural Development Inventory Resource Guide*. Berlin, MD: IDI, LLC.

Hammer, M., Bennett, M. and Wiseman, R. (2003) Measuring intercultural sensitivity: The Intercultural Development Inventory. *International Journal of Intercultural Relations* 27 (4), 421–443.

Hammer Holdings Inc. (2022) IDI general information. https://idiinventory.com/generalinformation/.

Institute of International Education (2021a) 'Fields of study of U.S. study abroad students, 2000/01-2019/20'. *Open Doors* report on international educational exchange. https://opendoorsdata.org/data/us-study-abroad/fields-of-study/.

Institute of International Education (2021b) 'Host regions of U.S. study abroad students, 2005/06-2019/20'. *Open Doors* report on international educational exchange. http://www.opendoorsdata.org.

Knight, J. (2003) Updated definition of 'internationalization'. *International Higher Education* 33 (Fall), 2–3.

Kuh, L., LeeKeenan, D., Given, H. and Beneke, M. (2016) Preschool through grade 2: Moving beyond anti-bias activities: Supporting the development of anti-bias practices. *Young Children* 71 (1), 58–65.

Ladson-Billings, G. (1995) Toward a theory of culturally relevant pedagogy. *American Educational Research Journal* 32 (3), 465–491.

Ladson-Billings, G. (2006) From the achievement gap to the education debt: Understanding achievement in US schools. *Educational Researcher* 35 (7), 3–12. See https://doi.org/10.3102/0013189X035007003.

Longview Foundation for Education in World Affairs and International Understanding, Inc. (2008) *Teacher Preparation for the Global Age: The Imperative for Change*. Silver Spring, MD: Longview Foundation.

Lou, K. and Bosley, G. (2012) Facilitating intercultural learning abroad: The intentional, targeted intervention model. In M. Vande Berg, R.M. Paige and K. Lou (eds) *Student Learning Abroad: What Our Students Are Learning, What They're Not, and What We Can Do About It* (pp. 335–358). Sterling, VA: Stylus Publishing.

Marx, H. and Moss, D.M. (2011) Please mind the culture gap: Intercultural development during a teacher education study abroad program. *Journal of Teacher Education* 62 (1), 35–47.

Medina, A.L. and Kiefel, K. (2021) Global literature in tandem with study abroad: Cultivating intercultural competence for preservice teachers. *Frontiers: The International Journal of Study Abroad* 33 (2), 61–78.

Medina, A.L., Hathaway, J.I. and Pilonieta, P. (2015) How preservice teachers' study abroad experiences lead to changes in perceptions of English language learners. *Frontiers: The Interdisciplinary Journal of Study Abroad* 25 (1), 73–90.

Medina, A.L. and Kiefel, K. (2021) Global literature in tandem with study abroad: Cultivating intercultural competence for preservice teachers. *Frontiers: The International Journal of Study Abroad* 33 (2), 61–78.

Morley, A., Braun, A., Rohrer, L. and Lamb, D. (2019) Study abroad for preservice teachers: A critical literature review with considerations for research and practice. *Global Education Review* 6 (3), 4–29.

Nieto, S. (2010) *Language, Culture, and Teaching*. London: Routledge.

Onyenekwu, I., Angeli, J.M., Pinto, R. and Douglas, T. (2017) (Mis)representation among U.S. study abroad programs traveling to the African continent: A critical content analysis of a Teach Abroad program. *Frontiers: The Interdisciplinary Journal of Study Abroad* XXIX (1), 68–84. Retrieved from https://frontiersjournal.org/wpcontent/uploads/2017/04/XXIX-1- (Accessed 12 June 2022).

Osborn, T.A. (2006) *Teaching World Languages for Social Justice: A Sourcebook of Principles and Practices*. Hove: Lawrence Erlbaum.

Paige, R.M. (1993) On the nature of intercultural experiences and intercultural education. In R.M. Paige (ed.) *Education for the Intercultural Experience* (pp. 1–19). Yarmouth, ME: Intercultural Press.

Paris, D. (2012) Culturally sustaining pedagogy: A needed change in stance, terminology, and practice. *Educational Researcher* 41 (3), 99–97.

Pilonieta, P., Medina, A.L. and Hathaway, J.I. (2017) The impact of a study abroad experience on preservice teachers' disposition and plans for teaching English language learners. *The Teacher Educator* 52 (1), 22–38.

QSR International (2019) *Nvivo 12 Software*. Victoria: QSR International.

Saava, M. (2017) Learning to teach culturally and linguistically diverse students through cross-cultural experiences. *Intercultural Education* 28 (3), 269–282. https://doi.org/10.1080/14675986.2017.1333689.

Shiveley, J. and Misco, T. (2015) Long-term impacts of short-term study abroad: Teacher perceptions of preservice study abroad experiences. *Frontiers: The Interdisciplinary Journal of Study Abroad* 26 (1), 107–120.

Short, K.G., Day, D. and Schroeder, J. (eds) (2016) *Teaching Globally: Reading the World Through Literature*. Portland, ME: Stenhouse Publishers.

Spenader, A. and Retka, P. (2015) The role of pedagogical variables in intercultural development: A study of faculty-led programs. *Frontiers: The Interdisciplinary Journal of Study Abroad* 25 (1), 20–36.

Strauss, A. and Corbin, J. (1998) *Basics of Qualitative Research: Techniques and Procedures for Developing Grounded Theory* (2nd edn). Thousand Oaks, CA: Sage.

Taranath, A. (2019) *Beyond Guilt Trips: Mindful Travel in an Unequal World*. Toronto, ON: Between the Lines.

Terzuolo, E. (2018) Intercultural development in study abroad: Influence of student and program characteristics. *International Journal of Intercultural Relations* 65 (1), 86–95.

Vande Berg, M., Paige, R.M. and Lou, K. (eds) (2012) *Student Learning Abroad: What Our Students Are Learning, What They're Not, and What We Can Do About It*. Sterling, VA: Stylus Publishing.

Wagner, M. and Byram, M. (2017) Intercultural citizenship. In Y.Y. Kim and K.L. McKay-Semmler (eds) *International Encyclopedia of Intercultural Communication* (pp. 1–6). Hoboken, NJ: Wiley.

Wagner, M., Cardetti, F. and Byram, M. (2019) *Teaching Intercultural Citizenship Across the Curriculum: The Role of Language Education*. Alexandria, VA: American Council on the Teaching of Foreign Languages (ACTFL).

6 Promoting Intercultural Citizenship in Study Abroad through Contemplative Pedagogy

Ana Conboy and Kevin Clancy

Recent scholarship has demonstrated the need for intercultural citizenship education in colleges and universities (Byram 2008, 2012; Wagner & Byram, 2017). The concept of intercultural citizenship as two-fold, with a dual focus on self-reflection and analysis on the one hand, and on social action on the other, aims to create change in the individual that will, in turn, impact the global community (Byram, 2008; Guilherme, 2007).

While intercultural citizenship has been widely researched within language education, there remains a lacuna within the field of international education and study abroad. The experiential nature and intercultural learning opportunities offered by study abroad programs should make them natural environments for the promotion of intercultural citizenship. However, to achieve this goal, it is essential to incorporate metacognition and critical reflection in the curriculum (Jackson, 2011).

This chapter is significant in that it places the landscape of intercultural citizenship within the context of international education. It proposes the use of contemplative pedagogy as a praxis for encouraging intercultural citizenship within study abroad, both as content and as outcome. In the case study presented, a group of 13 students from the College of Saint Benedict and Saint John's University (Minnesota), participated in a program in the south of France, in the fall of 2018. All students took a course in French language, according to their level, and all students also enrolled in the seminar 'Experiencing Contemporary French Culture through the Five Senses (and Beyond...)'. The seminar, taught by faculty from the home institution, used the lens of contemplative pedagogy to guide students in experiencing and exploring the host culture, using the five senses and interoception and proprioception (see note 5). Aligning with the reflective nature of intercultural citizenship, students were guided through carefully designed and purposefully systematic activities. Students reflected intentionally on their lived experience, in the present moment, and constructed knowledge about themselves and those around them.

We describe the fall 2018 program learning goals and present sample assignments and written work from the students, to showcase students' broadened sense of multiculturalism and awareness as well as respect of Self and Other. Moreover, we reference student engagement in the local and global communities during and after their sojourn, to illustrate increased intercultural citizenship. Through content analysis of students' reflections and responses to questionnaires, we posit how a seminar rooted in contemplative pedagogy perspectives, with clear learning goals, appropriate readings and carefully scaffolded assignments, might lead students to a progressively heightened metacognition and sense of intercultural citizenship.

Experiential Learning and Metacognition in Study Abroad

Recent global education scholarship espouses an approach to study abroad programming and development that is grounded in experiential learning theory. This experiential approach to education states that learning transactions are constructed between individuals and their interaction with the environment. Learning is thus described as 'the process whereby knowledge is created through the transformation of experience' (Kolb, 1984: 41). This experiential model is rooted within a constructivist epistemology that takes 'the theoretical position that the world we know is constructed in our mind through our ongoing perception of and interaction with external reality' (Stuart, 2012: 61). In keeping with the tenets of constructivism, scholars believe that metacognitive reflection is the key component of intercultural learning on study abroad programs (Bennett, 2012; Zull, 2012). Vande Berg et al. (2012) highlight the importance of metacognitive reflection on study abroad programs:

> ... the data show that students learn and develop considerably more when educators prepare them to become more self-reflective, culturally self-aware, and aware of 'how they know what they know.' In developing a meta-awareness of their own processes of perceiving and knowing, students come to understand both how they habitually experience and make meaning of events, and how they can use that newfound understanding to help them engage more effectively and appropriately with culturally different others. (Vande Berg et al., 2012: 21)

While higher levels of metacognitive reflection are ultimately the goal of experiential learning, scholars continue to debate the most appropriate teaching pedagogies to facilitate metacognitive learning within the space of study abroad. 'I am not sure any of us understands what we mean by the expression "life-transforming," or even if students know that they intend', writes Selby (200: 1). As such, a growing number of international education researchers and practitioners (Deardorff, 2009; Fantini, 2009; Leung *et al.*, 2014; Paige *et al.*, 2003) are exploring intercultural competence as a construct to assess and define student transformation and intercultural development on study abroad programs.

There is a plethora of different approaches to the definition of intercultural competence. A review of intercultural competence scholarship found more than 30 models and 300 constructs (Leung *et al.*, 2014). Intercultural scholars continue to seek a more 'uniform' definition of intercultural competence. Notably, Deardorff (2006) gathered a panel of national and international intercultural scholars to find consensus around the term 'intercultural competence'. Within this study, a majority of the scholars pointed toward 'the ability to communicate effectively and appropriately in intercultural situations based on one's intercultural knowledge, skills, and attitudes' (Deardorff, 2006: 249) as key characteristics of intercultural competence. Intercultural scholar Janet Bennett (2009) affirms this definition as she reflects:

> ...despite the variety of perspectives used in examining this topic, there is an emerging consensus around what constitutes intercultural competence, which is most often viewed as a set of cognitive, affective, and behavioral skills and characteristics that support effective and appropriate interaction in a variety of cultural contexts. (Bennett, 2009: 97)

We believe there is shared DNA between study abroad scholars' conceptualization of intercultural competence and Byram's (1997) models of intercultural communicative competence (ICC) and intercultural citizenship (2008, 2012). Mirroring intercultural competence, the ICC model assesses aspects of the knowledge, skills and attitudes that learners need in order to act as 'intercultural speakers' of languages other than their first or native language (Byram, 2008). Moreover, metacognitive reflection, or critical cultural awareness, is a key component of the ICC model. Byram defines critical cultural awareness as the 'ability to evaluate critically and on the basis of explicit criteria perspectives, practices and products in one's own and other cultures and countries' (Byram, 1997: 53). In addition to the cognitive acquisition of knowledge, skills and attitudes, intercultural citizenship and intercultural competence research further emphasizes the importance of active engagement within multicultural and international communities (Vande Berg *et al.*, 2012; Wagner & Byram, 2017). Within both models of intercultural citizenship and intercultural competence, the role of the teacher is to facilitate and guide the learner to reflect metacognitively upon and to construct learning through their active multicultural and international engagement (Vande Berg, 2007; Wagner & Byram, 2017).

The Unproblematized Focus on the Self

There are clear threads of humanistic perspectives embedded within constructivist approaches to intercultural learning. Influenced by the industrialization and urbanization of mid-19th century America, John Dewey championed a progressive and humanistic approach to education (Merriam & Brockett, 1997). Dewey (1897) stated that education is a process in which learners continually reconstruct their experience. Furthermore, Dewey argued (1910) that reflective thought was a key goal of learning. Thus, the students (and how they process and construct knowledge) should be the focus of education research. The teacher, rather than an authority figure who only transmits knowledge, becomes the facilitator of learning for the student. This is very much in line with the American Council on the Teaching of Foreign Languages (ACTFL) World-Readiness Standards for Learning Languages (National Standards Collaborative Board, 2015), where the focus lies wholly on the learner and on the construction of knowledge using authentic materials and real-life scenarios.

Dewey's approach to education is rooted in a humanistic notion of self. Merriam and Brockett (1997) note that within this humanistic tradition, each learner 'has the potential for growth and development, for self-actualization'; moreover, these 'tenets mesh particularly well with American democratic values, which emphasize independence, individualism, and self-fulfillment' (Merriam & Brockett, 1997: 40). Consequently, Dewey's humanistic learning philosophy influenced generations of adult learning theorists such as Jack Mezirow (Transformative Learning Theory[1]), Malcom Knowles (the concept of andragogy[2]) and David Kolb (Experiential Learning Theory[3]).

Adult education scholar Patricia Cranton (2016) writes that adult learning can be visualized along a continuum, from individual to social. Humanists, she contends, fall toward the individual side of the continuum. Within the humanistic perspective, adult learning is focused on the self and the degree to which reflection on experience will alter the perception of one's reality. The challenge with this approach is that it privileges the role of the individual, while ignoring the role of the society ('other') in the education process. Brookfield (2012: 131–132) warns adult education scholars that if learning is to be transformative it must not fall into an 'unproblematized focus on the self'.

Similarly, intercultural competence constructs, influenced by a humanistic perspective, are largely focused on the individual student sojourner wherein their self-awareness (consciousness or meta-consciousness) becomes the unit of analysis within intercultural encounters. Constructivist intercultural competence concepts can thus unintentionally lead to the privileging of the individual at the expense of engaging in mutual relationships within intercultural encounters. Ono (2013) terms the predominant approach to intercultural communication constructs as the 'Western gaze', wherein 'those using this Western gaze may accept unequal power relations as a given and therefore may overlook important dimensions of the cultural relationship, as well as the positive dimension of the Other' (Ono, 2013: 91). Critical intercultural communication theorists thus warn that methodological concepts focused solely on the individual can ignore the role of dominant ideologies within intercultural encounters (Martin & Nakayama, 2000).

Critical Intercultural Communication Theory

Critical education theorist Paulo Freire (1973: 3) writes: 'To be human is to engage in relationships with others and with the world'. Critical intercultural communication theory is born out of the critical inquiry tradition, as critical communication scholars endeavor to 'understand the role of power and contextual constraints on communication in order ultimately to achieve a more equitable society' (Martin & Nakayama, 2000: 8). Critical intercultural communication scholars advocate for pedagogies (or praxis) that will promote change within the field of intercultural communication (Starosta & Chen, 2003) and guide students to more fully engage in their relationship with their environment. Critical scholars imagine 'the classroom as a potential site for social change' and 'argue that it is perhaps our pedagogical strategies for teaching intercultural communication that require our attention' (Moon, 2013: 43). Martin and Nakayama (2013), echoing Freire, write: 'one becomes fully human only in relation to another person... there is something unique in a relationship that goes beyond the sum of two individuals' (Martin & Nakayama, 2013: 66).

Critical intercultural communication theory and intercultural citizenship, grounded in critical theory, both move the concepts of intercultural competence and ICC beyond a privileging of the individual to a concept that underscores the importance of action and civic engagement with the host community. Wagner and Byram (2017) write that within intercultural citizenship, 'the learners as well as the teachers are urged to question underlying beliefs and compare and analyze evidence from a variety of perspectives in order to arrive at critical judgments' (2017: 4). Teachers, moreover, play a key role as they 'facilitate and provide tools to their students so that they can engage in intercultural activities with people from other cultures and languages in other countries or their own' (Wagner & Byram, 2017: 4).

Critical scholars contend that, in order to honor and understand the relationship that exists between the individual sojourner and 'the other', we must bring an intersubjective lens to learning. The primacy of relationships is affirmed by scholar Christian de Quincey, who believes that knowing (consciousness) and relationship are inextricably bound together (de Quincey, 2005). Physicist David Bohm (1996) maintained that new and creative spaces are created when one learns how to hold tensions of ideas together with others. Gunnlaugson (2014: 305) states that an intersubjective approach to learning inspires 'deeper shared and co-emergent contemplative states of knowing and generally move[s] individuals toward a more common focus and collective discernment in their learning process'. Accordingly, the intersubjective field sits between first-person and third-person perspectives and posits that at least three points of view emerge when two or more people are gathered: mine, yours and ours together (Orange, 1995). Thus, an intersubjective lens can provide for a construct where intercultural competence is not viewed as a solo endeavor but, rather, 'ours together'.

Contemplative Pedagogy: Towards a Relational Lens

We suggest that the emerging discipline of contemplative pedagogy (Bai *et al.*, 2009; Gunnlaugson *et al.*, 2014; Zajonc, 2013) provides such an intersubjective lens and approach to intercultural awareness and engagement. Contemplative pedagogy offers a critical praxis of education that 'serves in helping students develop, through contemplative practices, a deeper awareness of self, others, and the world, and through that a deeper sense of purpose, place, and connection with others, as well as surrounding communities, ecologies, and greater cosmos' (Gunnlaugson *et al.*, 2014: 6). Furthermore, the discipline of contemplative pedagogy aligns with the aspirations of experiential learning, as it provides a scaffolded experiential approach to metacognitive learning through forms of introspection that balance third-person study and critical first-person reflection. This third-person approach refers to the systematic study of the underlying philosophy, psychology and phenomenology of the human contemplative experience (Roth, 2006), whereas the critical first-person approach encourages students to engage directly with contemplative techniques (Roth, 2014).

While new to the field of international education, contemplative pedagogy has been used for more than 15 years across higher education disciplines by thousands of professors and academic administrators (Zajonc, 2013). The growth of contemplative practice in higher education has been championed by the Center for the Contemplative Mind in Society (www.contemplativemind.org) and the more recent Association for the Contemplative Mind in Higher Education (ACMHE) (http://www.contemplativemind.org/programs/acmhe). ACMHE was founded in 2009 as a forum for college and university professors and administrators to exchange research and ideas about the impact of contemplative pedagogy in the classroom (Craig, 2011). ACMHE declares what it believes to be the critical importance of contemplative pedagogy on their website:

> Though valuable to a point, conventional methods of scientific research, pedagogy, and scholarship need to be broadened, deepened, and divested of their oppressive legacies. The experiential methods developed within the contemplative traditions offer a rich set of tools for exploring the mind, body, spirit, heart, and relationship to the world. Contemplative practices augment and transform conventional educational and scientific practices towards enriched research methodologies and pedagogic models which can lead to lasting solutions to global challenges. (https://acmhe.org/about/)

Here, we see a clear parallel between the goals of contemplative pedagogy and those of intercultural citizenship education: both seek to broaden student perspectives while also motivating them to actively participate in the betterment of their communities. Scholars of contemplative pedagogy contend the ultimate goal of contemplative experiential methods is to uncover the hidden interrelationships and connections between oneself, the community and the environment. Zajonc (2010) writes:

> The forest stream, the opera, and the atom all have standing by virtue of their experiential aspect, which arises in relationship to us. *The implications of this view of reality for education are great* [Zajonc's emphasis]. It can pivot the entire mandate of university inquiry away from a privileged objectivist and material metaphysics to an egalitarian one of connection, relationship, and lived experience. The full scope of our humanity, which we seek to cultivate, is included in this orientation toward the world. (Zajonc, 2010: 68)

The Tree of Contemplative Practices (Figure 6.1), published by the Center for Contemplative Mind in Society (CMind, 2021), illustrates a large diversity of contemplative and experiential methods. Within the tree metaphor, communion and connection and awareness serve as the roots of the tree, with the branches representing different groups of practices within the contemplative tradition, including various forms of meditation, *Lectio Divina* and journaling.

Mindfulness is one key experiential method within contemplative pedagogy. Jon Kabat-Zinn (2009) defines mindfulness as 'moment-to-moment awareness' that is sought through a 'systematic approach to developing new kinds of control and wisdom in our lives, based on inner capacities

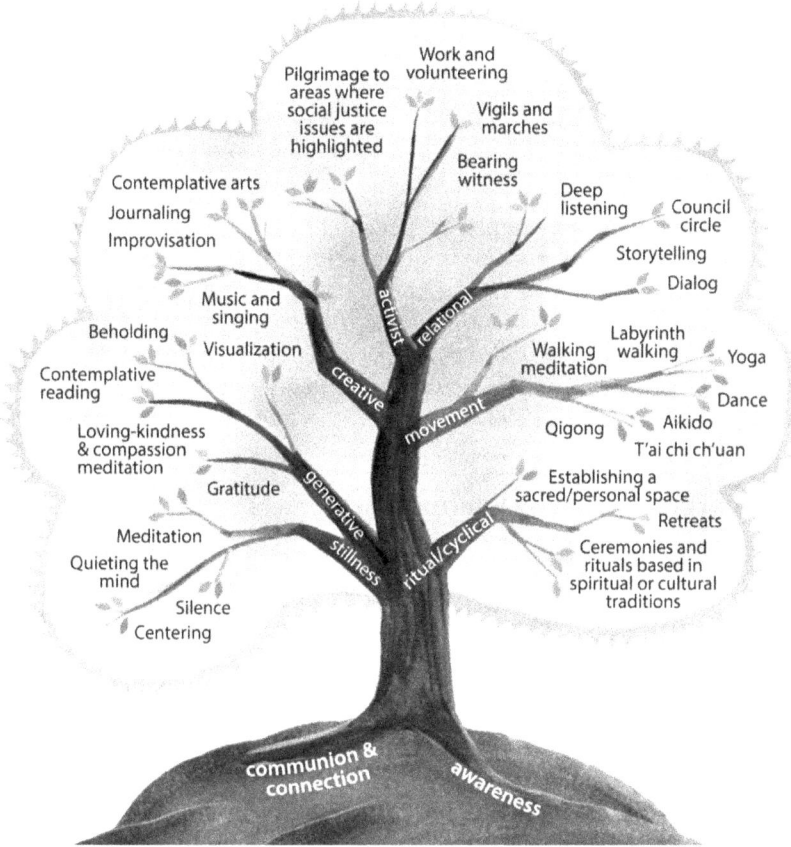

Figure 6.1 The Tree of Contemplative Practices. Reproduced with kind permission from The Center for Contemplative Mind in Society (CMind, 2021). https://www. contemplativemind.org/practices/tree

for relaxation, paying attention, awareness, and insight' (Kabat-Zinn, 2009: 2). In keeping with this definition, mindfulness in the higher education classroom is considered both a process (mindfulness practice) and an outcome (mindfulness awareness) (Barbezat & Bush, 2014). While the specific classroom approaches to mindfulness may vary, most applications of contemplative pedagogy involve forms of meditation and introspection. Barbezat and Bush posit that classroom introspective and contemplative exercises have four main objectives:

(a) Focus and attention building, mainly through focusing meditation and exercises that support mental stability;
(b) Contemplation and introspection into the content of the course, in which students discover the material in themselves and thus deepen their understanding of the material;

(c) Compassion, connection to others, and a deepening sense of the moral and spiritual aspect of education;
(d) Inquiry into the nature of their minds, personal meaning, creativity, and insight.

(Barbezat & Bush, 2014: 11)

These objectives of contemplative pedagogy consequently reiterate and complement many of those espoused within intercultural citizenship theory. Specifically, contemplative pedagogy's objective to foster 'compassion, connection to others, and a deepening sense of the moral and spiritual aspect of education' parallels intercultural citizenship's goal of developing one's civic awareness and communal engagement, to become intercultural workers.

Call to Action: Becoming Intercultural Workers

Contemplative pedagogy, and the associated practice of mindfulness, provides for an experiential and facilitated approach to guide student metacognitive reflection. The teacher, moreover, plays a key role in guiding the student through the contemplative practice and in helping the student link the practice to mindful awareness. It is important to note that this experiential approach is more than just passive reflection: rather, contemplative scholars contend that engagement and relationship with the environment must flow from the contemplative practice. To illustrate this point, Bai *et al.* (2014) advocate that contemplative practitioners and scholars should consider themselves 'intercultural workers'. These intercultural workers, 'need to participate in examining worldviews and values, and their enactment, assessing how they do or do not serve mutual flourishing and sustainability, and making suggestions and showing examples of different possibilities of imagining and handling reality' (Bai *et al.*, 2014: 637). In a similar call to action, Byram (2006: 127) writes: 'Education for citizenship leads to engagement and action, and education for intercultural citizenship should equally involve learners in engagement and action, at an international level as well as at a local, regional or national level'. Both contemplative pedagogy and intercultural citizenship education thus urge the student to reflect metacognitively and critically, engage in relationship with their environment and strive for change in the community.

Current global education scholarship underscores the paramount importance of rooting study abroad programming within experiential learning theory. Intercultural competence constructs are correspondingly used to assess and define student transformation and intercultural development (the acquisition of knowledge, skills and attitudes) on study abroad programs. Recent intercultural competence research further emphasizes the importance of active engagement within multicultural and international communities, reinforcing concepts of the intercultural citizenship model. We believe the burgeoning field of contemplative pedagogy offers a dynamic experiential praxis for study abroad, as it facilitates critical metacognitive reflection while simultaneously encouraging one to become an 'intercultural worker' within the host community, and thus an intercultural citizen.

In the following sections, we present a case study of a fall 2018 study abroad program in the south of France, where, through a curriculum founded on contemplative pedagogy, students were led to reflect critically on their lived experience. The chosen curriculum, we posit, helped students engage and act, first at the international level, in France, and then, after their return, at a more local level, so as to become intercultural citizens.

Study Abroad Curriculum: A Laboratory for Intercultural Citizenship

Study abroad programs, meant to be a transformative experience for students, can and should integrate intercultural citizenship pedagogies. Intercultural citizenship should be not only a goal of language education (Byram, 2008, 2012) but also a goal of the international education field, i.e. an outcome for our students studying in different parts of the world. The experiential nature and intercultural learning opportunities offered by study abroad programs make them ideal environments for the promotion and practice of intercultural citizenship. However, in order achieve this goal, it is crucial to incorporate experiential opportunities, metacognition and critical reflection in the study abroad curriculum.

The College of Saint Benedict and Saint John's University (CSB and SJU), in rural central Minnesota, boast several in-house study abroad programs that are led by faculty from the home institution. This model cultivates a greater sense of community and belonging and provides greater institutional support in each group of students studying abroad. Moreover, the faculty-led programs are preceded by robust pre-departure workshops and orientations during the semester prior to departure (up to four or five three-hour sessions, depending on the faculty member's preferences, availability and needs).

The formation of community is foundational for the functioning of our study abroad programs and the pre-departure workshops facilitate community-building. Before even setting foot in the host country, students are sensitized to one of the goals of intercultural citizenship education: that of building bonds and community among students. As a part of the interview process for the study abroad programs, for example, some faculty may choose to share one or two citations related to the definition of community and ask the interviewees to comment on them and provide their own definition of community. The aim of such an exercise is, first, to understand the student's view of life in community and, second, to come to a better understanding of how the different interviewees might interact and relate to each other in a small community setting while abroad.

The pre-departure workshops engender opportunities for meaningful dialogue and reflection about students' own biases, expectations of, assumptions about, and stereotypes associated with the host country or culture, creating the space to address and develop ICC skills. As students engage in critical reflection of their own assumptions or values, they are already engaging in what Byram tags as pre-political civic engagement (Byram, 2008; Byram *et al.*, 2017). Thus, a strong pre-departure orientation provides opportunities for discussions on students' expectations of themselves while abroad, or for the collective drafting of a group code of conduct, which they can be reminded of, and refer to often, throughout their time abroad. Furthermore, the pre-departure meetings are good venues to integrate, discuss and put into practice the institutional mission and values of CSB and SJU, rooted in the concepts of respect for persons, listening attentively and intentionally, hospitality, and community, among others. These values, which permeate the theory of intercultural competence and citizenship, continue to play a key role in students' learning overseas.

A Qualitative Case Study

In fall 2018, a group of 13 students from CSB and SJU took part in a study abroad program in the south of France. During the program, all students were placed in a French language class, appropriate to their language level (language level varied among the students: namely, two of the 13 were true beginners, five were placed in intermediate levels, and the six who were French majors or minors were placed in the higher levels). Additionally, all students participated in the seminar 'Experiencing Contemporary French Culture through the Five Senses (and Beyond...)', taught by the faculty director. The seminar, part of a curriculum focused on the present moment (Kabat-Zinn, 2012), and that of *cura personalis*, or whole person education, was designed to facilitate the transformative learning afforded by the study abroad experience.

One of the objectives of the course was for students to develop ICC and to gain a better understanding of contemporary French culture and society, and especially that of the region where the program was taking place (Cannes and the Alpes-Maritimes). The learning goals for the seminar included the then institutionally approved intercultural learning goals. As a part of the course, it was expected that students demonstrate:

(a) A level of understanding of another culture, including the awareness that it is neither monolithic nor static.

(b) An understanding that their perspective on the world is shaped in certain ways by their particular background.

(c) An awareness that when we encounter another culture, we filter the new experience through established perspectives, which makes it more difficult to uncover our common humanity and the reasons for our differences.[4]

The concept of mindfulness and its connection to the five senses, as well as with the senses of proprioception and interoception,[5] became the frame of reference for students' learning and development. Activities, readings and discussions were organized to help students develop sustained concentration, so as to gain greater clarity of mind and availability to insight. Students researched, learned and practiced multiple mindfulness strategies in order to improve their self-awareness and their awareness of surroundings and to gain a more fine-tuned perceptive acuity. The course was discussion based and was focused on the idea of transformation, be it of the surroundings or of the self. It also used a social/cultural anthropological approach: in experiential opportunities, readings or in-class discussions, students were asked to engage non-judgmentally and in the present moment, as active participant observers, and with the eye of the sojourner, as Byram (1997) proposes. With the aim of students' metacognitive development, they were always asked to reflect on their experiences, both in terms of themselves and of their own growth, and in terms of the actions/reactions of those around them. Following the tenets of mindfulness and Byram's description of the attitudes necessary for ICC, they were to reflect intentionally and to leave judgment and preconception behind: students were to act with 'curiosity and openness' and a 'readiness to suspend disbelief about other cultures and belief about one's own' (Byram, 2008: 163). The tools learned during the semester were additionally meant to supplement student reflection upon and discernment of personal vocation, of a sense of personal social responsibility and of purpose in life post-study abroad.

Seminar structure

The initial stages of the program aimed at students' attitudinal change: developing awareness of and respect for Other (and, in turn, for Self), and nurturing traits of culturally sensitive, humble and agile individuals, through the 'acquisition of the knowledge and skills that facilitate constructive, active participation in today's complex society' (Jackson, 2011: 82). The carefully designed and intentionally scaffolded study abroad seminar supported themes introduced in the pre-departure workshops. It also followed Byram's (2006) suggestion of using both cognitive and experiential approaches and aimed at promoting intercultural and experiential learning through guided critical reflection and metacognition, which would be transformative for students while in-country and, hopefully, continue its impact posteriorly. During the program abroad, in-class activities, discussions and formative writing assignments complemented outside-the-class activities and excursions, field debriefings and opportunities for journaling. In turn, excursions and project work were meant to challenge students to test and apply the classroom theory in real life settings.

Structurally, the course was divided into three main modules: Experience (learning about the Other through the senses); Reflection (learning of Self through the Other); and Action (using what was learned to engage in the future). Students were led to learn about their host culture and host community through hands-on experiences (some organized by the director, some others requiring student agency and autonomy). Experiences were discussed collectively and reflected upon individually, to enable student metacognitive development and greater self-awareness. The insights and construction of knowledge from the first two modules were integrated to allow students, towards the end of the semester, to discuss their sense of vocation, how they might continue the practices and learning from the study abroad program, and continuously find meaning and purpose in their lives.

The theoretical framework of the pre-departure orientations and of the first modules of the seminar centered around readings from Julie Barlow and Jean-Benoit Nadeau's *Sixty Million Frenchmen Can't Be Wrong: Why We Love France, but not the French,* Jon Kabat-Zinn's *Mindfulness for Beginners* and *Coming to Our Senses*, Thich Nhat-Hahn's *The Miracle of Mindfulness* and *Peace Is Every Step*, and Alain De Botton's *The Art of Travel*. Activities, discussions and written assignments during these stages included student presentations on ethnographic research, student-researched and student-led mindfulness techniques or strategies, a guided *Audio Divina* and *Visio Divina*,[6] a blind dinner, and sequential visits to the local market to focus on the different senses.

The third module integrated selected readings from Brené Brown's *The Gifts of Imperfection*, William Sullivan's *Liberal Learning as a Quest for Purpose*, Deepak Chopra's *The Seven Spiritual Laws of Success* and David Brooks's *The Road to Character*.

In the third module, students were asked to reflect purposefully and discuss the triad of questions: What brings me joy? What am I good at? What does my community need me to do?[7] These three questions encourage students in their development and in maturing into responsible, respectful and accountable intercultural citizens, by tapping into the knowledge of their personal gifts and abilities and in inviting them to explore ways in which to act, to engage, and to fully use their talents. The questions also echo the principle that intercultural citizenship education implicates 'creating learning/change in the individual: cognitive, attitudinal, behavioural change; change in self-perception; change in relationships with Others (i.e. people of a different social group); change that is based in the particular but is related to the universal' (Byram, 2008: 187). The ultimate use of students' gifts and that which provides a sense of meaning and purpose in their lives is the service provided to their local and global communities, which nurtures the common good beyond the study abroad program.

'Experiencing contemporary French culture through the five senses': A gateway to intercultural citizenship

Since critical self-analysis can lead to intercultural competence and citizenship (Jackson, 2011), at the end of the program, prior to departing France, students were asked to reflect on what might be the greatest takeaways from the program, and what practices or values they might adapt or adopt upon returning home. James[8] wrote:

> I find myself incorporating aspects of my host country into my every-day life back home. [...] These details haven't made me question my own beliefs and values, but rather added to my beliefs and values and helped give me an extra perspective of how things are done and helped me realize that there isn't exactly a right way of doing things, but there are many different ways instead. I wouldn't go as far as saying that there were any *ah-ha* moments, but *ah* moments. *Ah* as in *ah,* it makes sense why they do certain things different here than back home.

Beth wrote: 'I think it will be important to *readjust my frame of mind* with regard to my own culture and *adopt the same mindful, non-judgmental attitude that I have for my host culture*' (authors' emphasis). Charlie commented on the impact that the transnational peers (not only French but other international students) made on her personal life:

> Not only has the distance from my family changed me, but the people I've met here have also made a huge impact on my life. *My foreign friends have introduced me to a way of life that is liberating, accept-ing, and care-free.* I have finally started to love and accept my physical body, I'm more confident in the things I wear and the things I like, I'm less afraid to be myself, I've started caring less about what other people think, and more about my personal joy. In my opinion, one needs to love oneself before being able to truly love anyone else, so self-love was and still is very important for me. *I will take the lessons I've learned from my foreign friends with me for the rest of my life.* (Authors' emphasis)

These three students acknowledge personal change. Furthermore, they recognize on the one hand a greater sense of openness to, and understanding of, others, and on the other, a greater sense of self-awareness. These attitudes align directly with Byram's suggested attitudes necessary for development of ICC. Their transformation, as they perceive it, is influenced by their experience in context, by those around them, and has an impact beyond their time abroad.

At the end of the program, students thought critically about what their own impact in surrounding communities could and should be, following the study abroad program. This evokes the notion of *savoir s'engager*, and that of critical cultural awareness, one of the five elements in Byram's (1997) definition of ICC, and which has since been refined to incorporate notions of intercultural citizenship education. In various assignments during the study abroad program, students' assertions, in light of the mindfulness framework of the seminar, reflect elements of that early definition of ICC:

(a) *Savoir être:* '[Experiencing] France with curiosity, an open-mind and a generally conscious evaluation of my five senses transformed me into the more mindful and culturally-aware human being I am today. […] how beneficial and eye-opening it is to integrate into another's culture' (Florence).

(b) *Savoirs*: 'Overall, I've learned a lot about French culture, but *more than anything else, I've learned about American culture because of the way that my behaviors are suddenly contrasting to those around me*' (Sam; authors' emphasis).

(c) *Savoir apprendre/faire*: '[…] when I experience a cultural difference with respect to the French culture that may inconvenience me or be unpleasant, *I am more likely to take a deep breath and evaluate the situation with a mindful and culturally aware eye*' (Beth; authors' emphasis); 'Living in a new culture has made me a better person, both by *adopting certain views of my host culture, and by analyzing certain views of theirs that I don't agree with*. At the very least, I at last *understand the roots of those views better,* and thus, *I know myself better through this process of cultural reflection*' (Sam; authors' emphasis).

(d) *Savoir comprendre*: 'As a result of my cultural experiences this semester, *I am learning to view things from the "other" perspective more often*. I have always been a firm believer in a positive attitude, so *incorporating this mental technique [mindfulness] assists me with that*. Instead of being upset that [the French] do not dress lazily like me, I have begun appreciating how nicely everyone dresses and how much effort they put in to look nice each day' (Casey; authors' emphasis).

Manifestations of intercultural citizenship in student reflections

In echoing elements from Byram's definition of ICC, students also illustrate preliminary stages in the development of intercultural citizenship. While in-country, through activities encouraged by the faculty director and through independently motivated activities, the participants of the program personified the relational, critical and civic dimensions of intercultural citizenship, as related by Porto (2021):

(a) Relational dimension: Students interacted and got involved locally. All engaged in experiential opportunities associated with the seminar, such as: (i) sequential visits to the town market, where students were to pay attention to different senses at each visit and relate these to experiences at home; (ii) an assignment where students independently researched the public transportation system of Cannes, received a round-trip ticket for the bus, and decided on one location to go to, after which they presented a 'show and tell' in class; or (iii) a blind dinner, organized at the host institution, with two local chefs preparing the four-course meal. After 'blindly' experiencing the various elements of the meal, by focusing on senses other than sight, students had the opportunity to try the different courses again, now with their sense of sight restored, and in the company of the two chefs who answered students' questions, explained some of the traditions of Provençale food, and listened to students' perceptions and observations on the experience. Some of the students in the program became intercultural speakers (Byram, 2008) by volunteering to participate in a language exchange organized with French peers engaged in a practicum for the local hospitality industry. In experiential opportunities such as these, students grow in intercultural awareness, and they need to be emotionally intelligent intercultural speakers as they 'interpret linguistic and non-linguistic input critically in a comparative perspective' (Porto, 2021: 649). This is especially noteworthy when students observe behaviors they admire in their transnational peers and which they would like to adopt at home, as already noted above, and reiterated in Florence's comment: 'I think this practice [saying "Bonjour" and "Merci, au revoir" in stores and public transportation] shows respect for one another and *I value this norm very much [...] this is something I wish Americans would pick up on and practice more often*' (authors' emphasis).

(b) Critical dimension: Experiential opportunities were followed up by written assignments designed to consolidate knowledge and lead students to reflect critically on the experience. In a reflective essay where students were asked to analyze some of their experiences with the host culture at different stages during the program, Charlie exposed an astute insight on the distance between tables at restaurants in France: 'I wonder about the strategy behind closer tables. Perhaps it allows for more tables which allows for more customers and therefore makes the restaurant more money. Perhaps, the US values privacy more than the number of tables in a room, or maybe the US just hasn't thought of it yet!'. Even if Charlie was not comfortable or pleased with the shorter distance between tables in French restaurants, because of a perceived lack of privacy, there was critical reflection leading to a very plausible conclusion and comparison of cultural values and practices. In activities such as 'Become an Anthropologist', or 'France isn't what it used to be', students were asked to be participant observers or interact directly with their peers, and to reflect critically on what they observed or heard (see Appendix A for assignment prompts). Students demonstrated progress towards a greater understanding of cross-cultural differences and towards ethnorelativism, i.e. the sense that one's set of values and behaviors is just one of many possibilities (Bennett, 2004). Moreover, by questioning some of their own assumptions, values or practices, they experienced and interpreted their own culture in the context of the host culture. For example, Florence remarked:

> instances led me to think that Americans, or maybe Minnesotans, are timid when it comes to asking for something they want. This is a negative attribute I even possess, because I know if I don't ask, I will NEVER receive. [...] After seeing the French directness and fearlessness to ask for what they want, they do tend to get it in the end. [...] There is an amount of that ideology to follow, [...] I realized it is not a bad thing to ask for what you want in life. Instead of us just doing everything on our own, don't be afraid to be direct and ask for more!

Similarly, Casey noted: 'Prior to arriving in France, I had made a very ethnocentric and wrong assumption that practically everyone would know and speak English with me when they heard me struggling'. Here, she identifies personal ethnocentric perspectives and recognizes their effect on behavior, once again echoing Byram's description of the *savoir comprendre* element within ICC.

(c) Civic dimension: By taking initiative to be a conversation partner, to tutor students in English, or to enroll in flute lessons at the local music conservatory, some of the students engaged in social and civic action beyond the classroom and the school. In retrospect, when contacted in spring 2022, Sam mentions thinking that the language exchange 'would be a unique opportunity to improve my French'. Moreover, while spearheaded by the faculty director, all students in the program took an active role in collaborating with the host institution to organize, host and participate in a pre-Thanksgiving dinner concert. Traditionally, each fall, the host institution sponsors a Thanksgiving dinner in honor of the American students studying on-site, and also invites the school's administrative council and other influential partners. The organization of a Thanksgiving concert was a way of taking advantage of the school's chapel, a space in disuse, but, more importantly, it was a way of expressing gratitude for the hospitality received. The enthusiasm for the event was such that, even if most of the performers were students from the study abroad program, some of the staff and a couple of the other international students contributed equally, thus 'facilitating intercultural citizenship experience, and analysis and reflection on it and on the possibility of further social and/or political activity—i.e. activity which involves working with others to achieve an agreed end' (Byram, 2008: 187).

The study abroad course described, suits intercultural competence and citizenship pedagogies. As the group grew together as a community to cultivate a greater sense of attentiveness to the wonders of the surroundings, to continue using mindfulness in the quotidian and to be mindful listeners, respectful of peers, the hope was also to lead students to grow as enlightened, independent and critical thinkers, progressively more aware of their vocation, and to be morally responsible and engaged citizens in a world that understands, accepts and respects social and cultural difference. The length of the program and inability to continue working intentionally and intensively with the group of students upon return to the home institution made it difficult to follow up with them and develop the third module into a more continuous and practical one – one where the effects of students' potentially developed intercultural citizenship could be more readily identified.

Post-study abroad program follow-up: Long-term impact of intercultural citizenship pedagogies?

Students were contacted in summer 2020, 18 months after returning from the study abroad program, and after 11 of the 13 students had already graduated. They were asked to respond to an anonymous questionnaire related to their overall experience of contemplative pedagogy during and after the program, and how it had impacted their decisions and actions after returning from France.[9] Participation was voluntary, and 10 out of the 13 students submitted responses.

In spring 2022, we contacted the 13 students again, for feedback specifically related to their attitudes and experience of social and civic action during and after the program, until present day. At this time, all students had graduated and had experienced two years of the global pandemic. The goal was to gather evaluative data that might indicate the role played by the study abroad program and its components in the students' development of intercultural citizenship. In the email communication, students were asked four questions,[10] and had approximately a week to reflect on and respond to them intentionally. Of the 13 students who participated in the program in 2018, we received responses from five.

Summer 2020 feedback: Enhanced social awareness and personal transformation

From the 2020 responses, it is possible to discern elements of intercultural citizenship, even if that was not the primary intention of the questionnaire. One student describes how, after returning home, she engaged in society by tutoring immigrants in English as a Second Language (ESL) and used contemplative pedagogy in the approach: 'in my academic and professional life, mindfulness has reminded me to hone in on details and interact with others with as little judgment as possible, especially in cross-cultural and intergenerational interactions. I especially used mindfulness in my interactions with immigrants I taught English to at a non-profit last summer'. In this case, even though it is not evident what the impulse to tutor ESL was, it is clear that the study abroad program had an underlying impact on the student's approach, perspectives and actions following the decision to tutor immigrants. In the same 2020 questionnaire, another participant expresses social awareness and a desire to improve relations with those in closer circles, by referring to the use of mindfulness in personal interactions with family and friends:

> Mindfulness has helped me in relationships. We practiced going for walks and explaining to each other what all of our own five senses felt on the way. It helped us live in the moment and bond in a better way with each other and the world rather than being oblivious to the natural beauty around us and simply having a conversation about our day.

This participant extends the element of social awareness toward the greater community by way of her personal and academic choices: 'it is important to note that this experience with mindfulness while I studied abroad impacted me tremendously. So much so that I decided to complete my three-semester research capstone project on mindful eating'. This student's openness to personal transformation and growth impacted her academic choices, an expression of the relational dimension of intercultural citizenship. Plausibly, it also signifies her future engagement (and the civic dimension of intercultural citizenship) with others, which is linked to the previous experience abroad. Just as this student relates maturing while abroad, other students' voices during the program, after their return, and now into their early professional life, demonstrate personal growth and change – two important dimensions of intercultural citizenship: In 2020, one student reported: 'Being gone, for

4 months, I came back and did a lot of reshuffling and evaluation of my life. The person who went to France is not the same person who returned to the U.S.'. In a response to a different question, the same student wrote: 'I really do believe that the practice helped me develop positive outlook and attitudes about facing challenges and obstacles I may face. Character-wise, I look back on the level of independence I achieved which inspires me to this very day, push outside of my comfort zone'. Another student corroborates the personal transformation observed a year-and-a-half after the program: 'I know that my experience had an immediate impact on my life [...] and it [made] me the person I am today. More mindful, more calm and more peaceful'. Personal growth and social awareness – key elements of intercultural citizenship – were catalyzed, in part, by the contemplative practices learned and practiced during the study abroad program, and by the experience of being abroad.

Spring 2022 feedback: Life choices for civic engagement

Students' life choices after graduation illustrate the potential for the civic dimension of intercultural citizenship: several of the program participants chose to apply for, and accept placement in, the Teaching Assistantship Program in France (TAPIF) program after graduation (and in the middle of a pandemic). The information obtained from the five respondents in 2022 shows that their life choices also reveal a desire to work for the betterment of the community.

Stephanie refers to a desire to return to France after the study abroad experience to continue practicing the language and learning about the culture. Furthermore, she expresses a desire to pay it forward and continue working in the education field, engaging with students, and influencing their growth and learning, as she is 'considering pursuing [a] master's in teaching English to non-English speakers to potentially become an English teacher in France', because she 'found that [she] really enjoyed teaching high schoolers English [during TAPIF]'. Stephanie is currently working as an administrative associate at a small community-based mental health clinic. She recognizes that 'there is a great need for mental health professionals in [her] community', and she is pleased to be able to 'focus on helping people who are struggling and in need of mental health services'. Stephanie embodies social awareness in this response and is a part of the solution to a large social problem, specifically through her intentional civic action towards her peers. She goes on to say: 'it feels great to be a part of something that is so essential in today's world due to the Covid-19 Pandemic and rising health insurance costs in the United States'.

Other cases exemplifying the potential for the civic dimension of intercultural citizenship include Beth, who has chosen to complete graduate studies in the field of educational psychology, Sam, who has started a degree in Curriculum and Instruction, to become certified to teach English as a Second Language, and Florence, who is currently working in the field of nutrition and dietetics. Sam, for example, who hopes to be employed as a high school teacher after graduate studies, will be doing field work 'at a neighborhood community center before starting student teaching in the fall [2022]'. The four respondents' life choices further exemplify active participation and engagement in society and reflect steps towards intercultural citizenship.

Spring 2022 feedback: Greater self-confidence and activism for the common good

We posit that the study abroad experience, with its opportunities for experiential learning and metacognitive development, associated with a curriculum rooted in contemplative pedagogy, facilitates the preliminary stages of intercultural citizenship. Five students who participated in the fall 2018 study abroad program also report civic and political engagement in 2022, but there is no evident link to the time they spent in France four years prior. From the students' responses, it was evident that they are currently involved in social and political initiatives, such as food equality activism and efforts to promote nutritional access, serving the local homeless community, or participating in a grassroots group advocating for equitable educational reform. From their responses, however, it is not possible to directly correlate their current social and civic action to the study abroad curriculum and contemplative pedagogy.

It is possible, nevertheless, to posit that students' increased self-trust and confidence garnered during the study abroad experience, enhanced by the pedagogy chosen, may have empowered students to be more engaged citizens after their return: 'I became slightly more engaged in my community on campus when I returned from Cannes, [...] I became more confident after studying abroad and so I was less afraid of taking up space or speaking out in the smaller, niche groups that I belonged to (French department, clubs, sports teams, etc.)'. This statement by Sam is reflective of the general view among students at the end of the semester program, and in their responses to the 2020 questionnaire: that their experience abroad, with the intentional integration of contemplative pedagogy to interact and learn about the host culture, improved their sense of self-confidence and trust. Max corroborates this in stating: '[During the program,] I wanted to be immersed in unfamiliar and sometimes difficult situations. I knew those are the experiences we grow most from [...] without my experience abroad, I would not have had the confidence to throw myself into a new city in the middle of a global pandemic'. In turn, individuals who are more confident in, and comfortable with, themselves may be more likely to interact and impact those around them positively.

Overall, students report civic engagement linked to the study abroad program and curriculum more at the level of political, social and civic awareness – i.e. at the pre-political level, in Byram's terminology[11] – rather than specific action. Looking to the future, and in order to confirm a direct correlation between the two, it would be beneficial to (a) implement a more intentional curriculum for intercultural citizenship, and (b) create a more robust and sustained accompaniment of students upon their return to the home institution, ideally with continued programming for the group of students during the semester(s) after returning from study abroad – bookending the experience along with the pre-departure workshops. A recent change at the institutional level of our home institution regarding the study abroad curriculum may address the first of these two suggestions.

Cultural and Social Difference Courses: Potential for Intercultural Citizenship Education

A seminar such as 'Experiencing Contemporary French Culture through the Five Senses (and Beyond…)', rooted in contemplative pedagogy perspectives, may lead students to a progressively heightened metacognition and sense of intercultural citizenship. For such an outcome to be achieved, it is essential that the course have clear learning goals, appropriate readings, and scaffolded assignments that present students with experiential opportunities, guide them in their critical (self-)reflection, and encourage them to liaise and engage at the community level, be it local or more global.

Recent curricular changes at our institution have led to major modifications of the study abroad seminar, which may provide a clearer conduit for intercultural citizenship education. Starting in the academic year 2022–2023, all study abroad seminars taught by faculty directors will fall under the umbrella of Cultural and Social Difference: Systems courses. These courses are the second of a two-course series, the first of which is taken in the first three semesters of the students' college career. In the first course, students think critically about how gender, race and ethnicity intersect to shape identities dynamically and differently under specific social and cultural factors. They explore how those three dimensions, in isolation, are 'insufficient to conceptualize either individual or social identity'.

Cultural and Social Difference: Systems (CSD:S) courses deepen the knowledge constructed in the first CSD course and invite a focus on cultures outside the US, making it highly relevant and applicable to the study abroad context. The institutional goals suggest that, in these courses:

> students will demonstrate an understanding of how constructions of race, gender, and ethnicity shape cultural rules and biases and how these constructions vary across time, cultures, and societies. This class

may address gender, race, and ethnicity in any context, including the contemporary United States, other nations or cultures, and/or various points in history. (https://www.csbsju.edu/documents/Integrations%20 Curriculum/CSD%20Systems%20Teaching%20Guidelines%20 updated%20March%202021.pdf)

CSD:S courses further explore the theme of justice and systems of power, inviting students to reflect, develop a sense of social justice responsibility and, ideally, act towards achieving justice in their surroundings.

In fall 2023, students studying abroad in France enroll, not only in a French language course appropriate to their level of linguistic competence, but also in a CSD:S seminar where there is meaningful reflection and discussion on social, political and cultural matters pertinent to their transnational peers and on how multiple factors such as gender, class, age or religion intersect with each other in the French context. The learning outcomes associated with the course proposed are those of gender,[12] and race and ethnicity.[13] The content of the CSD:S course thus includes challenging and sometimes controversial topics. When complemented by out-of-class activities, reflective assignments and in-class discussion, the new format of the study abroad seminar will help develop students' meta-awareness as well as social and civic awareness and will encourage students to improve their communities by engaging in them at the social and civic level (see Appendix A for a potential assignment).

Since the new curriculum has only recently been implemented in study abroad programs, it is not yet clear whether the recent curricular changes associated with the study abroad seminar will, indeed, have perceptible results in terms of intercultural citizenship development for the students participating in the various in-house programs. Nevertheless, we join the CSB and SJU curriculum committees, the CSB and SJU Center for Global Education, and the on-site program directors, in trusting that the new organization of the study abroad seminar, with its clear learning goals and outcomes, will have a tangible impact on the students and on their future active engagement in society. Collecting evidence for it will require commitment from faculty, student participants and the institution as a whole, to maintain contact and continued communication with students after the respective study abroad programs end.

Conclusion and Recommendations

The study abroad curriculum and the opportunities it provides have the potential for encouraging greater civic and social action in the leaders of tomorrow. They are, therefore, gateways towards intercultural citizenship education. Rethinking the study abroad curriculum to intentionally include themes and conversations that might be difficult and polemic (such as those in the Cultural and Social Difference courses), supplemented by continued reflection and meta-reflection, may enhance intercultural citizenship pedagogies. It may also inspire long-term attitudinal changes in our students, i.e. changed comportment and decisions that reflect agency and empowerment in social and political engagement, both at the pre-political and political levels. Moreover, using the framework of contemplative pedagogy for such a curriculum and experiential opportunities may assist in the difficult conversations in the classroom, in that students will have the experience of quieting the mind to achieve greater clarity, attentive listening and respectful dialoguing, while exercising intentional and non-judgmental awareness of the present moment.

In the case study presented, students report continued use of contemplative pedagogy strategies learned during their time abroad, three-and-a-half years after returning from the program. Additionally, students convey greater social awareness, and report personal growth and increased self-confidence associated with the study abroad curriculum. In turn, these traits have translated into an empowerment to engage civically since the students' return. The curriculum of the study abroad seminar presented in this chapter did not intentionally seek to include elements associated with intercultural citizenship. Nevertheless, as students were guided through carefully designed and purposefully systematic activities, the content and organization of the seminar aligned with the reflective nature and different dimensions of intercultural citizenship. The student voices cited indicate a proclivity toward engagement and social awareness, following metacognitive analysis, both while in-country and after their return to the home institution. As such, we posit that the use of contemplative pedagogy can be a praxis for encouraging intercultural citizenship within the study abroad setting, especially at the pre-political level, even if the correlation between study abroad pedagogies and subsequent social and civic action is not explicit.

Given that our study is small scale and localized in a single study abroad site, with one group of students, the conclusions presented are observations specific to our circumstances rather than more general trends. What we present may resonate with other programs and other colleagues, in other contexts. We postulate that if we continue investigating and following up with students on this and other study abroad programs where contemplative pedagogy and intercultural citizenship education is integrated, we will observe reproducible results and be able to produce more generalizable conclusions about the influence of study abroad curricula on students' greater sense of intercultural citizenship and subsequent action. Nevertheless, we demonstrate here that the potential for intercultural citizenship development through a carefully structured study abroad curriculum is tangible, especially at the preliminary stages of civic and social awareness and at the pre-political level.

We recommend that colleagues in the field of international education, in college administration, and faculty directly involved in the implementation of study abroad programs, utilize the resources readily available to them in the host countries to promote intercultural citizenship education, and concomitant with language education for our college students studying overseas. Such action will contribute toward one of the main goals of education: that of students' personal growth and personal development so as to lead to the 'development of democratic societies and the evolution of individuals and societies' (Porto, 2021: 663). In this chapter we offer the description of our home institution's Cultural and Social Difference: Systems course as a way to inspire other international educators to consider incorporating similar learning goals into their study abroad curriculum so as to cultivate a greater sense of intercultural citizenship in the participants of their programs.

Ideally, intercultural citizenship education is should have a sustained impact. We recognize, though, that this may not be evident or easily discernible (Llewellyn *et al.*, 2010; Porto, 2021). Porto, concurring with Byram's previous assertions, suggests that in order for intercultural citizenship education to engender long-term civic or social action, there is a need for 'systematic and routinised intercultural citizenship experiences' (Porto, 2021: 663–664). The need for follow-up programming is, therefore, vital for (a) continued encouragement and development of student metacognition and social action, and (b) formative evaluation of the impact of intercultural citizenship and contemplative pedagogies on the students returning from study abroad programs. Due to multiple potential constraints, it may be difficult to have a robust, structured and institutionally sponsored program after returning from study abroad. Implicated faculty need to exercise initiative and find the time for follow up with the students, in order to ensure greater long-term effects of intercultural citizenship pedagogy. This remains an aspiration – but not an impossibility. Given the increasing challenges and demands that students must navigate, now is the time to build intercultural citizenship pedagogy into study abroad programs and cultivate the intercultural speakers and citizens who will work towards a more just society.

Appendix A: Examples of Student Assignments

'Become an anthropologist'

This activity was inspired by Richard Carlson's *Don't Sweat the Small Stuff*, and his segment on 'Become an Anthropologist' (Carlson,

1997: 111–112). The goal of the activity was for students to engage as a participant observer in the here and now, with the eye of the sojourner. Students were to find a place to sit and 'people watch'. They were to have a 'prepared mind', that is, as Kabat-Zinn describes it:

> [a] ready mind, an open mind, a mind that knows or maybe just intuits what it doesn't know, questions its own tacit assumptions, and is drawn to inquire—to look more deeply beneath the appearance of things and perhaps behind the conventional narrative about why things are or aren't the way they are. (Kabat-Zinn, 2012: 74)

When something caught their attention, students focused in on it, observed, then reflected, and journaled about what they observed. In their writing, students were asked to dig deeper: to be an active participant observer and follow Carlson's recommendation of 'being interested, without judgement, in the way other people choose to live and behave'. In their short reflection, they were to describe their experience in detail and make note of how and why they might be interpreting what they were observing and how those they observed may have interpreted the situation/behavior observed. As such, students were asked to reflect on possibly different perspectives at play. Finally, students were asked to reflect on and respond to how they may adapt their own reactions in accordance with what Carlson (1997) suggests, in order to cultivate a more peaceful and patient self, which would translate into more peaceful and patient comportment towards others. In terms of metacognition, the 'Become an Anthropologist' activity lends itself well to repetition, in different settings, and at different points of time during the sojourn abroad, as the relationship to the host culture is burgeoning. If it is done twice or three times, each time students can return to the previous reflections and write a few sentences about how they may have grown and changed since then.

'You know, France isn't what it used to be'

In the activity, 'You know, France isn't what it used to be', students were asked to re-read the Afterword of *Sixty Million Frenchmen Can't Be Wrong*, reflect on it in comparison with their own experience in France, and write a reflective essay after interviewing a peer they knew and were comfortable talking to. The prompt for the activity read: 'In your time in Cannes, you have likely heard/overheard someone say this already. Encounter, converse and listen attentively to the opinion of a Cannois on this subject. (Mindfully) (hand)write a reflective paper (2–3 pages) explaining who you spoke with, how old they are, what their background is, what they exposed and how you interpret what was shared with you, in light of what you have read/experienced from

French culture so far. What conclusions can you draw? Does it fit with what you have experienced? How? Why might their perspective be such? Do you agree?'

Cultural and Social Difference: Systems (CSD:S): Suggested assignment to reflect intercultural citizenship

Touching on the relational, critical and civic dimensions of intercultural citizenship, as related by Porto (2021), the CSD:S abroad seminar may include an assignment, for example, in which students interview someone in their close host community, such as a host family member, and with whom they are comfortable talking. They can have an active and respectful exchange with them to address their views on how factors such as race, ethnicity, gender, age, class, sexuality, disability, religion or nationality intersect with one another in the French context. Prior to the interview assignment, students may view Kimberlé Crenshaw's TED Talk on Intersectionality[14] as a way to introduce the concept and framework, and to jump start conversations in the classroom. In the exchange with their transnational peer, students voice their own understandings of intersectionality, and how certain factors intersect and influence each other in society, before asking the interviewee to voice a personal understanding and perspective, in the context of France. After the interview, students reflect on how what they learned from the interviewee might help them better understand something that had surprised/shocked them about gender/race/ethnicity dynamics observed during their time in the country. To consolidate knowledge and share collaboratively, students bring back their findings and conclusions from the interview to classmates during class, and lead discussion to reflect collectively as a community of learners.

Notes

(1) See Mezirow, J. (1991) *Transformative Dimensions of Adult Learning*. San Francisco, CA: Jossey-Bass.
(2) See Knowles, M. (1980) *The Modern Practice of Adult Education: From Pedagogy to Andragogy*. Cambridge: Cambridge University Press.
(3) See Kolb, D.A. (1984) *Experiential Learning: Experience as the Source of Learning and Development*. Englewood Cliffs, NJ: Prentice Hall.
(4) See https://www.csbsju.edu/common-curriculum/common-curriculum-learning-goals.
(5) Proprioception and interoception are both ways of sensing that exist beyond the traditional five senses of taste, smell, sight, touch and hearing. Proprioception, as the name indicates, is the perception of self, the sense of 'knowing and feeling the body's position in space both statically and in motion'. Interoception is the experience and awareness of the internal processes happening inside our bodies, 'an internal, embodied *feeling*, a felt sense', or more simply put, it is the awareness of homeostasis (Kabat-Zinn, 2012: 56, his emphasis).
(6) *Audio Divina* and *Visio Divina* are contemplative traditions from the Benedictine monastic order. Both ask that the participant be open and available to the unexpected and reflect on the experience. Traditionally, the practices are conducted in multiple

stages and are associated with discernment of a divine presence in the participant's life. In the context of the study abroad program, however, the practices were adapted to hone sensorial acuity. In a first preparation phase, students settle into silence and stillness, becoming more aware and connected with the present moment. Students focus on their breath and let go of any distractions as they breathe out, in order to shift focus from the head to the heart and become open to what the experience might offer. In a more passive second phase of listening (*Audio Divina*) or observing (*Visio Divina*), the students let their senses be filled by what they hear or see, non-judgmentally, and note the effects the experience might have or if there are certain elements they find more striking. In a reflective stage, students focus more deeply on the element(s) that were most striking and discern any movements, memories, feelings or emotions (pleasant or unpleasant) that may arise as a consequence. They make note, as well, of any assumptions they may have brought into the experience. The students conclude the exercises by journaling on the experience, writing down their reflections. If time and the experience allow, following a moment of silence, and to savor the first experience, there can be a second and third listening or observation, in which, building on what came before, and centering on what response is evoked by the experience, students ponder how the awakening of those memories or feelings may be an invitation to act in the future, or an indication of previously unidentified desires, in the students' personal life context. While the *Visio Divina* was done in the context of a museum, where students could move at their own pace, and therefore take time to do second and third observations, in the case of the *Audio Divina* this was not possible, as students attended a concert, where the music was not repeated.

(7) These questions were adapted from Rev Michael Himes's instructional video *The 3 Key Questions*, available at https://www.youtube.com/watch?v=P-4lKCENdnw.

(8) Names used in this chapter are pseudonyms. Student excerpts in this chapter are mostly verbatim but minor grammatical changes may have been made for the purpose of clarification and understanding for the reader.

(9) Students were asked to 'Take 30 min or so of your time to sit, reflect intentionally, and honestly respond to the questions:
   (a) What is the first thing that comes to mind [when you think of your study abroad experience with mindfulness]? What was memorable?
   (b) Are you still applying what you learned? What? How?
   (c) Has it had an impact (positive or negative) on your academic, professional or personal life? How? Please elaborate, providing examples where appropriate.
   (d) Do you think it will have an impact in the immediate future/long-term for you? If so, what do you envision?
   (e) Is there anything further you would like to share about your experience with mindfulness?'

(10) The four questions were:
   (a) While you were in France, were there activities you engaged in within the community (e.g. tutoring, weekly conversations with a local)? Why did you choose to do that/What inspired you to pursue those activities?
   (b) Did your experience in Cannes impact your post-college decisions? If so, how?
   (c) Did you continue/start with active community engagement after returning from Cannes? If so, how? What inspired you to do so?
   (d) How are you engaging, or taking action (social/political) within your local or more global communities at this time?

(11) This follows Porto's conclusions in a 2021 study that looks at long-term impact of intercultural citizenship education in several transnational programs (Porto, 2021).

(12) 'Students analyze how historical and/or contemporary constructions of gender shape and are shaped by cultural systems of power. Students analyze how factors such as race, ethnicity, age, class, sexuality, disability, religion, or nationality intersect with gender'.

(13) 'Students demonstrate how historical and/or contemporary constructions of race and/or ethnicity shape and are shaped by cultural systems of power. Students analyze how factors such as gender, age, class, sexuality, disability, religion, or nationality intersect with race and/or ethnicity'.

(14) https://www.ted.com/talks/kimberle_crenshaw_the_urgency_of_intersectionality?language=en.

References

Bai, H., Scott, C. and Donald, B. (2009) Contemplative pedagogy and revitalization of teacher education. *Alberta Journal of Educational Research* 55 (3), 319–334. See https://doi.org/10.11575/ajer.v55i3.55330.

Bai, H., Eppert, C., Scott, C., Tait, S. and Nguyen, T. (2014) Towards intercultural philosophy of education. *Studies in Philosophy and Education* 34 (6), 635–649. See https://doi.org/10.1007/s11217-014-9444-1.

Barbezat, D.P. and Bush, M. (2014) *Contemplative Practices in Higher Education: Powerful Methods to Transform Teaching and Learning.* San Francisco, CA: Jossey-Bass.

Barlow, J. and Nadeau, J. (2003) *Sixty Million Frenchmen Can't Be Wrong: Why We Love France but not the French.* Naperville, IL: Sourcebooks.

Bennett, J.M. (2009) Transforming training: Designing programs for culture learning. In M.A. Moodian (ed.) *Contemporary Leadership and Intercultural Competence: Understanding and Utilizing Cultural Diversity to Build Successful Organizations* (pp. 95–110). Thousand Oaks, CA: Sage.

Bennett, M.J. (2012) Paradigmatic assumptions and a developmental approach to intercultural learning. In M. Vande Berg, R.M. Paige and K.H. Lou (eds) *Student Learning Abroad: What Our Students Are Learning, What They're Not, and What We Can Do About It* (pp. 90–114). Sterling, VA: Stylus Publishing.

Bohm, D. (1996) *On Dialogue.* London: Routledge.

Brookfield, S.D. (2012) Critical theory and transformative learning. In E.W. Taylor and P. Cranton (eds) *The Handbook of Transformative Learning: Theory, Research, and Practice* (pp. 131–146). San Francisco, CA: Jossey-Bass.

Brooks, D. (2015) *The Road to Character.* New York, NY: Random House.

Brown, B. (2010) *The Gifts of Imperfection.* Center City, MN: Hazelden Publishing.

Byram, M. (1997) *Teaching and Assessing Intercultural Communicative Competence.* Clevedon: Multilingual Matters.

Byram, M. (2006) Developing a concept of intercultural citizenship. In G. Alred, M. Byram and M. Fleming (eds) *Education for Intercultural Citizenship: Concepts and Comparisons* (pp. 109–129). Clevedon: Multilingual Matters.

Byram, M. (2008) *From Foreign Language Education to Education for Intercultural Citizenship: Essays and Reflections.* Clevedon: Multilingual Matters.

Byram, M. (2012) Conceptualizing intercultural (communicative) competence and intercultural citizenship. In J. Jackson (ed.) *The Routledge Handbook of Language and Intercultural Communication* (pp. 85–97). London: Routledge. See https://doi.org/10.4324/9780203805640.ch5.

Byram, M., Golubeva, I., Han, H. and Wagner, M. (eds) (2017) *From Principles to Practice in Education for Intercultural Citizenship.* Bristol: Multilingual Matters.

Carlson, R. (1997) *Don't Sweat the Small Stuff… and It's All Small Stuff.* New York, NY: Hyperion.

Chopra, D. (1994) *The Seven Spiritual Laws of Success.* San Rafael, CA: Amber-Allen Publishing.

CMind (2021) The Tree of Contemplative Practices [Illustration]. *The Center for Contemplative Mind in Society.* See https://www.contemplativemind.org/practices/tree.

Craig, B.A. (2011) Contemplative practice in higher education: An assessment of the contemplative practice fellowhship program, 1997–2009. http://www.contemplativemind.org/archives/785.

Cranton, P. (2016) *Understanding and Promoting Transformative Learning: A Guide to Theory and Practice* (3rd edn). Sterling, VA: Stylus Publishing.

De Botton, A. (2002) *The Art of Travel*. New York, NY: Random House.

de Quincey, C. (2005) *Radical Knowing: Understanding Consciousness through Relationship*. Rochester, VT: Park Street Press.

Deardorff, D.K. (2006) Identification and assessment of intercultural competence as a student outcome of internationalization. *Journal of Studies in International Education* 10 (3), 241–266. See https://doi.org/10.1177/1028315306287002.

Deardorff, D.K. (ed.) (2009) *Intercultural Competence*. Thousand Oaks, CA: Sage.

Dewey, J. (1897) My pedagodic creed. *The School Journal* LIV (3), 77–80.

Dewey, J. (1910) *How We Think*. New York, NY: Heath.

Fantini, A.E. (2009) Assessing intercultural competence: Issues and tools. In D.K. Deardorff (ed) *The SAGE Handbook of Intercultural Competence* (pp. 456–476). Thousand Oaks, CA: Sage.

Freire, P. (1973) *Education for Critical Consciousness*. New York, NY: Continuum.

Guilherme, M. (2007) English as a global language and education for cosmopolitan citizenship. *Language and Intercultural Communication* 7 (1), 72–90.

Gunnlaugson, O. (2014) Considerations for collective leadership: A threefold contemplative curriculum for engaging the intersubjective filed of learning. In O. Gunnlaugson, E.W. Sarath, C. Scott and H. Bai (eds) *Contemplative Learning and Inquiry Across Disciplines* (pp. 305–324). Albany, NY: State University of New York Press.

Gunnlaugson, O., Sarath, E.W., Scott, C. and Bai, H. (2014) An introduction to contemplative learning and inquiry across disciplines. In O. Gunnlaugson, E.W. Sarath, C. Scott and H. Bai (eds) *Contemplative Learning and Inquiry Across Disciplines* (pp. 1–11). Albany, NY: State University of New York Press.

Himes, M. [Center for Student Formation] (2016) The 3 Key Questions [Video]. *YouTube*, 20 April. See https://www.youtube.com/watch?v=P-4lKCENdnw.

Jackson, J. (2011) Cultivating cosmopolitan, intercultural citizenship through critical reflection and international, experiential learning. *Language and Intercultural Communication* 11 (2), 80–96.

Kabat-Zinn, J. (2005) *Coming to Our Senses: Healing Ourselves and the World through Mindfulness*. New York, NY: Hyperion.

Kabat-Zinn, J. (2009) *Full Catastrophe Living: Using the Wisdom of your Body and Mind to Face Stress, Pain, and Illness* (15th Anniversary reprint). New York, NY: Bantam Dell.

Kabat-Zinn, J. (2012) *Mindfulness for Beginners: Reclaiming the Present Moment—and Your Life*. Boulder, CO: Sounds True.

Kolb, D.A. (1984) *Experiential Learning: Experience as the Source of Learning and Development*. Engelwood Cliffs, NJ: Prentice Hall.

Leung, K., Ang, S. and Tan, M.L. (2014) Intercultural competence. *Annual Review of Organizational Psychology and Organizational Behavior* 1 (1), 489–519. See https://doi.org/10.1146/annurev-orgpsych-031413-091229.

Llewellyn, K., Cook, S. and Molina, A. (2010) Civic learning: Moving from the apolitical to the socially just. *Journal of Curriculum Studies* 42 (6), 791–812.

Martin, J.N. and Nakayama, T.K. (2000) *Intercultural Communication in Contexts* (2nd edn). Mountain View, CA: Mayfield.

Martin, J.N. and Nakayama, T.K. (2013) Intercultural communication and dialectics revisted. In T. Nakayama and R.T. Halualani (eds) *The Handbook of Critical Intercultural Communication* (pp. 59–83). Malden, MA: Wiley-Blackwell.

Merriam, S.B. and Brockett, R.G. (1997) *The Profession and Practice of Adult Education: An Introduction*. San Francisco, CA: Jossey-Bass.

Moon, D.G. (2013) Critical reflections on culture and critical intercultural commu-
nication. In T. Nakayama and R.T. Halualani (eds) *The Handbook of Critical
Intercultural Communication* (pp. 34–52). Malden, MA: Wiley-Blackwell.
National Standards Collaborative Board (2015) *World-Readiness Standards for Learning
Languages* (4th edn). Alexandria, VA: National Standards in Foreign Language
Education project.
Nhat Hanh, T. (1975) *The Miracle of Mindfulness*. Boston, MA: Beacon Press.
Nhat Hanh, T. (1991) *Peace is Every Step: The Path of Mindfulness in Everyday Life*. New
York, NY: Bantam.
Ono, K.A. (2013) Reflections on problematizing 'Nation' in intercultural communica-
tion research. In T. Nakayama and R.T. Halualani (eds) *The Handbook of Critical
Intercultural Communication* (pp. 84–97). Malden, MA: Wiley-Blackwell.
Orange, D. (1995) *Emotional Understanding: Studies in Psychoanalytic Epistemology*.
New York, NY: Guilford Press.
Paige, R.M., Jacobs-Cassuto, M., Yershova, Y.A. and DeJaeghere, J. (2003) Assessing
intercultural sensitivity: An empirical analysis of the Hammer and Bennett
Intercultural Development Inventory. *International Journal of Intercultural Relations*
27 (4), 467–486. See https://doi.org/10.1016/S0147-1767(03)00034-8.
Porto, M. (2021) Long-term impact of four intercultural citizenship projects in the higher
education foreign language classroom. *The Language Learning Journal* 49 (6), 648–667.
Roth, H.D. (2006) Contemplative studies: Prospects for a new field. *Teachers College
Record* 108 (9), 1787–1815. See https://doi.org/10.1111/j.1467-9620.2006.00762.x.
Roth, H.D. (2014) A pedagogy for the new field of contemplative studies. In O. Gunnlaugson,
E.W. Sarath, C. Scott and H. Bai (eds) *Contemplative Learning and Inquiry Across
Disciplines* (pp. 305–324). Albany, NY: State University of New York Press.
Selby, R. (2008) Designing transformation in international education. In V. Savicki (ed.)
*Developing Intercultural Competence and Transformation: Theory, Research, and
Application in International Education* (pp. 1–10). Sterling, VA: Stylus Publishing.
Starosta, W.J. and Chen, G.-M. (2003) *Ferment in the Intercultural Field: Axiology, Value,
Praxis*. Thousand Oaks, CA: Sage.
Stuart, D.K. (2012) Taking stage development theory seriously. In M. Vande Berg, R.M.
Paige and K. Hemming Lou (eds) *Student Learning Abroad: What Our Students Are
Learning, What They're Not, and What We Can Do About It* (pp. 61–89). Sterling,
VA: Stylus Publishing.
Sullivan, W. (2016) *Liberal Learning as a Quest for Purpose*. Oxford: Oxford University
Press.
Vande Berg, M. (2007) Intervening in the learning of U.S. students abroad. *Journal
of Studies in International Education* 11 (3–4), 392–399. See https://doi.
org/10.1177/1028315307303924.
Vande Berg, M., Paige, R.M. and Hemming Lou, K. (2012) Student learning abroad:
Paradigms and assumptions. In M. Vande Berg, R.M. Paige and K. Hemming Lou
(eds) *Student Learning Abroad: What Our Students Are Learning, What They're Not,
and What We Can Do About It* (pp. 3–28). Sterling, VA: Stylus Publishing.
Wagner, M. and Byram, M. (2017) Intercultural citizenship. *The International
Encyclopedia of Intercultural Communication*. Hoboken, NJ: Wiley.
Zajonc, A. (2010) Beyond the divided academic life. In P.J. Palmer and A. Zajonc (eds)
The Heart of Higher Education: A Call to Renewal (pp. 53–75). San Francisco, CA:
Jossey-Bass.
Zajonc, A. (2013) Contemplative pedagogy: A quiet revolution in higher education. *New
Directions for Teaching and Learning* 134, 83–94. https://doi.org/10.1002/tl.20057.
Zull, J.E. (2012) The brain, learning, and study abroad. In M. Vande Berg, R.M. Paige and
K. Hemming Lou (eds) *Student Learning Abroad: What Our Students Are Learning,
What They're Not, and What We Can Do About It* (pp. 162–187). Sterling, VA: Stylus
Publishing.

Index

For Product Safety Concerns and Information please contact our EU Authorised Representative:

Easy Access System Europe

Mustamäe tee 50

10621 Tallinn

Estonia

gpsr.requests@easproject.com

www.ingramcontent.com/pod-product-compliance
Lightning Source LLC
Chambersburg PA
CBHW050438280326
41932CB00013BA/2166